WITHDRAWN BY THE
UNIVERSITY OF MICHIGAN

Mark Hobart and Robert H. Taylor, Editors

CONTEXT MEANING AND POWER IN SOUTHEAST ASIA

STUDIES ON SOUTHEAST ASIA

Southeast Asia Program
120 Uris Hall
Cornell University, Ithaca, New York
1986

Editor in Chief
    Benedict Anderson

Editorial Board
    George Kahin
    Stanley O'Connor
    Oliver Wolters

© 1986 Cornell Southeast Asia Program
ISBN 0-87727-701-X

CONTENTS

Preface	5
1. Introduction: Context, Meaning, and Power *Mark Hobart*	7
2. The *Wayang* Controversy in Indonesian Communism *Ruth McVey*	21

3. "Good Omens" versus "Worth": The Poetic Dialogue
   between Ton Tho Tuong and Phan Van Tri
   Jeremy H. C. S. Davidson
	53

4. Burmese Concepts of Revolution *Robert H. Taylor*	79
5. *Kānpatthanā:* Thai Views of Development *Harvey Demaine*	93

6. The Deliberate Use of Foreign Vocabulary by the Khmer:
   Changing Fashions, Methods, and Sources
   Judith M. Jacob
	115

7. Thinker, Thespian, Soldier, Slave? Assumptions about
   Human Nature in the Study of Balinese Society
   Mark Hobart
	131

Preface

The essays collected in this volume were first given in a series of seminars held in 1983 at the Centre of South East Asian Studies, School of Oriental and African Studies, under the title "Context, Meaning and Change in South East Asia." At that time all of the contributors were on the staff of SOAS, teaching either a Southeast Asian language or one of the mainstream disciplines (anthropology, politics or geography) with particular reference to the region. One of the strengths of both teaching and research at SOAS has been the importance placed upon a thorough understanding of language in the comprehension of social phenomena in Southeast Asian societies and in other regions of Asia and Africa. It was the intention of the seminar series to illustrate the value of linguistic study to an appreciation of various aspects of the political and social life of Southeast Asian peoples. We are convinced that Southeast Asian studies, in whatever field, cannot adequately illuminate the richness and complexities of their subject without an appreciation of the linguistic and contextual nature of thought and action.

We are grateful to the Director and staff of the Cornell University Southeast Asia Program for their careful and efficient publication of this volume. They have done more than can be reasonably expected from the publishers of a volume of this nature to ensure its readability and accuracy. Any shortcomings or errors are solely the responsibility of the editors and contributors.

The Editors

1

INTRODUCTION: CONTEXT, MEANING, AND POWER

Mark Hobart

A discussion of meaning involves questions of context and power in several senses. The recent debate about "Orientalism" has largely been about how Westerners in various ways created a mysterious world of "the Orient."[1] In so doing they came to assume a power over the peoples they described by imposing meanings from alien contexts upon them. In contrast to the objective, scientific, rational West a strange, mystical, irrational Orient was born. The essays in this volume attempt to break away from the assumptions behind this approach, and explore possible styles of research which do less injustice to the peoples with whom—rather than on whom—we work.

The sweeping and misleading generalizations too often made by students of Southeast Asian societies commonly have their roots in a superficial understanding of the history, culture, and linguistic complexities of what they profess to explain. A scarcely less dangerous tendency has been to constitute an imaginary "object of study" which displaces Southeast Asians to some timeless, distant world.[2] So we have focused on the impact their neighbors, the colonial powers, contemporary economic and political relations, and their own historical experiences have had, the better to understand the forms which the discourses of Southeast Asian peoples have assumed.

The title of the volume is itself suggestive of the type of problem we are addressing. "Southeast Asia" does not "exist" any more than terms like "context" or "meaning" have any very clear or unambiguous sense, other than within a particular framework. Southeast Asia is a recent, externally defined, political invention and denotes no exclusive internally bounded entity, geographically, ethnically or culturally.[3] It is merely a convenient label to refer to one part of the globe in relation to others.

This said, however, there are senses in which such a regional focus is not entirely arbitrary. Long before Jayavarman II returned from Java to found the Angkor dynasty in Cambodia, there seems to have been extensive travel, mutual influence through trade and conquest, and cultural adaptation around the South China and nearby seas. There has been a long history of conscious borrowing, within as well as without the region, as Jacob makes clear in her essay. Such influences may perhaps best be seen as in opposition, or as supplementary, to the dynamics of local cultures. With the growth of Western imperialism and global trade, more distant centers of power tried to impose their ideas upon Southeast Asian societies and change these societies to further what they perceived as their own or sometimes the colonized peoples' interests. The idea of the region, more recently, has served the aim of some Southeast Asian governments to represent themselves as having something in common. Others have sought to stress broader extra-regional (and often ideological) links, or have taken refuge in more narrowly interpreted "national identities." It is in the shaping of these processes that we are interested.

If the notion of a "region" is a fiction (in the sense of "something made"), so may be its constituent "societies" or "cultures," which are in no small part outsiders' constructions of an amalgam of processes, interpreted and disputed in different ways by those involved. Such hypostatization follows easily from the common-sense model of language, whereby words and sentences have meaning by corresponding to the actual state of affairs in the world. The problem is that much of what people say and do gains meaning, not by reference to the world, but by reference to other things which have been said and done. In other words significance depends upon context. So Correspondence Theory has a rival, or complement, in Coherence or Contextual Theory. Instead of analyzing a subject in search of its essential nature, the appeal to context implies a focus on relationships, and potentially different perspectives. If the former is of use in practical science, the latter comes into its own in interpreting cultural statements and actions, which often make little sense in terms of any simple correspondence with the world. The difficulty is simply that, whereas it is possible in principle to lay down fairly strict conditions for meaning in Correspondence Theory, how is one to circumscribe all the possible contexts relevant to a contextual approach?

Contextualizing also raises the delicate issue of the relation between analysts' and indigenous frames of reference, and poses the questions: whose formulation of relations, and whose criteria of relevance, are at stake? People have different representations (in Goodman's sense)[4] of relevant context, not just between, but within, cultures. Such representations involve power and knowledge in two ways, as Davidson's essay shows. The ability to assert, and have one's assertions accepted as legitimate knowledge, are important aspects of power, as Jacob and Taylor suggest and as I argue below. At the same time, the knowledge available to different groups or persons in a society delimits the forms of power which are recognized and may be used.

The question of context becomes more complex when it is recognized that, in importing "foreign" ideas, or having them imposed, the political and cultural possibilities are extended. In allowing greater choice in how to contextualize, there emerges a double relationship between knowledge and power. In adopting academically fashionable criteria for selecting relevant contexts in preference to those used by the participants themselves, we may be guilty simultaneously of an act of distortion and a subtle kind of epistemological domination. The illustration of these points is an implicit theme running through this book.

At first sight, the six essays may seem to address somewhat different topics. Some readers may wish to look only at those which seem pertinent to their own fields. To do so would be to miss how far the themes complement and illuminate each other. To classify the essays—this one on Burmese politics, that one about Vietnamese poetry—is to split a complex reality into compartments, an approach from which it was our purpose to suggest an escape. The reason for people interested in literature, politics, economic development, and culture coming together was the shared realization of how similar were the kinds of questions we were asking. We feel it would be a mistake to lose the richness of the plurality of these views for the sake of producing short-lived hypotheses with a semblance of "scientific" comparability.

This introduction will not therefore attempt to generalize about what might seem a common theme, namely how borrowed languages and symbols came, through adaptation, to bring about change in Southeast Asia. Generalization of this kind would misrepresent what the contributors have sought to achieve. For we have eschewed the naive model of "social change" (or "political change") which implies a static system to which "change" happens. Societies, polities, and languages are dynamic and continually being reinterpreted and reevaluated in different contexts. Perhaps one should ask not how, or why, change happens but what underlies the impression of continuity.

All the essays make use of linguistic materials in their analyses. A word of warning is therefore necessary against a potential misunderstanding. One can slip into the comfortable mistake of seeing language as a transparent medium for picturing truth and meaning—language as a kind of container, a conduit for the communication of the essence of thought or reality.[5] However, as Edelman observes:

> Language . . . is not to be conceived as something which conveys meaning by itself. Its meanings are always a function of the context from which it issues, of the disparate needs and interests of the audiences involved, and of their respective modes of perception. The realistic study of political language and its meaning is necessarily a probing not only of dictionaries, nor of word counts, but of the diverse response to particular modes of expression of audiences in disparate social settings.[6]

Thus language may indeed refer; but it may also express a speaker's attitude or feelings; it may be prescriptive; it may express shared contact; it may be used to check for misunderstanding; and it may be reflexive commentary.[7] How the different functions of language may be subtly mixed emerges in the various papers. Whatever language does, it does not just describe. For descriptions do not just "happen": they are asserted, denied, questioned, mused over, and more besides, by people in specific situations.

If the meaning of language is complicated, so *a fortiori* is its use in symbolism. One of the legacies of the structuralist analysis of symbols, as Sperber has pointed out, is that it has "established, all unknowing, that symbols work without meaning."[8] Worse, symbolism is often appealed to when the analyst can find no criteria which, by his or her standards, are rational. It tends thus to be a residual category, an inheritance of the Romantics' critique of the Enlightenment's vision.[9] We would do well to refrain from imposing this type of category on peoples who have their own, and different, traditions of argumentation.

The essays collected here offer complementary perspectives which suggest an interesting, if unexpected, picture. To draw out what I see as their implications, I shall discuss them briefly in an order convenient for exposition.

Development, the current soubriquet for planned social change, is a Western notion shot through with universalist assumptions about evolution, as Demaine brings out in his discussion of Thailand. There, successive National Development Plans were couched in the to us familiar language of economic development theories. These plans, however, have come adrift in the context of Thai economic and political relations, which in practice are articulated in terms of cultural presuppositions quite different from what those who drafted the plans imagined. Projects and funds are administered through ministries which operate as semiautonomous fiefdoms; and relations, whatever the formal constitution, are organized in a manner reminiscent of "traditional" ties of patronage.[10] A striking characteristic of the elite responsible for implementing the development plans is its remoteness from the supposed beneficiaries and its image of the latter as "stupid" peasants. Failure of the plans is therefore easily accounted for by superiors in terms of their model of their society's membership. Miscommunication, and conflicting paradigms, seem to occur at each point in the chain of command.

The "objective," or "scientific," language of economic and social development planners tends to conceal how critical different epistemological points of view and cultural presuppositions are to communication, or (more often) its lack. At its simplest, "development" involves divergent and ambiguous Western models of others' imagined societies and how these must evolve to emulate their creators' self-image or, still more condescendingly, attain the lesser goals thought fit for them. Further, ideals or plans are interpreted and "adapted" by interest groups, typically drawn from potentially rival segments of an elite who proceed according to their idiosyncratic constructions or assertions of what their own society is, or ought to be, about. The miscommunication which often ensues and still passes for "development" stems from the imposition, by virtue of economic and political power, of alien models of invented Others (to use Foucault's trenchant term).

Just how the discourse of development has been shaped by existing power relations, and modified in the light of apparent failure, is clearly drawn out by Demaine. As he notes, "development" is in itself an ambiguous notion, capable of disseminating all sorts of readings. According to the earlier economic version, resources are its focus, and success is judged by increases in gross national product. When this model failed to achieve the ends sought by some Thai, attention shifted slowly—by way of curious hybrids like "human resource development"—to human and social "progress." This idea treated "development" as "a series of stages in the process of man's attempt to realize his potential."

Demaine demonstrates the extent to which these two interpretations of "development" in Thailand do not come as isolated concepts but are part of a set of more or less coherent ideas. Each interpretation includes ontological preferences (in other words, what aspect of reality or human action should be treated as primary: material resources or the satisfaction of needs); a theory of human nature and society; and a view of history. Each model postulates some kind of teleological account of the way in which society or Man must—if helped by a little pushing—naturally evolve. Discreetly tucked away in most such models is a metaphorical image, which has a habit of taking on a life of its own.[11] So wealth "trickles down" or threatens to "polarize" rich and poor. In the language of progress, ideas like "development" and "society" rapidly become reified: a trend with critical political implications.

Two of the essays examine the borrowing of foreign words and its implications. Jacob shows that there is nothing new in Cambodians importing and adapting vocabulary from others, often by conscious and deliberate borrowing. In pre-Angkorean and Angkorean times, Sanskrit was already used "as the language of prestige and of literature. Loan words relating to law, religion, and politics, and abstract ideas in general, were absorbed into Khmer." By contrast, later borrowings from Thai included "everyday words obviously chosen for literary effect." In the colonial period, certain words seem to have been used more out of necessity than choice, to judge from the strenuous efforts of the Cultural Commission set up by the government after independence to remove French words from the language. Such steps were justified by the state as necessary for the preservation and advancement of what it portrayed as "Khmer culture." They were also a sign of the independent state's attempt to claim to be the arbiter of meaning and the origin of power over language as over everything else.

While Jacob notes the motives behind the borrowing of terms, she is careful not to conjecture about worlds of "meaning" which such borrowings could be thought to imply.[12] Instead she states that "meaning" is used to indicate "the effect which the deliberate use of a foreign term may have or have had" at the given time. Such a loosely

"Wittgensteinian" approach has the advantage of not committing one *a priori* to any particular function of language. It also avoids the assumption that, in importing alien lexical items, the Khmer were necessarily importing ideas with them.[13] For such terms were not always used with their original referents and could develop quite distinct connotations. For example, where Khmer words were available, to the extent that Sanskrit offered a language of prestige, it was not that one could say something different *in* Sanskrit so much as *with* Sanskrit. A language of prestige is, of course, a language which implies privileged knowledge and therefore power for those who use it as opposed to those who do not. Significance seems to lie metalingually in the choice of codes as much as in the "meaning" (in a correspondence or referential sense of the word). Similar observations could, without doubt, be made for other Southeast Asian peoples.

The other essay which concentrates on the borrowing of lexical terms and alien concepts, is that by Taylor, whose problem is the translation or interpretation of "revolution" in recent Burmese politics. Jacob's and Taylor's contributions point to a process which is in some respects the antithesis of Demaine's Thai example. Whereas in the Thai instance the focus is on an internal Thai discussion of "development" in the context of Western conceptual trends and of the political complexities of the country, the Burmese and Khmer studies note the purposeful attempts of the indigenous authorities to seek to avoid foreign control, or models, in this and other regards.

In both Cambodia and Burma, political elites were at pains to create what Parkin has called an "internal cultural debate."[14] The point of focusing on a debate defined in this manner is that its effects are singularly political. "Internal" implies a legitimate forum, from which others are excluded; "cultural" gives the proceedings an air of identity and asserts the existence of culture: "debate" suggests that conflicts are constructive and do not threaten the proposed boundaries or definition of the culture. Parkin implies this is a strategy adopted by a people who feel concern at being swamped by influences represented as external. Of course, should one party in the internal debate gain sufficient control over the state apparatus, it is likely to try to steer the future evolution of the debate by asserting, in indigenous terms, the "right," or "real," meaning of political language. The results, however, may be surprising, because such strategies are usually based on a naive vision of language. One might add that the identification of a political group with "the people," "the culture," or "the state," and the constructions placed upon conceptions like the state itself, are claims which are part of this notional debate. Before we consider such debates, we should note the extent to which the parameters of discussion are already preempted.

The problems confronting revolutionary nationalist groups in Burma before and after independence from colonial rule included how to present to their intended audience the kind of radical change they wished to bring about. Taylor shows how, for aspirants to power, the image of revolution was designed to give form to an idea of moral and social change; and how, for incumbents, it was used to justify state policy. He further notes that:

> Since 1948, however, the concept of revolution has become the metaphor which leaders who intend not only to control but to transform radically the nature of the polity use to convey to their followers the essence of political purpose.

As Taylor develops clearly the implications behind the changing notions of revolution, I need only make two small points about his argument here. The assertion that an idea or concept has an essential meaning introduces questions of power. If this is claimed by an aspiring elite, the implication is that it is they, rather than any alternative elite, who are qualified to state what the essential truth is, and thereby claim that others must follow their interpretations and orders.[15] Further, the transformation of a term like "revolution" to the status of a key metaphor in political argument is significant. For metaphors represent neither accurately nor fully—they portray something as something else. In other words they are persuasive rather than descriptive. In this way Taylor introduces us to the complex functions of political language. It is emotive in so far as it suggests the speaker's attitude to what he or she is saying; it is conative in so far as it implies appropriate action; it is assertive in so far as it claims to portray how things really are.[16]

The different ways in which words can mean things comes out clearly in the history of Burmese expressions for revolution. Significantly, at the start Marxist thinkers did not worry about the issue, which only became important as sectarian conflicts grew. For the democratic socialists the preferred expression, *ayēi-daw-bon*, came to indicate "a people's movement" rather than "a revolution to overthrow established authority and to redistribute values and power," the latter being encapsulated in the less well-rooted phrase *taw-hlan-yēi*. Where the former included a "struggle for power" among its senses, the latter implied treating "a superior with disrespect or insolence, to be in rebellion." In creating neologisms with different connotations, the politicians drew on existing semantic uses, but in such a way as to constitute a discourse which at times undermined their own roles and their attempts to restructure popular perceptions of the state and its functions.

Once again we are back not just to what words "mean" but what people do in using them. The critical point in the shift from a theory of connotation and denotation to one of reference is that one now focuses not on an elusive eternal, and essential, meaning but on the ways in which people use language in different contexts with varying effects. As Taylor suggests, to ask out of context what revolution is is largely meaningless.

If Burma's political leaders exerted conscious control over the kinds of picture they wished to present of themselves and their aims, they seem to have had less control over other aspects of their ideas. Revolution is not a concept *in vacuo*. It has its own context of ideas, and relates to such issues as views of history, human nature, and the relations between human beings and society. The two socialist factions found themselves arguing implicitly, but consistently, for radically different views of the world. Whether these wider issues are presupposed, rather than entailed, in the Burmese instance is not the immediate point:[17] from the evidence presented, it would seem that Buddhist ideas of time were presupposed, the nature of human beings entailed. What is relevant however is the extent to which we mislead ourselves in looking at "symbolism" (here a consciously constructed one at that) rather than at the implications ideas have for one another and the extent to which people find it necessary to appeal to such general issues as history, society and human nature in the course of political and daily life.

McVey's paper also deals with the problems of introducing alien ideologies to indigenous populations. But where in Burma the debate was between rival views of revolution, in Java the discussion focused on how far Marxism should adapt to existing, and seemingly well entrenched, cultural ideas, enshrined in part in the Javanese shadow play. Perhaps because of Indonesia's sheer size and diversity, the problems of the Communist Party (PKI) were less with translating foreign imports into culturally acceptable form (although those existed too) as with overlapping, and incompatible, identities. For, while Java is politically and demographically the dominant island in the archipelago, other large islands like Sumatra are economically important and are locked in the struggle for national influence. Cultural, ethnic, religious, and political differences mesh in an intricate kaleidoscope, and make the formation of coherent mass movements extremely difficult. McVey looks at the complex implications of being simultaneously Javanese and Communist and shows how far the two paradigms were incompatible, not just at the level of formal ideological postulates, but in their philosophical assumptions.

The puzzle with which McVey starts is why a leading Communist, in his last public statement, should identify himself and his colleagues with the "feudal" heroes of the Mahabharata, the epic on which most shadow play *(wayang)* is based. She observes that:

> there is a deep difference between the philosophical vision of Marxism and the classical shadow-play. *Wayang* teaches that contradictions are not overcome; they may only be understood and thereby borne ... (whereas) in Marxist thought, history is the process of man's realization of himself. ... Marxism is optimistic where *wayang* is not; Marxism teaches that understanding dictates struggle, *wayang* that it enjoins acceptance.

Marxism and shadow theater embody radically different views of social history, conflict and the human condition. In the world portrayed by the shadow theatre, the past is purer and so serves to suggest precedents, "for in its vision all time coexists." In Marxism, on the other hand, the past is something to be transcended. History is pictured in both views by a spatial metaphor of "direction." But one looks back, the other forward.

One of the assumptions in much Marxist theory is that its assertions reflect and correspond to dialectically changing states of affairs in the world, both past and future. Otherwise it would be incapable of the generalization beyond immediate context which its predictions of historical inevitability require. In practice, however, Marxism adapts. Apart from being a timely reminder that we need to contextualize general terms like "Marxism," this observation highlights an interesting problem encountered by the Javanese Communist elite (and other Western-derived ideological groupings too). The difficulty was that there was a disjuncture between the image of the Common Man, in the abstract, and what actual common men tended to do.

The Javanese seem to have set about ordering their relations with cultural ideals quite differently. As McVey writes:

> the inclination of Javanese [is] to see individuals and events in terms of *wayang* characters and *lakon* (plays) and to choose as exemplars for themselves those *wayang* figures perceived to be most in accordance with each perceiver's character and situation.

Here interpretation is doubly contextual: both according to the specific situation and according to what is seen as fitting for one's personality. The confrontation of Marxism and Javanese culture is not between two symmetrical ideologies or paradigms, as in the Burmese political debate, but between two quite different kinds of metaphysical system, articulated in terms of different theories of meaning and truth.

The question still remains of whether or not we should attribute the importance of shadow theater in Java to its capacity to provide the constituent, or meaningful, symbolism of Javanese life. So phrased the question skews discussion *a priori*. To suppose that the need to understand and order the incomprehensible through symbols is fundamental to human nature begs the question. The intricate polysemy which the

Javanese seem to enjoy so much may be described in terms other than symbolism. There is something to be said, if only for a change of perspective, for thinking in terms of a notion like "text," where this is understood not as a particular work but as field of possibilities permitted at any time by the presuppositions and ideas of style of those who produce (here puppeteers), and those who watch, a play.

Other peoples' kinds of textuality may differ from ours and we are only too liable to misunderstand what the words that are created say and do (as many who have wished to mold shadow theater have found to their cost). We tend to assume that language is there to communicate some truth about the world, whereas it may just as well be seen as instantiating, exemplifying, or hinting at, the ineffable.[18] Reference is only a part of what shadow plays do. The language permits plays on homonymy and folk etymology, and the use of Javanese is valued as a unique and differentiating code. Shadow theater also provides a paradigm of the nature of reality; it serves as a reflexive commentary on Javanese life and customs, as well as on the nature of language and human beings.[19] Rather than being a transparent medium, language in Java, and *a fortiori* the shadow play, provide a reservoir of terms and situations which have been preconstrained by previous use and in terms of which new situations may be ordered. By the same token, new uses modify the appropriateness of established signs. The problem in understanding wayang stems from imposing alien ideas of communication on a set of practices which are far from fully studied.

How intricate cultural conventions of textuality may be comes out in Davidson's detailed analysis of the dialogue between two Vietnamese poets at the time the French were striving to extend their political control over the country. One scholar and poet, Ton Tho Tuong, had sided with the colonialists. In a famous poem, *Tu Thuat* ("Being Autobiographical"), he set out to justify his allegiance and to persuade others to follow him. His verses were capped by a more patriotic and, as it turned out, a subtler poet, Phan Van Tri, in a long exchange which was at once literary and political. For under discussion were the moral duties of scholar-bureaucrats, ideas about what it meant to be Vietnamese, a confrontation between the ideals and practice of Confucianism and political modernism, and much else besides. Where Javanese shadow plays must reach their audience in a largely *ad lib* performance on a single night, no such constraints operated on these poetic exchanges and so they show the full complexity that literary and artistic forms may attain in Southeast Asia.[20]

Poetry is the Achilles heel of essentialist theories of language. For words and phrases do so much at any one moment that it is vainglorious to try to say what it is that language is "really" about. "Meaning" here is the revealed intention of the poet, and the better the poem, the more it implies. One could run the gamut of the functions of language in the analysis of the Tuong-Tri poetic dialogue but it would only hint at a few of the tools they used; and one would be saying next to nothing about style and textuality. Nor is it easy to pin down the references of the poems. An allusive use of metaphor can suggest an open set of possible contexts, some of them as yet unrealized. So Davidson concludes with two prophetic lines of Phan Van Tri suggesting that an idea which seemed doubtful when penned, could turn out more powerful and percipient than the gun boats that had served so often as metaphors at the beginning of their poetic dialogue:

> The nation, one tomorrow, will change its destiny to one of peace,
> The South in common will enjoy reunion in peaceful equilibrium.

In passing one might note the connection between metaphor and context, and why poetry is so hard to classify linguistically. What a sentence denotes (sentence meaning) is different analytically from what it is used to refer to on a given occasion (utterance meaning). So context is already relevant to understanding exchanges like the poets' dialogue. Even in literal sentences, where arguably the sentence and the speaker's meaning coincide, "the sentence only determines a definite set of truth conditions relative to a particular context."[21] On this view context cannot be eliminated from even simple description.

How metaphor works is a much disputed topic, but by most accounts it involves the existence of one or more contexts beyond that implied in the sentence meaning; and what it hints at is usually reached by considering the full context of the utterance. Guessing what someone "has in mind" is a tricky business because of the amount of information needed, and because people vary in their allusive skills. So metaphor resists attempts to circumscribe its potential range of implications and its contexts of application.[22]

To gauge just how contexts are alluded to in much discourse, the reader can do no better than to follow Davidson in his unravelling of the stanzas of the poets' exchanges. For example, at one point Phan Van Tri compares Ton Tuo Tuong to an opera actor. In one phrase he draws upon actors' duplicitous reputations and unfitness for high bureaucratic office, takes a sideswipe at the nobility among whom opera was popular, and opens the way for an extended double play between actors on stage and Tuong in politics.

Another important aspect of metaphor is the stress it allows on perspective. By viewing one situation in terms of another, it permits parallels to be asserted in a fluid classificatory field. The argument between Ton Tho Tuong and Phan Van Tri was whether the former was a true patriot in urging collaboration with a formidable foreign state, so as to learn the secrets of its power, or whether he was simply an opportunist and traitor. Through the sustained use of metaphor Tuong sought similarities in the classical literature to his actions; while Tri, playing on homonymy and the different potential contexts of key words, offered a radically different perspective. The situation as such offered no clearcut interpretation. Determining its nature depended on the rival poets' deployment of comparison and contrast, and their implications. Metaphor here is political: and it was in part through Tri's greater skill and subtlety in matching and rephrasing Tuong's claims that his view came to be accepted.

Furthermore, poetic dialogues in Vietnam were not a rarified communion between scholars of little relevance to anything else. Where we tend to treat power and poetry as antithetical and substantively different, the Vietnamese did not. Davidson remarks that "in Vietnam, poetry and politics have never been very far apart." Not only were the literati in charge of the country's administration, so that power underwrote knowledge and knowledge power; but what kinds of power there were, and how they were to be managed were delineated by discursive rules. For it was expertise in Confucian texts which defined a person as fit for power and also defined what powers were recognized.

My own essay discusses explicitly the relation of meaning, context and power. It considers how the definition of context in Bali turns on questions of power. This point leads to an examination of the theories of human nature which observers have imputed to the Balinese to explain their culture and actions; and how the Balinese represent the position in quite different—and incommensurate—ways. I suggest that most accounts, whether they see the Balinese as "constructing," "dramatizing," or "negotiating" their culture are *prima facie* wrong, because the models of human nature invoked are quite alien to those the Balinese themselves use in accounting for their actions.

All the contributors are concerned to avoid grand generalizations of the kind which positivism made popular. Theorizing is the easier the less one knows about the history and culture of the people under study. Detailed knowledge of context is vital to an understanding of the kinds of issues with which we are interested. Part of the relevance of context in Southeast Asia arises from the weakness of correspondence theories of truth and meaning which, my essay suggests, may also be alien to at least one such society's style of argument. It is true that one drawback of coherence, or contextual, theories is that they make it hard to generalize. This difficulty may be no bad thing if we consider how far the alternatives have led to hypostatizing what happens and turning labels into realities.

Correspondence theory rests on a referential view of language which the authors in this book show to be inadequate for finely detailed research. The theory presupposes the existence of essences in things, events or states, such that words can depict, or denote, what is relevant or essential with reasonable accuracy. It is far from clear, however, that the peoples we are discussing share this view of language and the world. In any case, culture is not a "thing": it is asserted, challenged, and misunderstood by people on different occasions. The stress on metaphor in several of the essays is a way of looking at how language is used in actual situations. The link is at once semantic and political. People recognize different styles of argument and ways of producing texts; and knowledge is not just power to influence interpretations but also the ability to state, or even instantiate, whatever culture is, or what the correct context should be.

It is the potentially infinite range of relevant contexts which makes it so hard to define their implications in practice. The contributors, however, have attempted, more or less directly, to explore at least some of the possibilities suggested by the interplay of semantic contexts and social, political, and other situations.[23]

The degree to which ascertaining, or arguing, the relevant context is a matter of daily concern is discussed in my own contribution. Even so apparently simple a matter as the jural definition of "the village" depends upon context, in the sense that different interest groups may argue for the relevance of different sets of relationships. The ability to interpret events by defining what kind of situation is at stake and what ties are germane is a vital part of all political activity in Bali. We often take too narrow a view of power by confining it to the mobilizing of support for winning confrontations. Yet to be able to classify how events are to be considered, i.e., the relevant context, is crucial in political power in Bali and probably elsewhere.

It is, of course, also possible to discover, or invent, new ideas and uses of power: definitions of new offenses against the state or person, positing extended areas of personal responsibility (over sexuality, one's intentions and so on) or simply refined techniques of surveillance.[24] Part of the difficulty in seeing the part which knowledge plays in forming (new) power comes from our tendency to regard the terms as denoting quite different sorts of substantive entities.

Strictly speaking, then, the title of this book might refer simply to contexts and meanings.[25] It is of little import so long as it is clear the words are simply labels for kinds of relationships. Each of the contributors has been looking at the ways in which meanings and powers are recognized and incorporated (Jacob), argued over (Taylor, McVey), reinterpreted (Demaine), and constituted or expressed in different forms (Davidson, Hobart). We are not talking about meaning as being some separate realm, intuited through symbols or enshrined only in language; nor is power conceived of as linked exclusively to the state, law, violence, and so on. Besides these phenomena there are other powers which may be summoned up and bring complexity, uncertainty, and potentiality to people's lives. After all, in some circumstances a grasp of meanings is a form of power, while powers are culturally celebrated and challenged in poetry, theater, and everyday life. And new possibilities always threaten to disturb the comfortable predictions of scholars.

What categories like religion, theater, and literature have in common is that they are about knowledge, a knowledge which is made manifest or attains its potentiality by people using it in different contexts. Neither knowledge, meaning, nor power exist *in vitreo*. If knowledge concerns the potentialities of situations, power may usefully be seen as the uses, or exemplifications, of such potentialities. In a way, knowledge and power are two aspects of the same kinds of process, or better the same process seen from two different perspectives. So perhaps it is fitting that the provenance of this book, its context if you like, is an institution whose motto is:

KNOWLEDGE IS POWER

---

1. The controversy was started off largely by Edward Said's book, *Orientalism* (New York: Pantheon, 1978). The lasting brunt of Said's criticism of the grounding of traditional Orientalist studies has been succinctly stated by an historian of India.

"Orientalist discourse presents itself as a form of knowledge that is both different from and superior to the knowledge that the Orientals have had of themselves ... the knowledge of the Orientalist, known nowadays as an 'area studies' specialist, appears as rational, logical, scientific, realistic, and objective. The knowledge of the Orientals, by contrast, often seems irrational, illogical, unscientific, unrealistic, and subjective. The knowledge of the Orientalist is privileged ... (and) has appropriated the power to represent the Oriental, to translate and explain his (and her) thoughts and acts not only to Europeans and Americans but also the Orientals themselves. ... In many respects the intellectual activities of the Orientalists have even produced in Asia the very Orient which it constructed in its own discourse." (Ronald Inden, "Orientalist Constructions of India," *Journal of Modern Asian Studies*, forthcoming.)

I am grateful to Ron Inden for letting me use his forthcoming article on Orientalism, and for many stimulating conversations, of which this introduction is in part an offshoot. I am also grateful to the other contributors who made many helpful suggestions. Special thanks goes to Bob Taylor who took the trouble to redraft and greatly improve the original version of this essay.

2. Cf. Johannes Fabian, *Time and the Other* (New York: Columbia University Press, 1983).

3. Donald K. Emmerson, " 'Southeast Asia': What's in a Name?" *Journal of Southeast Asian Studies*, 15: 1 (1984), pp. 1–21.

4. Nelson Goodman, *Languages of Art* (Brighton: Harvester, 1981), pp. 27–31.

5. See Michael Reddy, "The Conduit Metaphor," in *Metaphor and Thought*, ed. Andrew Ortony (Cambridge: Cambridge University Press, 1979), pp. 284–324.

6. Murray Edelman, *The Symbolic Uses of Politics* (Urbana: University of Illinois Press, 1964), p. 130.

7. These are, respectively, the referential, emotive, conative, phatic, metalingual, and poetic functions (see Roman Jakobson, "Concluding Statement: Linguistics and Poetics," in *Style and Language*, ed. Thomas A. Sebeok [Cambridge, Mass.: MIT Press, 1960], pp. 353–58). No doubt, these distinctions will be superseded. As they are the product of a particular culture at a particular time, any reference to their applicability to Southeast Asian societies is provisional, pending more detailed studies of indigenous ideas about language use.

8. Dan Sperber, *Rethinking Symbolism*, trans. Alice L. Morton (Cambridge: Cambridge University Press, 1975), p. 52.

9. For a telling criticism of the symbol-as-irrational, as well as a useful distinction between the internal and external motivation of "symbols" (roughly, what is significant by virtue of its place within a set of ideas, and what by virtue of reference to a perceived world), see Nigel Frederick Barley, *Symbolic Structures: An Exploration of the Culture of the Dowayos* (Cambridge: Cambridge University Press, 1983). On the history of Western ideas about symbolism and sign theory, see especially Tzvetan Todorov's *Theories of the Symbol*, trans.

Catherine Porter (Oxford: Blackwell, 1982) and his *Symbolism and Interpretation*, trans. Catherine Porter (London: Routledge & Kegan Paul, 1983).

10. There is a regrettable tendency to find behind current behavior an unverifiable, earlier *fons et origo* from which the present is presumed to devolve by some massive inertia. One of the oldest, but hardiest, fallacies about "the Other" is that it is bound by illogical habit whereas we are rational and adaptable. We have very little detailed knowledge about what the Thai bureaucracy was like in the past.

11. See Thomas S. Kuhn, *The Structure of Scientific Revolutions* (London: University of Chicago Press, 1962); and the commentary on Kuhn's ideas in Margaret Masterman, "The Nature of a Paradigm," in *Criticism and the Growth of Knowledge*, ed. Imre Lakatos and Alan Musgrave (London: Cambridge University Press, 1970), pp. 59–89.

12. Her reticence contrasts sharply with David P. Chandler's "Songs at the Edge of the Forest: Perception of Order in Three Cambodian Texts," in *Moral Order and the Question of Change: Essays on Southeast Asian Thought*, ed. David K. Wyatt and Alexander Woodside (New Haven: Yale University, Southeast Asia Studies, Monograph Series No. 24 (1982), pp. 53–77.

13. The best known version of such a view is the Sapir-Whorf hypothesis (Lee Whorf, *Language, Thought and Reality: Selected Writings of Benjamin Lee Whorf*, ed. J. B. Carroll [Cambridge, Mass.: MIT Press, 1956]). The strong interpretation that, roughly, language determines available meaning and so thought, is as absurd as is the contrary that there is no connection at all. This suggests that there is something wrong in the formulation of the problem and its constitutive concepts. If "language" and "meaning" are ambiguous and misleadingly coherent ideas, then "thought" is just as vague. Latter-day essentialism requires the conscious experiencing subject as a cornerstone of any theory, dubious as this assumption may be (see Ian Hacking, *Why Does Language Matter to Philosophy?* [Cambridge: Cambridge University Press, 1975]). Where I refer to thought or ideas here I mean them in the sense of *ex post facto* assertions about what has happened.

14. David J. Parkin, *The Cultural Definition of Political Response: Lineal Destiny among the Luo* (London: Academic Press, 1978), pp. 286–330.

15. The constitution of an audience as those to be governed, an electorate, or the masses is one of the more interesting and ignored aspects of the modern political process. For a good discussion, see Jean Baudrillard, *In the Shadow of the Silent Majorities... or the End of the Social*, trans. Paul Foss, Paul Patton, and John Johnston (New York: Semiotext[e], 1983).

16. In keeping with my point that the language of academic argument involves representation as much as any other, the use of metaphor in this introduction needs comment. "Borrowing," "importing," or "adapting," which I have used to describe how certain terms or ideas were taken up in parts of Southeast Asia, are mercantile, or material, metaphors, just as references to "clarity" or "perspective" are visual. It is questionable whether trying to find some neutral language would solve any problems. Our stress in this book is on how much epistemological usages, including our own efforts, are part of a long history of relations between peoples. At least we can be aware (in part) of the consequences of our own categories!

17. See the discussion in Ruth M. Kempson, *Presupposition and the Delimitations of Semantics* (Cambridge: Cambridge University Press, Cambridge Studies in Linguistics 15, 1975).

18. See Nelson Goodman, *Of Mind and Other Matters* (Cambridge, Mass.: Harvard University Press, 1984), pp. 59–60.

19. Speaking of the complex blend of religions, philosophy, and practice known as Agama Jawa, McVey comments that "the Agama Jawa is powerfully syncretic, capable of turning something alien into an avatar and confirmation of itself." *Wayang* is the classical vehicle for expressing, or embodying, Agama Jawa.

20. Where Vietnamese poetry involves two media, speech (or song) and music, shadow theater further introduces iconography (as well as movement) between which a lively play is possible.

21. John Searle, "Metaphor," in *Metaphor and Thought*, ed. Ortony, pp. 92–123, at p. 94.

22. See Goodman, *Languages*, pp. 68–80. As this Introduction explores the potential uses of Goodman's approach to representation—

which attempts to formulate an alternative to correspondence or copy theories—I have followed his nominalism in avoiding postulating more than is necessary. Accordingly, I have not sought to draw any hard and fast line between "context" and "situation." (Cf. the use of "context of situation" in Bronislaw Malinowski, "The Problem of Meaning in Primitive Language," supplement in *The Meaning of Meaning*, ed. Charles Kay Ogden and Ivor Armstrong Richards [London: Kegan Paul, 1923], pp. 451–510, at pp. 506–10.)

23. Here it may be useful to mention the unjustly ignored, pioneering texts of Malinowski: "The Problem of Meaning"; and *Coral Gardens and Their Magic* (London: Allen and Unwin, 1935), vol. 2. My concern here is not to formulate a theory of context as such; I have discussed the problems involved in "Meaning or Moaning? An Ethnographic Note on a Little Understood Tribe," in *Semantic Anthropology*, ed. David J. Parkin (London: Academic Press, ASA Monographs in Social Anthropology No. 22, 1982), pp. 39–63, and "Texte est un con," in *Contexts and Levels: Essays on Hierarchy*, ed. Robert H. Barnes, Daniel de Coppet, and Robert J. Parkin (Oxford: Journal of the Anthropological Society, Occasional Paper No. 4, 1985), pp. 33–53. See also my essay in the present volume.

24. See Michel Foucault's *Discipline and Punish*, trans. Alan Sheridan (Harmondsworth: Allen Lane, 1977) and *The History of Sexuality*, vol. 1, trans. Robert Hurley (Harmondsworth: Allen Lane, 1979).

25. Following Foucault, who prefers to speak of "truths" rather than "Truth," one might also speak of "powers," keeping "Power" for those systems of representation which portray diverse powers as part of some transcendental construct. See the texts cited in the note above, as well as his "Truth and Power," in *Michel Foucault: Power, Truth, Strategy*, ed. Meaghan Morris and Paul Patton (Sydney: Feral Publications, 1979); and Paul Patton, "Of Power and Prisons" in the same volume.

2

THE *WAYANG* CONTROVERSY IN INDONESIAN COMMUNISM

Ruth McVey

*The four of them are I, and I am the four of them.
Communist solidarity demands that I unite my stance
with theirs and choose the "path of death."
With the four of them, I have been five-in-one.*

This statement was made by Sudisman, the last surviving member of the inner core of the Indonesian Communist leadership, to the Extraordinary Military Tribunal which condemned him to death in July 1967.[1] The four to whom he referred were the other principal members of the standing committee of the party's presidium: Aidit, Njoto, Lukman, and Sakirman. The "five-in-one" are the Pandawa, brother-heroes of the Mahabharata cycle in the *wayang purwa*, the classical shadow-play of Java.

Strange metaphor for a Communist: the Pandawa are princes, and their adventures reflect courtly life and the ethics of the *satria*, the knightly warrior. The central plays of the *wayang purwa* repertory are drawn from the Indian Mahabharata and Ramayana cycles, part of an ancient cultural borrowing by Javanese chiefs who saw in Indic ideas of the state a means to strengthen their own claims to power. Through the *wayang* plays, ideas of royal power, hierarchy, and appropriate behavior have been transmitted from court to village, a process which has continued long after colonialism effectively destroyed their royal source. *Wayang* is par excellence the expression of Javanese "feudal" values, the chains of tradition and subservience which Indonesian Communism was dedicated to break.

In addition to this hostility toward an ancient and unacceptable social order, there is a deep difference between the philosophical vision of Marxism and that of the classical shadow-play. *Wayang* teaches that contradictions are not overcome; they may only be understood and thereby borne. The victory of the Pandawa over the Kurawa does not mean the triumph of good over evil, for justice and nobility are not exclusive to their side and, however rightful the Pandawa's struggle to reclaim their kingdom and however predestined the final battle, the slaying of their Kurawa relatives is a sin from which they cannot escape unscathed. Ambivalence and imperfect choice condition all existence, and one can only act in accordance with the values appropriate to one's allotted role.[2]

Marxism does not harbor such doubts. For it, as for most modern Western thought, history progresses. The past is overcome, a higher stage of civilization is reached. In Marxist thought, history is the process of man's realization of himself. In this effort man is at once active—in control of his destiny—and carried forward by the working of large social forces: man makes himself through arduous endeavor, but he is bound in the end to make himself well. Marxism is optimistic where *wayang* is not; Marxism teaches that understanding dictates struggle, *wayang* that it enjoins acceptance.

Yet Sudisman seems to have found no real contradiction between the two visions. He was certainly serious in his *wayang* reference: the speech from which I have quoted was his last opportunity to state his beliefs publicly, and he was clearly conscious of this circumstance. Nor would many Javanese Communists of his generation and background have found the metaphor strange; on the contrary, it would have indicated to them his profound commitment to his party's cause. Indonesian Communist strength was, in fact, concentrated in that part of the population for which *wayang* had particular meaning. Sometimes called *abangan*, they were Muslims whose beliefs were heavily influenced by the island's older faiths—Hinduism, Buddhism, and more ancient ideas often called animism but more deeply concerned with man's relationship with his immortal ancestors. For this amalgam—the Agama Jawa, or the Religion of Java—*wayang* was the supreme expression.[3]

For *abangan* Javanese, *wayang* is in the first place the symbol of a great cultural heritage. However, it does not simply recall the past; if that were its only purpose, it would very likely have gone the way of other Southeast Asian high arts in this century, retreating into an ever narrower cultural and social space. It has maintained its relevance because it does not exist on just one level of meaning or time. As Alton Becker has pointed out, the various categories of *wayang* puppet—knights, gods, clowns, demons—represent different epistemological worlds, each taking part in the general action in terms of its own order of meaning and using the language appropriate to its world: Old Javanese (Kawi), Sanskrit, modern Javanese, and now also Indonesian.[4] The central point of the action is the clash between these worlds, usually set off by what appears to be happenstance, but in fact occurring to demonstrate the character of their opposition.

There is no time past in the *wayang*'s terms, for in its vision all time coexists. The world of the heroes is not removed from the present but precedes it in the sense of setting a precedent, a prior, because purer, case which serves as a criterion for action now.[5] Hence the inclination of Javanese to see individuals and events in terms of *wayang* characters and *lakon* (plays), and to choose as exemplars for themselves those *wayang* figures perceived to be most in accordance with each perceiver's character and situation. The habit—as Sudisman's speech showed—was by no means abandoned by Javanese who came to believe in Communism.[6]

The very contrast between the *wayang* vision and that of Communism may have been a source of their joint appeal for *abangan* Javanese, for Marxism-Leninism provided, as the *wayang* world did not, a sense of competence to deal with problems of the modern world, something sorely missed by a people who had suffered much from colonial rule and from involvement in a world market economy. Ideological consistency is something felt inwardly and is not necessarily reflected in a formally coherent vision—certainly not for a people whose culture endorses the containment of opposites.[7] In any event the attraction was there, and this, in the period of the Communist movement's legality before the coup of 1965, raised the question of what the party should do about it.

If *wayang* suffered severe ideological disabilities from the Communist viewpoint, it also offered opportunities. Its assumption of a moral model and its denial of barriers created by time gave it a didactic potential; indeed, the inculcation of values had been one of its historic purposes.[8] The emphasis on a clash of epistemological worlds could easily be adapted to the portrayal of class conflict and competing social philosophies. Moreover, *wayang* could be used to comment on current affairs. It is common for contemporary references to be inserted into the classical tale narrated by the puppet-master *(dalang)*. Though strikingly anomalous to the observer used to mainstream Western theatrical conventions, these references are important from the philosophical viewpoint of *wayang*, for they link the Javanese of today with the world of the ancestors, and thereby serve a central concern of the Agama Jawa. Precisely those elements are taken from the contemporary and the mundane which seem to grate most harshly when juxtaposed to the past, for it is part of the *wayang's* function to resolve such contradictions by placing them in the larger, eternal pattern.

The *dalang* is expected to remark on contemporary affairs and problems of relevance to his audience. The puppet-master who performs a play without interpolation—a "book *dalang*"—is considered an artist of only minor ability.[9] He makes such comments most openly through the clown figures, but also through veiled allusions *(sindiran)* throughout the play.[10] In a country where adverse comment on those in power has rarely been permitted, *wayang* performances have often been the only source of critical observations on public affairs, and interpreting the *dalang's* allusions is a favorite game of the *wayang* audience.

In particular, the popular and important role of the clowns *(punakawan)* has great potential for communicating a social message. The clowns appear to be an entirely Javanese addition to the Indian myth cycles on which the dramas are based, and they play a role which is more than mere comic relief. For the Mahabharata cycle the main clown-figures are Semar and his sons, servants to the five Pandawa.[11] They are grotesque in appearance, crude in behavior, and comic in effect. They dress in peasant clothes and carry bill-hooks rather than krisses. They are the lowliest of the low, but they are also something more, for Semar is a god.[12] He has been assigned quasi-human form and menial status, but he remains divine. When the god Kresna appears to advise the Pandawa, Semar of all the company speaks to him familiarly, for he alone can address a god as an equal. When the Pandawa consult him their plans go well; when he is absent or ignored they meet disaster. Thus a cultural instrument for transmitting courtly values also conveys the idea that a peasant may be ultimately higher than the king, the outwardly coarse may be divine, and the poor wiser than those placed above them. The celebration of such principles in the *wayang purwa* relieves the tensions of a highly stratified social structure, reminding common folk of their value but also of their duty of service, and those in power of their fallibility and their dependence on the loyalty of their retainers. In the *wayang* plays themselves the clowns, while essential, do not exist without the heroes, and they are rarely relieved of their menial position.[13] However, with very little change a quite different point could be made.

One might imagine, therefore, that the Indonesian Communist Party (Partai Komunis Indonesia, PKI) would have bent its efforts to capturing the *wayang* for its own ends. In this, it would have followed a long line of rulers and movements which sought to assert through *wayang* their particular claims on the Javanese heart.[14] In fact, however, *wayang* proved a singularly sensitive subject for the Communists in their period of post-independence legality (1950–65). It was the center of an open, if sporadic, battle among the party leadership, occasioning the only major inner-party controversy to be waged publicly during the first half of the 1960s, a time when the PKI otherwise sought to present a monolithic front under Sukarno's Guided Democracy. Ranged on one side were such powerful contenders as Ir. Sakirman and (we may assume, though he played no public role in the debate) Sudisman; on the other, such weighty persons as D. N. Aidit, party chairman, and Joebaar Ajoeb, head of the cultural front Lekra (Lembaga Kebudayaan Rakyat—Institute of People's Culture).

There was, of course, a certain danger in attempting to grasp an instrument with such deep cultural ties. The Agama Jawa is powerfully syncretic, capable of turning something alien into an avatar and confirmation of itself. It had not mattered to the *wayang purwa* that new dynasts had introduced new cycles with their own styles of puppet and *gamelan* orchestra. Through these innovations such leaders had fortified their rule by establishing its ancestry in the ancient past; yet their efforts also acknowledged the essential *wayang* vision of things, while none of the new cycles flourished more than locally or temporarily, let alone replaced the *wayang purwa* as the central myth. Even Islam had been absorbed: the Javanese had accepted that religion (some lightly, some deeply) in spite of the difference of its vision, which, like Marxism, saw the world in terms of the unidirectional working-out of a great idea, and in spite of the contradiction between the Hindu element in the *wayang purwa* and Muslim religious thought. Certain *lakon* were reinterpreted to reflect the new faith, and some of the more popular plays of the *wayang purwa*'s secondary tradition *(lakon-lakon carangan)* were said to be inspired by ideas derived from Sufi mysticism. New cycles were developed around Islamic themes, and their introduction was attributed to the holy messengers *(wali)* who were supposed to have brought Islam to Java.[15] Yet none of this had threatened the *wayang purwa*'s position; if anything, it had helped remove doubts that there was any ultimate contradiction between *wayang* and Islam. There seemed no reason to think that Communist elements could not in due course be similarly absorbed and transformed, thereby rejuvenating and reaffirming the Javanese world.

Marxism, however, is not syncretic; it does not tolerate visions other than its own. Lenin particularly stressed the need for discipline, for high ideological boundaries and strict organizational control to give maximum coherence to the party as the spearhead of the revolution. A syncretic view meant, at the end of the day, divided loyalties. If the Javanese did not see everything in Communism, what *did* they see in it? If it was merely a variation on what was basically an *abangan* cultural theme, could one really press issues which went against traditional Javanese values?[16]

Indonesian Communism was by no means the first ideology to confront this dilemma. Islam, likewise an exclusionist faith, had at first penetrated Java by accommodating to existing traditions and power structures. In the nineteenth century, however, the political pressures and cultural disorientation resulting from colonial subjection had brought to a head the latent tension in the relationship between Islam and the Agama Jawa. Reforming groups arose to call for the purification of Muslim observance, an end to confusion of Islam with older beliefs, and rejection of social hierarchs now compromised by their collaboration with the Dutch. These groups were concerned with creating barriers, in the first place against the foreigners and their alien faith, but also against those groups and practices which were seen as the cause of weakness and confusion, preventing an effective response to colonial rule.[17]

The ideological self-confidence that resulted from this new discipline provided a moral armament against the uncertainties and humiliations of colonialism. Yet it also helped to create a division between those who oriented themselves primarily towards Islam and those who did not, between those who found in the old observances a source of weakness and those who still saw in them the essence of what it was to be Javanese. A fissure opened between strict Muslims (often called *santri*) and the more ambiguously Islamic *abangan*. The *selamatan* (ritual communal feast) and the *wayang* play accompanied by *gamelan* orchestra were essential rites of *abangan* life; now, good *santri* rejected them. *Wayang*, it was said, violated Islam's prohibition on the representation of the human form, so that even the myth cycles with Islamic themes were unacceptable. The *gamelan*, compromised by its association with the *wayang* and old Javanese court culture, was replaced in strong *santri* communities by musical instruments and styles derived from the Middle East. As the difference in culture accelerated, so too did the potential for hostility between *santri* and *abangan* groups—a potential that was encouraged both in colonial and postcolonial times by political movements and powerholders who thought to profit by it. Even if *santri* and *abangan* lived in the same village, they were, by the mid-twentieth century, very likely to inhabit different hamlets, to dress somewhat differently, and to express themselves culturally and politically in different ways.[18]

The Communists could observe the political advantages of such apartness during the parliamentary democracy of the 1950s. While the PKI attracted the disillusioned among the *abangan* masses, drawing them away from the Nationalist Party (PNI), which many found too identified with the traditional bureaucratic elite *(priyayi)*, it made very little headway among the *santri* population. Poor Javanese *santri* remained solidly behind their religious-political leaders, impervious to the Communists' generalized appeal to the *rakyat*, the common man. Whatever doubts the *santri* may have had concerning Islam's ability to provide answers for postrevolutionary Indonesia, they accepted their religion's claims to exclusive ideological commitment and gave their political loyalties to parties which spoke for Islam.

But the democratic experiment also showed clearly the limitations of such exclusiveness. The erection of barriers between *santri* and *Islam statistik*—nominal Muslims—meant that although ninety percent of Indonesia's population was formally Islamic, the religion was politically a minority orientation, excluded from any real power by Indonesia's postrevolutionary elite, whose sentiments were secular and *abangan*. Members of this elite viewed devout Muslims as dangerous and aggressive *Islam fanatik*, to be handled delicately but under no circumstances to be allowed to prevail. Moreover, the democratic period illustrated the fact that insistence on doctrinal purity easily creates internal dispute within a religious community. The Javanese *santri* were deeply divided between those who adhered to an orthodoxy based on local Muslim tradition, gathered politically around the Nahdatul Ulama party, and those who looked to the modernist religious ideas represented by the Masyumi. Since for these groups correct faith was the most important issue, their primary antagonisms were with each other, and this presented secular politicians with an excellent means of controlling the forces of Islam.

At the same time, the Communists were by no means as well placed as Muslim zealots to impose discipline on their following. Their faith had penetrated Javanese life much more recently and superficially. True, Marxist vocabulary had become part of the general nationalist discourse, but the number of people willing to commit themselves to a world view shaped wholly by Marxist-Leninist ideology was undoubtedly very small indeed. Had the PKI leadership stressed discipline and orthodoxy above all else the party would have remained (like many other Communist movements faced with this choice) an insignificant sect waiting for failure of the existing order to turn the populace towards a new social discipline. No doubt there were PKI cadres who would have found such a course congenial and prudent, but those who led the party from 1951 to 1965 had embarked on a radically different strategy, which achieved such apparent success that no effective objections to it were raised. They sought as much mass support as they could gather, and this strategy meant blurring boundaries and stressing cultural compatibility. Moreover, their own understanding of Communism was heavily penetrated by nationalist ideology, to the extent that they even tacitly denied some fundamental Marxist-Leninist assumptions.[19] One might have thought, therefore, that they would have seized upon *wayang* as a means of conveying their message and at the same time reaffirming their national character, or, at the least, that they would have found the art not a serious issue at that stage of their movement's development. As we have seen, however, they found the matter more difficult.

A problem of identity did indeed lie at the bottom of their debate over *wayang*, but it was one of national rather than ideological boundaries. The problem is illustrated very clearly in Sudisman's speech, which concluded:[20]

> I am a Communist who was born in Java; and therefore it is my duty, in accordance with the custom of the Javanese, to take my leave by saying:
> First: *matur nuwun*, I thank all those who feel that they have helped me in the course of the struggle.
> Second: *njuwun gunging pangaksama*, a thousand times I ask forgiveness, above all to the progressive and revolutionary masses who feel that I have harmed them in the course of the struggle.
> Third: *njuwun pangestu*, I ask for blessings, especially from my family, my wife and my children, as I leave to undergo the verdict of the law.
> Long live the Republic of Indonesia!
> Long live the PKI!

This is far from the stereotypical style of Marxist-Leninist oration favored by the PKI for its public discourse. Sudisman was not attempting to present himself as socialist man, as an internationally recognizable martyr in the Communist cause, or as the defiant revolutionary conceding nothing to his enemies. Rather, he took upon himself the image of the *wayang* hero of high morality, obeying the *satria* code by assuming responsibility for all that resulted from his deeds, acting out his destiny, and accepting his fate. The liberation of his language from the straitjacket of normal PKI discourse results in imagery which is moving, but which cannot be understood except as an oration by a Javanese to people who shared his cultural assumptions. It is clear that he did not intend this as a qualification of his Communist belief; rather that, in his last opportunity to make himself known, he found the emotionally deeper discourse of his existence as a Javanese the most meaningful way to express his faith. Nor, clearly, did he intend the fact that he identified himself above all as Javanese to limit his Indonesian-ness. For him, as for most Javanese, there was no incompatibility between the two: to be Javanese was one way, very likely the best way, to be Indonesian.

And here was the rub. Three of Sudisman's four comrades-in-leadership might have fancied themselves with him as fellow Pandawa, but the Sumatran Aidit certainly did not, and he was party chairman. To a very great extent, the quarrel in the PKI over the *wayang* was thus an argument between Javanese and Outer Islanders. In many ways the PKI was a Javanese party, though it gave non-Javanese many high posts and determinedly (and, from the late 1950s, quite successfully) expanded its regional base. The party's formal discourse did not express this cultural leaning, for it kept to the highly stylized speech of Marxism-Leninism, reduced, for purposes of general comprehension and acceptance, to the simplest ideological vocabulary. Yet this rigid and impoverished language had little to offer for informal talk among party cadres, and the frequent use of *wayang* references in everyday communication was a reminder to the Outer Islanders that they were, however high their posts, in a certain sense outsiders.[21]

The problem was not limited to the PKI, for *abangan* Javanese domination of politics more generally meant that Outer Islanders had to adjust to Javanese ways. This cultural weight grew heavier under Sukarno's Guided Democracy (and would increase still more under Suharto's New Order), when the Indonesian political vocabulary became suffused with Javanese images and words. Those who would participate in the national elite had to conform, but the non-Javanese disliked it; their resentment—when not expressed in regional rebellion—frequently took the form of identifying Javanese culture with the "feudal" values which accounted for Indonesia's backwardness.

The PKI's debate on the *wayang* reflected and exacerbated these resentments. To illustrate: when in 1965—a time when the controversy was in full swing—I asked Aidit to explain the matter of the "reform" of the *wayang*, he was quite abrupt. Though he had been willing to discourse at length, if not necessarily with frankness, on many politically sensitive topics, he immediately dismissed the *wayang* issue with the recommendation that I see the man in charge of the party's cultural activities, Banda Harahap. So I did; but that gentleman, a Batak, reacted with acerbity, declaring that as a non-Javanese he knew, and wanted to know, nothing of *wayang*. As the two leaders were heavily involved in the debate one could scarcely escape the impression that they suffered from a surfeit rather than from ignorance of the subject.

But the *wayang* controversy was not simply an argument between Javanese and Outer Islanders. Among those party members who called for the reform of *wayang* there were also Javanese. They were a mere handful and they were far less well-placed in the party than *wayang*'s defenders. But they had one great advantage, which was what caused their opponents to make any concessions at all: they appeared to represent the future.

They were, even more than most of the PKI leaders, part of a culture which formed the way of life for Indonesia's postrevolutionary ruling elite. This semi-Westernized style—which has been given the somewhat awkward title of Indonesia's "metropolitan superculture"—became established early in this century in the great cities of the Netherlands Indies, as a substantial number of Indonesians obtained a Western-style education and employment in the modern sector of the economy and administration (the colonial regime itself, the professions, or European business).[22] To members of this emerging elite "modernity," as evidenced in European (and from the 1950s American) industrial civilization, was both a cultural goal and a political weapon. Insofar as they acquired the trappings of modernity, it legitimized their claims to replace the Dutch as the rulers of Indonesia, for it was by their expertise in dealing with the modern world that the Netherlanders had argued their tutelary right. It also legitimized the new nationalist leaders' precedence over the traditional ruling elites of Java and the Outer Islands, for the old chiefly families could be portrayed as *feodal* and outmoded, incapable of meeting the challenge of the West or coping with the socio-economic change colonialism had brought about.

But however useful modernity was as a mystique, it created the problem of establishing a sense of cultural self that was something more than a hybrid of European and local traits. Hence the great concern—psychological as well as political—for establishing an Indonesian national identity, and the intense ambivalence towards things deemed "Western" and "foreign."

The problem acquired another dimension after the Revolution, when the emergent urban life-style became the culture of the new ruling class. "Modernity" now became the national cultural goal, though the method of achieving it remained in dispute. For the general population, modernity became the image of the new official high culture, as represented by the urban elite. The venue of the cultural model had changed, from the court centers of Central Java to Jakarta, but as in pre-colonial days it was embodied primarily in the ruler, his entourage, and officialdom. Because that elite was heavily Javanese and—increasingly, under Sukarno—sought to reinsure its claims for pre-eminence by adopting certain attributes of the traditional ruling class, westernization and older ideas of refinement became intertwined: it was *modèren* (modern)[23] to speak proper Indonesian or *halus* (refined) Javanese, to live in a middle-class urban house, and to belong to the class of officials. At the same time, ideas of refinement changed away from a respectful regard for all that was *kuno* (old, ancient). *Kuno* was now elided into *kolot*—old-fashioned, in a rather stubborn and countrified sense. The new word of praise was *maju*: progressive, and ipso facto new. To be *modèren* was to be urban, middle-class, cosmopolitan: the common people were thus not *modèren*, and attitudes and events that touched them but were not recognized by the elite or by official ideology did not enter the *modèren* sphere.

The activists of the Communist party were socialized into some version of *modèren* culture, their choice of the PKI indicating that they did not wish to pursue the cause of the common man by rejecting modernity as a goal.[24] Rather, they hoped to separate the idea of modernity from its identification with the postrevolutionary Establishment in order to capture its spiritual power for themselves. The PKI thus faced not only the nationalists' task of creating a goal culture that was different from the modernity of the foreigners, but also the problem of somehow divorcing itself from the *modèren* style of the Jakarta elite. This was no mean task: there was a recognizable and admired international style of ascetic Communist modernity, at the time modeled especially by the Chinese; but insofar as the PKI adopted such attributes it risked the accusation of foreignizing. A delicate balance was required between exogenous and indigenous models, between using and criticizing familiar ways, in order both to endorse modernity defined as an Indonesian quality and to assert the PKI's particular claim to it.

Accordingly, the Institute of People's Culture (Lekra) devoted itself, following its foundation in 1951, to separating a socialist aesthetic modernity from a Western-influenced "Establishment" one, opposing "Art for the People's Sake" to "Art for Art's Sake."[25] The Lekra's founders were urban intellectuals, very much new men, at odds with the Westernizers politically but not culturally. So it is perhaps not surprising that the institute's first manifesto ignored the traditional popular arts and considered the ancient high arts only insofar as their indigenous and aesthetic advantage could be separated from their "feudal" content:[26]

> The elements of foreign culture will be accepted critically, on the basis of the practical interests of the Indonesian people. Similarly, *kuno* Indonesian culture will not be rejected in its entirety but will also not be adopted unquestioningly. Ancient Indonesian culture will be accepted critically, in order to elevate a new Indonesian Culture, a People's Democratic Culture.

This might have served had the PKI sought its support basically in the urban and *modèren* sphere, but its leaders were particularly concerned to spread Communist influence among the rural masses, and these still lived very much in a traditional symbolic world. A party leadership with a modern political message had to consider carefully the means of reaching this *kolot* crowd, and the folk arts seemed all the more logical a vehicle in view of their ancient political use. For some time, however, the PKI's cultural arbiters avoided *wayang*, preferring to address themselves to those forms which they considered more oriented toward the masses. *Wayang* was thus slighted in the executive report to the Lekra's first congress in 1959, which emphasized instead the liberation of the more popular forms of entertainment from domination by the high arts: "The time is now past when the term 'artist' is reserved for famous writers and painters, while artists of film and drama, let alone *ketoprak* and *ludruk*, are referred to as derivatives of the *wayang*."[27]

The nettle had to be grasped, however, for the *wayang purwa* was too important in Javanese and not all-Indonesian character, its aristocratic and not working-class orientation, its "feudal" and not modern spirit. From the viewpoint of national leaders in a suing this aim, three major openings for attack presented themselves: *wayang*'s Javanese and not all- Indonesian character, its aristocratic and not working-class orientation, its "feudal" and not modern spirit. From the viewpoint of national leaders in a period when regionalism acutely threatened Indonesian unity, the first of these seemed the most obvious and unexceptionable target. Equally reasonable seemed the suggestion that *wayang* plays be performed in the Indonesian language. This would not only "nationalize" them but, by avoiding Javanese speech levels and archaic language, would make them both more democratic and more usable for communicating modern ideas. Yet so apparently reasonable a proposal aroused such a storm that at its 1960 plenum the Lekra leadership was forced to give the idea a very cool endorsement:[28]

> *Now, the question of an "Indonesian-language wayang."* For about six months, down to this very day, there has been a lively discussion on the matter of an "Indonesian-language *wayang*." Many questions concerning the problem have been addressed to the Secretariat, and the Secretariat has discussed the matter thoroughly. Its conclusion is that in principle Lekra approves efforts to perform the *wayang* in the Indonesian language, but this does not in the least imply an intent to divert attention and activity from *wayang* in Javanese. We are fully conscious that it is no easy thing to perform *wayang* in Indonesian.

A principal reason for this reticence was the relationship of language to the innermost meaning of the *wayang*. Ultimately, the performance of the *wayang purwa* is not an entertainment or an instruction but the enactment of a mystery.[29] Conveying sacred truths through a profane tongue and homely imagery, exchanging spiritual resonance for secular relevance, had little appeal to Javanese who were not so far separated from their traditions as to wish to delatinize their mass. These cultural conservatives included high leaders from the Communist party, who, because they had internationalized both symbol-systems, were perhaps less keenly aware of any encroaching irrelevance for the *wayang*.

The people who led the campaign to Indonesianize the *wayang* and carry out other fundamental reforms which basically aimed at secularizing the art and converting it into a didactic instrument of the PKI were, by and large, younger Javanese thoroughly acculturated into the *modèren* sphere and people from largely Sundanese West Java, where the *wayang*, usually performed with wooden *golèk* puppets rather than the flat leather *(kulit)* ones of *wayang purwa*, was more purely an entertainment and was correspondingly more flexible. These reformers were less caught up in the *wayang* world, but they were also less "inside" the party than *wayang*'s principal defenders. There was no significant age difference, since the senior party leaders had been young men themselves during the 1945–49 Revolution, but there was a marked difference in background, *wayang*'s proponents coming from more traditional lower-class (and in a few cases upper-class) Javanese backgrounds than the largely middle-class urban reformers. Moreover, in the matter of Indonesianizing *wayang* the Javanese conservatives had the support of many Outer Islanders, who saw the Indonesianization effort not as nationalizing and demystifying the *wayang* but as a new form of Javanese cultural imperialism.

As the argument heated up, a major defense of *wayang* was essayed by Politburo member Sakirman, who in 1961 published under Lekra auspices a statement of the conservative position. The greater part of his essay was devoted to the argument that, in spite of the Indian origin of its major myth cycles, *wayang* was truly Javanese in content as well as form. Critics of *wayang* had found a vulnerable point in its foreign ancestry and demanded that the old *lakon* be rejected as alien imports. To ward off this campaign, Sakirman supplied erudite references to Dutch authorities on the autochthonous origins of the *wayang;* Dutch scholars might be reactionary imperialists, but they could be thought neutral on the matter of *wayang*'s ancestry.

Having established *wayang*'s claim to Javanese authenticity it followed, for Sakirman, that it was part of Indonesia's cultural treasury and must accordingly be cherished; for him, as for Sudisman, to be Javanese was a perfect expression of being Indonesian. In the end, however, he was willing to concede that certain improvements might be made. Himself also a participant in Indonesia's *modèren* culture, he could not escape the feeling that *wayang* might need to keep up with the times, and that those who said it must change in order to survive might ultimately be right. Rather gingerly, he suggested:[30]

1) The possibility of shortening *wayang* performances from an entire night to, at the latest, two a.m.
2) The possibility of increasing understanding and popularity of the *wayang purwa* among other culture groups.
3) Reforming and perfecting interpretation of the *wayang purwa*, so that it becomes really capable of fulfilling the requirements of Revolution and Development.
4) Creating as many new *lakon* as possible, aiming on the one hand at enhancing the classical standards of the *wayang purwa* and on the other at giving democratic and patriotic instruction to the people on the basis of the lines laid down by President Sukarno in the Political Manifesto of 1959.
5) Expanding the role of Semar-Petruk-Nalagareng-Bagong [the clowns] as embodiments of popular elements *(unsur-unsur kerakjatan)* in every play.

Basically, this remained the position on reform of those who did not want to see *wayang* fundamentally changed. It conceded very little—or so it would seem—and in 1964 Aidit indicated that his patience was being sorely tried. At a party Conference on Revolutionary Art and Culture, the chairman put forward what was to be the most authoritative response to the conservative position:[31]

> There are still some of our comrades who pigheadedly reject reform, for example in the matter of *wayang*. They evidently sincerely love and cherish *wayang*. But in fact their old-fashioned *[kolot]* view will kill it off, because without renewal the present generation—not to speak of generations to come—will not be drawn to *wayang;* its audience will dwindle till only the old people are left. And when those oldsters have died, that will be the end of the *wayang* audience. The blind love of these *kolot* comrades must be fought, not by interfering with their pleasure but by adding new *lakon* to those existing and by attracting them, willy-nilly, to the new. Therefore, the new and revised *lakon* must be better, more beautiful, and of a higher artistic standard than the old.

For Aidit, Outer Islander and new man, it was very easy to believe that the new could be more beautiful than the old; indeed, it was probably hard to feel otherwise. The old, to him, was dead: the dialectic of history demanded the improvement of all forms, and *"the question is not whether or not there can be reform, but how we will carry it out. Once again I emphasize, the reform of all popular folk arts cannot be ignored."*[32]

Nor was Aidit willing to admit the kind of compromise that would pour the new message into old forms, using classical figures to symbolize modern forces. This, to his mind, simply created a chimera, disturbing to the eye as well as the ideology. It went against reality, prevented people from gaining a true historical materialist view of the origin of events, and implied, in short, a vulgar concept of renewal. New figures were needed, but, as people were used to puppets of great artistic refinement, it would be necessary to create them at a high aesthetic level.[33]

In arguing for the voluntary conversion of the party's cultural die-hards to a reform of the *wayang*, Aidit allowed for the coexistence of both forms under party auspices. But it was easy to see where the leader's heart lay, and in the months that followed the cultural conference much vigor was displayed by the reformers in proposing improvements to the art. These innovations were of two main kinds, technical and ideological. The first included shortening the playing time (a change on which almost everyone could agree), the use of electric light rather than the flickering *bléncong* oil-lamp to illuminate the screen, the use of a stage without a screen, the use of more than one *dalang*, and abandoning the customary requirement that the *dalang* wear traditional Javanese dress.

These technical changes were not conceived as having ideological implications, although some were given a Marxist justification by their proponents—for instance, by arguing that the use of several *dalang* represented a "mass line."[34] Basically, they were aimed at ease in performance: the use of several *dalang*, for example, demanded less knowledge and physical endurance on the part of each individual puppeteer. They also fitted the reformers' image of what was modern. Hence they mimicked Western stage and cinema (by abandoning the shadow-screen *[kelir]*, for example) and also notions of time: modern man, tied to office and factory schedules, cannot afford to spend all night at a performance.

The PKI reformers' recommendations were by no means original: they were, in fact, quite in line with the innovations being urged by *wayang* reformers outside the party. Non-Communist advocates of renovation, if more solidly middle-class and less radical in their politics, were very much the same kind of people as the Communist proponents of *wayang* reform, and the coincidence of their perception reflected their joint participation in *modèren* culture.

Ever since the early 1920s Javanese cultural modernizers had been concerned to use *wayang* for the purpose of enlightening the *rakyat*, and the more radical among them saw this as most practicable if new forms were developed portraying ordinary people (or real leaders) in modern dress, acting out the political and social dramas of the day.[35] During the unsettled times of the Japanese occupation and the Revolution there was a spate of efforts at creating new puppet styles for "realistic" shadow-plays, using only human characters, a common language, and a single kind of time. In 1944 the Javanese educationalist R. M. Said introduced the *wayang suluh*, the puppets of which represented human figures in contemporary dress.[36] Its purpose was to convey moral and political instruction as part of the national awakening, especially by portraying the lives and deeds of exemplary leaders. During the Revolution the *wayang perjuangan* was developed by the Republic's official information service following a resolution by the 1946 Youth Congress that there be created a *wayang* form which would convey the message of struggle to the people. *Wayang perjuangan* also used puppets in contemporary dress, representing naturalistically the leaders of the independence movement and their opponents.

A compromise between such unambiguous forms and the *wayang purwa* was the *wayang pancasila*, created during the Revolution by Empu Hadi, an employee of the Republican information service in Yogyakarta. His creation used traditional *wayang purwa* figures but renamed them to indicate through allusion and wordplay the chief figures in the Revolution—just the kind of solution Aidit found particularly objectionable. The possibility of using the traditional *wayang purwa* figures had a clear advantage, since new ones did not have to be provided, identities could be changed to match the needs of the day, and the *dalang*'s imagination could make play with the relationship between classical puppet and political figure. However, there were also puppets made specially for this form, consisting of *wayang purwa* figures given accoutrements that pinned them firmly to the present: thus Patih (Chief Minister) Prahasta, portraying the Dutch general Spoor, packs a pistol.[37]

None of these *wayang* forms gained a popular foothold. In spite of official promotion they survived into the postrevolutionary period only as curiosities, for the reality they portrayed was not that of the common man. We can discover that reality, for it was expressed in various *wayang*-derived popular art forms of the time. They tell us a good deal about the relationship between the *rakyat*, *modèren* culture, and the PKI.

There were three forms of popular drama which developed out of the *wayang* under the influence of Western theater, their emergence reflecting the gradual spread of Western cultural influence to broader and lower levels of society and also an increasing departure from the *wayang purwa*'s content. The first of these was the *wayang orang* (or *wayang wong*), which uses human actors to play the puppet roles and which generally follows the stories of the *wayang purwa*. From the late nineteenth century it became popular in the Javanese heartland of Yogyakarta and Surakarta, as a result of promotion by the royal Mangkunegaran house which had originated it.[38] While its greatest troupes have continued to be based in that region—though now as commercial organizations rather than as royal protégés—it has become widely popular throughout Java and attracts audiences of all social classes. Aside from the use of human actors, and a stage instead of a screen, *wayang orang* departs from the *wayang purwa* in the direction of Western theater by limiting its purpose to entertainment, reducing the duration of its performance from all night to four or five hours and eliminating much of the religious and instructional content together with what now has come to seem dramatically extraneous material.[39] With some notable exceptions, *wayang orang* troupes tended to the PNI (Nationalist Party) side as the pressures of the 1950s and early 1960s impelled cultural groups to seek political patrons.

At second remove from the *wayang purwa* is *ketoprak*, which became popular in Yogyakarta in the 1920s.[40] Though it can appeal to a rural audience, it has basically an urban lower-class and lower middle-class following. It draws its material from the *wayang purwa*, and from the *babad* (chronicles) and legends which figure in the Javanese historical consciousness and in the lesser cycles of the shadow play. The actors appear in "classical" costumes like those of *wayang orang*. However, any sense of high art is gone: the intrigues, amours, and battles of the supposed Javanese past are played for all the thrills and comedy they are worth, and nothing more. The past is thus desacralized, and the sense of hierarchy it enshrined. The world of the ancestors has an immediacy for our world not because it provides a high example but because it exhibits all the defects of ordinary, contemporary society. The language is modern Javanese, with coarse *ngoko* (low Javanese) having pride of place. The comic and dramatic elements are very broad, so that even the heroes appear as caricatures of themselves, and the whole slant of the exposition and allusions is anti-Establishment.[41] The atmosphere of the performances is noisy, anarchic: *ketoprak* provides a release from order, both that imposed by social subordination in a highly stratified society and that imposed by the narrowness of life as a member of the crowd.[42]

Nonetheless, from the viewpoint of the elite, *ketoprak* is not unrescuable. It is seen as a folk art, derived from the high art of Java and so capable—when cleaned up and redirected—of reminding people of their differences with foreign ways and their ties to their own elite. In the Guided Democracy period, Nationalists as well as Communists bid for the allegiance of *ketoprak* troupes; army units, whose officers were often of little more than lower middle-class origin, sponsored them. Under the New Order, efforts were made to develop *ketoprak* as a means of conveying official ideas to the populace.[43]

Ludruk, the third, most recent, and probably (given the rapidity with which cinema and television have engaged popular attention) the last of these dramatic forms,[44] emerged in the 1930s among the proletariat of Surabaya, then Indonesia's major port and industrial center. If *ketoprak* made a large step away from the *wayang purwa* by overturning and undermining its values, *ludruk* took another in moving completely away from its concern to link present with past. Although its repertory also contains "historical" plays, most *ludruk* dramas move only in present time; their characters are exclusively "real" people, and their incidents are exclusively those which ordinary folk might imaginably experience. They offer a worm's eye view of postrevolutionary Indonesia: social superiors are not exemplary leaders of the struggle against colonialism but corrupt petty officials, greedy moneylending *haji* (pilgrims returned from Mecca), and unscrupulous bosses. The plots are florid: tropical versions of the Victorian pennydreadful. They are, however, realistic in that they show the kinds of crises that the urban poor may have to meet and the kinds of glamor to which they are likely to aspire. Like *ketoprak*, *ludruk* is implicitly anti-order, anti-hierarchy, and escapist.[45]

Containing almost no redeeming reflection of traditional high art, and with its audience limited almost exclusively to the urban working class, *ludruk* is even more uncouth than *ketoprak*. Consequently it found no official favor except in the final, radical-populist phase of Guided Democracy. Only the PKI could really love it, its proletarian origins and latent lower class hostility redeeming its regrettable tendency to find a solution to life's problems in the discovery of some long-lost rich relation rather than in purposeful political struggle. The affection was returned; the political loyalty of *ludruk* troupes, like that of their audiences, went overwhelmingly to Communism.[46]

The proletarian character of *ludruk* and its concern with contemporary social problems encouraged Lekra leaders to employ the genre to a certain extent as a model, urging *ludruk*-izing changes on other art forms. At the same time, they could not escape the urge to improve it.[47] PKI leaders may have been more sympathetic to the plight of the ordinary man than most of Indonesia's postrevolutionary elite, but they shared its general assumption that the *rakyat* were *masih bodoh* (still ignorant) and in need of uplift. Therefore, at the same time that the PKI encouraged *ludruk*-izing changes on less proletarian art forms, it attempted to raise the cultural tone of *ludruk* and other lower-class arts by moving them towards a *modèren* and *halus* style.[48]

We can also see this improving principle at work in the reforms of the *wayang purwa*'s content undertaken by the PKI. These innovations aimed first of all at eliminating scatological elements in the *lakon* and stressing their didactic side—matters on which almost all the involved party cadres could agree. The PKI was, after all, a puritan party.

It attracted elements which were anti-order—such as those expressed in the *réog* and *ludruk*—because of its opposition to established hierarchy, but it was itself determined to impose an order of its own. In consequence, party cadres had little patience with indiscipline and the mocking of social norms. Insofar as they participated in a petty-bourgeois version of *modèren* culture they simply found such behavior in bad taste. They had to tolerate excess in *ketoprak* and *ludruk* in order to retain their audience, but they aimed at turning attention away from riotous release and toward a new discipline. It went without saying that such *ludruk*-izing tendencies as the party encouraged in the *wayang purwa* for the sake of increasing its proletarian aspect did not include *ludruk*'s racy and violent qualities.

The PKI also wanted art to be optimistic, to expose social injustice yet point the way to victory. In the *wayang purwa*'s case a particular opportunity for this was offered, as we have seen, in the role of the clowns, particularly Semar, the servant-god. The clowns' place in the *wayang*-derived forms is instructive in this respect. In all three genres the clown roles are important, not simply because comic elements are generally stressed but also because the clowns are serious figures.[49] In *ketoprak* and *wayang orang*, the clowns break into Indonesian (a *maju* language), particularly for some aside on current events, or put on this or that bit of modern clothing in contrast to the others' stylized classical dress. These traits, like their critical comments on current events in *ludruk*, show that the clowns are not simply bumpkinish *kolot* figures. They are certainly not *modèren* in the sense that this term represents urban elite culture and official ideology, but they are in important respects *modern:* a gap thus opens up between the modernity represented by the cultural model of the ruling class and a modernity of lower-class criticism.

Here we find the distinction between lower-class and elite modernity which the PKI needed to make. The party itself was far from successful in setting forth the distinction, partly because it was, at least at the leadership level, a participant in *modèren* culture, and partly because politically it could not afford it. The latter fact is vividly illustrated by what the party did *not* do with the role of the clowns. As we have seen, the PKI's recommendations for reform of the *wayang purwa* called for enlarging the clowns' roles, not only as social commentators and representatives of the common folk, but also as beings on whom the heroes ultimately depend. However, at no time in the PKI's efforts to implement the artistic reforms was the tradition strained so far that the clowns shook off their servile functions. Such a reversal would undoubtedly have aroused serious controversy among an elite increasingly nervous at the prospect of the PKI's coming to power. Indeed, in modern times the Javanese elite has generally grown more wary of the social revolutionary potential of the clowns' divinity: in earlier times Semar did not make the *sembah* gesture of obeisance to his Pandawa masters which he now does. Moreover, the role of essential but loyal servant was one the party itself had assumed vis-à-vis the Sukarno, and it was not eager to give its enemies evidence that this stance was a mask. Thus the exigencies of the day made for avoiding the single most important change in the *wayang*'s content that might have been made from the viewpoint of furthering Marxist ideology.[50]

For all its role as champion of the masses, the PKI was politically as well as culturally part of Indonesia's postrevolutionary order, in the sense that it shared a great many of that order's assumptions and generally played the political game according to its rules. In the Guided Democracy period of 1959–65 this tendency was especially evident. The party was locked into a situation where it depended for its advancement on the favor of those in power, especially Sukarno; such efforts as it made to reject this subordination led to reprisals it was by no means equipped to ward off. Increasingly, it denied the gap between its own modernity and the *modèren* culture of the ruling elite, while doing its best to persuade the ideologues of Guided Democracy to place more stress on "popular" elements in Indonesian culture and to eliminate the influence of the West. For all that the PKI seemed to conservatives to embody the threat of revolution from below, it was, by the late Guided Democracy period, trying to capture Indonesia from the top, and this meant that its "revolutionary optimism" had to be a version of the regime's official optimism.[51]

This optimism was in stark contrast to the reality seen by the common folk. Their view was vividly illustrated in *ludruk*, where the difference is embodied in the two central roles of transvestite and clown singers. The transvestite is a *modèren, maju* figure; he is *halus* in demeanor, sings in high Javanese, and the social content of his songs focuses on objects of official culture and ideology; in the late Sukarno period he was, as described by Peacock, nationalist and optimistic.[52] In 1963, when the eruption of the Balinese volcano Gunung Agung spread misery as far as East Java, not one of the transvestite songs mentioned the disaster. It did not fit into the way those in power wished to portray the world, for insofar as natural disasters were traditionally thought to reflect the malfunctioning of the state, the eruption was a subversive event. On the other hand, all the clowns sang of the explosion, for in *ludruk* the clowns are common folk. They are not *halus* but *kasar* (crude) in their language and behavior, and critical of social injustice and officials; they comment bitterly on the lot of the poor, are pessimistic in their outlook, and refer—indirectly, if this is politically necessary—to the events of the day. They deal, in short, with experienced rather than official reality.[53]

The split between official and experienced reality realized so vividly in *ludruk* portrays the contradiction which arises when art is expected both to communicate a message from above to the masses and also to express the views of the populace itself. That art should have a message is certainly not a new idea. As we have seen, the *wayang purwa* had an ancient role in conveying the Javanese courtly world view to ordinary folk. Most likely (as can be seen more clearly in contemporary Bali) it had deep roots in local life, only gradually—and at the village level partially—becoming the spokesman for a distant court.[54] The fit between high culture purpose and folk appreciation demanded several conditions, however: first, an effective looseness of supervision by the high culture over the low, so that whether from self-confidence or from lack of information the rulers did not impose their model too strictly; second, an evident legitimacy of the ruling class in popular eyes, so that the indoctrinating aspects of the art appeared as assurances of right order; and third, a lack of major alternative sources of entertainment and ideas.

In Java, these conditions began to dissolve in the nineteenth century. The *wayang purwa*, like the other courtly arts, reached its greatest elaboration in the process of "cultural involution" with which the Javanese aristocracy sought to defend itself against the encroachments of colonial power; but this elaboration only made it more remote from a people who were losing faith in the royal centers and were beginning to be attracted by new sources of leadership and entertainment. Improved communications and surveillance methods also made it easier to observe the extent to which folk performances deviated from the court model; the result was a spate of denunciations by spokesmen for the high culture of the grievous state to which (as they saw it) the *wayang purwa* had declined, and recommendations for restoring standards by stricter ideological and artistic supervision. Ultimately, as we shall see, royal sponsors turned to modern methods of cultural control for this purpose, establishing schools to train puppetmasters who would convey the cultural message in the way the courts conceived it.

By the time the royal *dalang* schools were established, the Javanese courts were in no way able to control popular consumption of the arts. Their concern, however, was inherited by those of the emergent national elite who believed that the popular arts had a social role to play. For though the growing emphasis on entertainment in the *wayang purwa* and the vulgarity and irreverence of the new *wayang*-derived genres might be charged to deculturation and commercial abuse, they were also clearly what the people wanted. They were a consequence of democratization, the gradual movement of the common man towards center stage.[55] Indeed, the fact that *ketoprak* and *ludruk* became recognized genres was part of this emergence: urbanization and commercialization, combined with ideological change, allowed forms which might otherwise have remained rustic skits to spread, to acquire a consistent style and audience, and to be perceived and pondered on by the elite.

Commercial considerations, lack of control, and confusion between, on the one hand, the idea that the will of the people was the touchstone of legitimacy and, on the other, the conviction that the *rakyat* were *masih bodoh*, led successive Indonesian leaderships to much the same response as modern ruling elites elsewhere: they concentrated on preserving the high-culture arts as "classics" for the decoration and delectation of the elite, while allowing the popular arts to go where they would within the allotted bounds of security and propriety. Few regimes—in our day, chiefly Marxist-Leninist ones—have had the will and the reach to deal decisively with the matter of whether the people should be given what they want or what is good for them. Save in brief ultrarevolutionary periods even these Marxist-Leninist regimes have shared the concern of their bourgeois counterparts to encourage "classical" art as a dignity mark of the political center. Popular art, however, has been firmly subjected to official perceptions of reality: the people are allowed to see themselves only as their leaders would have them, lest they be confused as to the true path to improvement. The problem of the sovereignty of the popular will is solved by arguing that, as the Party is the vanguard of the people, its decisions reflect popular opinion in its highest form. In this version of court-sponsored art, what is presented to the masses is not conceived as a transmission of high art downwards but as an expression of the people themselves. The humble genre, lifted from its lowly origins by a political center which recognizes its artistic potential and social worth, is polished into a form which realizes its possibilities and is returned as a model to the masses. That this perfected art should appeal to the populace is taken for granted: after all, it came from them.

Had the cultural reformers in the PKI leadership been able to impose their ideas on the art forms the party influenced, they would very likely have moved them towards that divorce of popular art from People's Art typical of established socialist regimes. *Ludruk* would have been made presentable, positive, and meaningless so far as its original audience was concerned, and it would have portrayed a single, official reality. Thus a Lekra-sponsored National Ludruk Congress held in Surabaya in June 1965 noted with approval that the art had already improved its social acceptability to the point that university students were forming *ludruk* groups, and its morals to the point that female roles were now beginning to be taken by real women instead of men in drag. It was hoped that patriotic and revolutionary themes would be developed for *ludruk* plots as well as the usual social satire.[56]

As things stood in 1965, however, the party hierarchs were not in a position to enforce on *ludruk* their vision of what it should be. For one thing, not having achieved power, they needed to attract broad lower-class support—which meant giving the people what they wanted rather than what would improve them—and for another, they did not have sufficient control at the lower levels. If the higher party cadres were participants in a version of *modèren* culture, those at the local level frequently were not;

they tended to see Communism more directly as the representative of ordinary folk than did party heads striving for respectability and advancement in Jakarta. For the *ludruk* troupes, as for other practitioners of the popular arts, the issue was above all what the audience wanted: Lekra advice and financial support were welcome, but not if they alienated the public on which (since the party purse was limited) the troupes depended for survival.[57] Consequently, the party leadership's reforming ideas had only a marginal effect.

Such was also the case with the PKI's attempts to change the *wayang purwa*. In fact, the reorientation to which Aidit was least sympathetic—the use of existing puppets and tales of adventure to illustrate contemporary themes, the approach of the *wayang pancasila*—was the one which most often entered practice, partly as a result of its convenience and partly because it was one which seemed most likely to win popular favor. Efforts in this direction involved the inclusion of issues important largely at the leadership level (for example, figures from the Mahabharata cycle were exploited to dramatize Indonesia's Confrontation with Malaysia), but the main application of the "*wayang PKI*" as it was performed in parts of Central Java was to address the problem which had particular meaning at the mass level: the struggle of poor peasants (the Pandawa) against the "village devils" (the Kurawa) who had usurped their right to the land.[58]

The line of *wayang* reform Aidit most favored called, we will remember, for the use of wholly new puppets, and plots reflecting the times and the PKI's message. Communist-sponsored efforts in this direction differed from the *wayang suluh* and *wayang perjuangan* in that no specific leaders were portrayed and the emphasis was on lower-class actors. In practice, it amounted to an attempt to extend to the *wayang purwa* the "*ludruk*-izing" tendency the PKI also promoted in *ketoprak* and *wayang orang*: taking plots and characters from popular *ludruk* plays which were thought to have positive ideological meaning and inserting them into the repertoires of other art forms. The main problem seen by the advocates of this approach was the likelihood that the new puppets would be less aesthetically satisfying than the old; we have seen how Aidit, in encouraging this development at the 1964 cultural congress, stressed that it must show a high aesthetic level.[59] As a result, models were proffered in the party newspaper of elaborately carved, *halus* puppets portraying workers and peasants.

The solution is revealing. The refined puppets represent the *rakyat* with a capital R; they are icons, political constructs not really imagined to be related to the man in the street. They show that the PKI leaders were affected no less than the nationalist elite by the contradiction between the fact that the common man, seen in the abstract, was a progressive, *maju* figure, the source of political legitimation and the goal of revolutionary endeavor, while in the concrete he was backward and unrefined. If *ludruk*-izing tendencies were meant to bring the *wayang*'s scene of action down to the present day and the popular level, the creation of *halus* representations of the common man was intended to have the opposite effect. They raised him to the mythical plane, made him part of official rather than experienced reality, the common man as his leaders would like to have him—a portrayal as removed from social reality as the delicate mantis-figure of Arjuna. The *halus* worker-puppet was thus a hybrid, combining the assumptions of socialist realism with the representational techniques of the *wayang purwa*.

These formal efforts at revising *wayang* did not get beyond the experimental stage, as the PKI was eliminated as a legal movement following the coup of 1965. Had they not been so halted, however, there is very little likelihood that they would have threatened the *wayang purwa*; they would simply have brought new *wayang* forms into existence, as had happened before. The introduction of new *wayang* species for legitimating purposes continued in the post-1965 New Order: military *wayang* aimed at conveying the importance of the army's role and values, *wayang* for popularizing the regime's birth control program, and so on.[60] The real threat to the *wayang purwa* lay not in such departures but in an outwardly unexceptionable kind of change, to which even the PKI's cultural conservatives had felt they had to agree—the "technical" reforms aimed at making the art easier to perform and responsive to the exigencies of modern life.

To understand why this was so, we must bear in mind that the distinction between form and content is basically a modern one. For a traditional and sacral art such as the *wayang purwa* all elements of the performance are symbolically laden, and such changes as the substitution (now almost universally practiced) of petromax or electric light for the flickering *bléncong* diminish *wayang*'s meaning. Moreover, some changes viewed as technical are in fact ideological, reflecting new ideas as to proper cultural models and thus denying *wayang*'s centrality: for example, the use of a regular proscenium stage, rather than the *kelir*, in imitation of Western theater and cinema.

The technical reform that most gravely threatened the *wayang purwa*'s meaning was shortening its playing time. The classical *wayang* performance moves in a highly formalized progression from dusk to dawn, the location and basic content of its scenes unvarying.[61] This extreme stylization is important because, given *wayang*'s fluidity with regard to language, time, and sphere of action, it is the structural linchpin that holds the *lakon* together.[62] It is dramatically possible because *wayang* sees all action as part of the same cosmic dance. Shortening the playing time means selection, and, under the influence of popular modern taste, this has been in the direction of throwing out the boring (philosophical and ritual) bits and keeping the action and the jokes. Thus truncated, the *wayang purwa* becomes a puppet version of *wayang orang*, losing nearly all its deeper meaning.[63] The PKI's cultural conservatives were certainly aware of this danger, yet it was something to which, as we have seen, they felt they must submit: there seemed nothing to be done about the fact that modern urban man could not sit up all night as could a peasant during the agricultural slack season. While they might point out to *wayang*'s would-be reformers that the *wayang purwa* had survived many changes and that attempts to transform it ideologically had only created transient new forms, they had to admit that modern times were different, that Java had entered a new historical stage the demands of which could not be denied. They could, moreover, see that the changes they feared were not just a matter of intraparty debate but were part of a cultural transformation of far older and broader force.

Let us now look at this larger history of "technical" change in *wayang*, because it will help locate the party's debate within the development of elite ideology, both before and after 1965. We shall concentrate on the role and training of the *dalang*, both because they were an important issue for the reformers and because they are central to the *wayang purwa* itself.

Classically, the puppet-master is far more than just a performer. Together with the *dukun* (spiritual adviser), the *dalang* is the nearest the Agama Jawa has to a priest.[64] The mastery of puppets is a craft usually passed down from father to son; it is assumed to require spiritual inspiration, which may be inherited. Simply to perform the dark-to-dawn *malam suntuk* of the classical *wayang* performance requires enormous concentration and stamina: the *dalang* must sit, cross-legged, for nine or more hours, working the puppets, directing the *gamelan*, narrating and singing, remembering the classic verses in their various languages but improvising according to the needs of the occasion, his only refreshment the odd draw of cigarette or sip of water in the brief intervals when a female singer *(pesindèn)* takes a turn or when the *gamelan* plays alone. The *dal-*

ang prepares himself spiritually before such an effort and often performs partly in trance. The *dalang* should be a morally superior man, a person of wisdom who has a particularly close relationship to the spiritual world; as such, his word has particular weight. He may not directly ask a fee for his performance (but accepts gifts reflecting the gratitude and liberality of its sponsor). By reason of this semi-priestly position the *dalang* has been relatively free to comment on affairs of the day; and at the same time those in power have been alert to the political implications of his allusions and choice of play.[65]

The first people to sponsor changes leading to a reduction in the *dalang*'s position were not political modernizers but princes of the royal courts of Central Java. In 1923, the Sunanate of Surakarta began a school for *dalang*, an example followed two years later by the Sultanate of Yogyakarta. These initiatives were part of the effort of an old elite gravely uncertain of its position to refine and elaborate the traditional arts, both to entice a population seen as drifting away from classical values and to demonstrate a cultural level which would be acknowledged by the Europeans. But the fact of teaching the art in a school, which issued certificates to its graduates, implied that it was more a matter of technique than of spiritual qualities. This change was a first step toward denying the *dalang*'s claim to have a particular relationship with the world of the spirit and thus to deserve special regard from society.[66]

The Revolution and the coming to power of a new middle class gave further impulse to this direction. Young members of the new elite, students at Gajah Mada University in Yogyakarta, interested in exploring their cultural roots as well as in mastering modern science, undertook to learn the *dalang*'s craft. In 1953 a *dalang* course was opened for them as an extracurricular activity. They were neither willing nor able to perform an entire *malam suntuk*, and so they introduced the innovation of a four-hour *wayang purwa* performance. What was retained was the action and what was dropped were elements which, in the judgment of sponsors concerned for narrative but not for philosophical qualities, were superfluous to enjoying the performance; as we have already noted, this change went far towards demystifying the *wayang* and making it solely a matter of entertainment and indoctrination. At the time, the four-hour *wayang* was much disapproved of, but in 1955 the cultural office of the Department of Education gave it an official endorsement, together with approval of those *lakon* which had been adapted or invented for its performance. Thereafter it gradually spread to the major Javanese cities and, via broadcast performances on the national radio, became a generally recognized alternative.

Akin to such changes were those involving the organization of people concerned with *wayang*. Insofar as organizations brought *dalang* together to exchange thoughts about their craft, about improving conditions of work, and about urging the state to promote their art, they functioned as professional or labor unions and hence threatened to define the puppeteers as workers. Few saw themselves this way, and they found little virtue in the modern principle of strength through organization. The PKI acknowledged this problem by confining its unionizing efforts primarily to the lower genres of the traditional performing arts.[67] Of more importance as far as *wayang* was concerned was the founding in 1953 of the nonpolitical association of *dalang*, Panunggaling Dalang Republik Indonesia (Padri). It led to the convening of the first congress of *dalang* in 1958 at the Mangkunegaran palace in Surakarta. In spite of the conservative element in their sponsorship, such modern activities helped to move *dalang* from a frame of reference in which their role was culturally central to one in which—in their own perception and the public's—it was a craft peripheral to contemporary society and consequently in need of renovation and protection.

The *dalang* congress also brought together people who were not themselves performers, but who felt concerned to promote the art. They represented an influential segment of the urban elite, with much influence on state patronage and policy regarding the arts, and fearful that *wayang* might not find a place in modern Indonesia.[68] They sought to ensure its future by embedding it in *modèren* culture, and by acquiring for it official sponsorship and the dignity marks recognized by the national elite as a whole. The projects which the congress recommended reflected these concerns: more courses to train *dalang*, publication of a *wayang* encyclopedia, foundation of a *wayang* institute, and formation of an Akademi Pedalangan Indonesia which would provide higher education for practitioners of the *dalang*'s art.[69]

Such sponsors became particularly active after the 1965 coup, which effectively ended political party involvement with the arts and brought an upsurge of interest in cultural roots on the part of the ruling military-bureaucratic elite. A first Indonesian Wayang Week (Pekan Wayang Indonesia) was held in 1969, and other national and regional festivals followed. A national *wayang* foundation was set up, and a national *wayang* secretariat, while a Wayang Museum was established in Jakarta. All these aimed at promoting *wayang* but also at transforming it, for while the sponsors generally felt it desirable to preserve the classic tradition of *wayang purwa* performance as an aesthetic and historical model, they believed that the art must adapt to the times and respond to social needs. Needless to say, these needs were conceived in terms of official ideology. Thus a conference on the *wayang purwa* sponsored in 1968 by the University of Indonesia and the Ministry of Education determined that "The *dalang*, aside from providing entertainment, must also be an information officer for the public with regard to the development of the Nation and State." Even though "we now live in a time of scientific and technological progress," the conference continued, "*wayang* can function as an element of National Culture and can be used to further the sense of Indonesian Identity." *Wayang* performances could serve "as a mass-media" for government campaigns, but in order to do so effectively new forms of *wayang* should be developed which had a popular content and which used Indonesian and other non-Javanese languages.[70]

The argument was carried further at the second Wayang Week, in 1974, when a group of prominent Indonesian intellectuals demanded that *wayang* be expanded into a "vehicle for folk tales from all over Indonesia" and that the genre be broadened in form, content, and function. Not only should *wayang* be presented in Indonesian but, they urged, an English-language form should be created—a measure of the extent to which they equated international acceptance with cultural value. While the more radical proposals of the group met objections from the main body of the participants, most could agree that the *wayang purwa* could at least be Indonesianized by translating its classic *lakon* into the national language.[71]

Some of these recommendations were peculiar to the political climate of the New Order, but the general lines concur notably with the PKI *wayang* reformers' vision of what needed to be done, and simply extend the ideas much further. This coincidence of politically opposed views has arisen in part from a shared participation in *modèren* culture and the assumption by both Communist left and military-led right that culture should serve power.[72] In addition, it reflects the broad belief in modern Indonesian political thought, inherited from the independence movement, that the *rakyat* is the ultimate source of legitimacy and that therefore art's relevance to social needs is essential. Though such concern has often been largely a matter of rhetoric for those in power, it has kept a continuing ideological salience, providing a source of both internal tension and continuity between regimes.

Of course we should not mistake the ideas of the *wayang* reformers for the view of the *wayang* audience; for the mass of habitual onlookers, the reformers' ideas probably seem as intellectually remote as the most archaic elements of the shadow-play. Nonetheless, glacial changes have been taking place in the way in which the *wayang purwa* has been performed and apprehended, reflecting a long-term process of ideological transformation that has affected the whole of Indonesian society. It was an apprehension of this larger change that lay behind the PKI cultural conservatives' reluctant belief that time lay on the modernizers' side. Over the years there has been a gradual but noticeable decline in the leeway allowed the *dalang* for criticism, a result not just of increased official surveillance but also of diminished regard for the *dalang*'s role.[73] In performances, ambiguity has faded; the moral problems posed by choice of action receive less stress. Now the Kurawa are frequently seen simply as the bad side and the Pandawa as the good. Their conflict becomes one of black-hats versus white-hats, and the emphasis is increasingly on action, cleverness of dialogue, and jests. The religious aspect of the *wayang* has declined; indeed, from the viewpoint of most members of the modern big-city elite it is effectively dead. The *wayang purwa* is fast becoming straightforward entertainment; even in rural areas, performances on traditional ritual occasions become more matters of custom and enjoyment than of spiritual significance.[74]

As this process of secularization continues, *wayang* performances in the traditional manner are likely to be preserved among the urban elite as a cultural product appropriate to the few—like "classical" music or "serious" theater. What counts in such circumstances is imitation of the past—the *wayang* of the "book *dalang*," which is in fact increasing—not the linking of past and present through improvisation and allusion.[75] At the same time, there has been a notable increase in interest in the *wayang purwa* within the urban elite, in contrast to the 1950s, when many younger middle-class Javanese disdained it. Then the art had represented a past and a "feudal" hierarchy still too close, and they wanted cultural manifestations which reflected their hard-won modernity. A generation later, the New Order elite makes much of the *wayang purwa* and of traditional ceremonies and dress. This interest has gone together with an enthusiastic adoption of international consumer culture, but the anomaly is only apparent. Traditional culture no longer has the same meaning: more and more it is simply a decoration, something to set off and lend flavor to the new. The general of humble background may marry his children off in ceremonies appropriate to a royal court because he finds them impressive and fitting to his power and purse; but he need no longer be troubled by the thought that he has overstepped proper social order and that others will find him laughable. On the contrary, he will be likely to see the art's celebration of hierarchy and the *satria* ethic as endorsing the social order he represents, and to suspect those who make light of the *wayang purwa* of subversive intentions.[76]

Whatever else the future may bring, it is unlikely that *wayang* will recede, like so many of the Southeast Asian performing arts, into something simply preserved for tourists and state cultural functions. As long as the Javanese remain the preponderant cultural element in Indonesia, symbols based on *wayang* will inform the elite's vocabulary. Urban Javanese and those who otherwise have not had much opportunity to watch traditional performances can become familiar with *wayang* images and ideas through radio and television performances of shortened *lakon*, cassette tapes of favorite scenes performed by famous *dalang*, and so on. These images and ideas will not have the same coherence as in the past, however, nor will they form the basis of a moral world and a guide to action. Sudisman's speech, coherent and moving in its own time, was perhaps only possible then, a liminal period in which one could credibly be both fully committed to a modern ideology and to an ancient conceptual world. In not too many years such a statement may seem quixotic, as sincere and meaningless as Mishima's suicide. We should bear in mind, however, that the pace of ideological change is often deceptive, and that people turn to older ideas as well as new ones when faced with crisis. Should there be a collapse of order in Indonesia we may well find an upsurge not only of political radicalism but of reference to *wayang* as a moral guide—that combination out of which, in the course of the independence struggle, Sudisman's own commitment arose.

---

1. Sudisman, *Analysis of Responsibility*, translated by Ben Anderson (Melbourne: The Works Co-Operative, 1975), p. 4.

2. Benedict R. O'G. Anderson, *Mythology and the Tolerance of the Javanese* (Ithaca: Cornell Modern Indonesia Project, Monograph Series, 1965), pp. 4–27.

3. Mangkunagara VII, K.G.P.A.A., *On the Wayang Kulit (Purwa) and Its Symbolic and Mystical Elements*, translated by Claire Holt (Ithaca: Cornell Southeast Asia Program Data Paper No. 27, 1957); P. J. Zoetmulder, S.J., "The Wajang as a Philosophical Theme," *Indonesia*, 12 (1971), pp. 85–96; Clifford Geertz, *The Religion of Java* (Glencoe: The Free Press, 1960), pp. 261–78; Moebirman, *Wayang Purwa: The Shadow Play of Indonesia* (Jakarta: Yayasan Pelita Wisata, 1973), pp. 11–13.

4. Alton Becker, "Text-Building, Epistemology, and Aesthetics in Javanese Shadow Theater," in *The Imagination of Reality*, ed. Alton Becker and Aram Yengoyan (Norwood: Ablex, 1979), pp. 211–43, at p. 236. This separation of orders of meaning through language is probably related to the importance of speech level distinctions in Javanese, which has a strong sense of language appropriate to status and arena of discourse. Of course, the representation of different epistemological orders by different orders of being is not limited to the *wayang* genre of theater. To take one European example, we can see it in Wagner's *Ring* cycle.

5. For relevant materials concerning Javanese ideas of time, see Anthony Day, "Ranggawarsita's Prophecy of Mystery," in *Moral Order and the Question of Change: Essays in Southeast Asian Thought*, ed. Alexander Woodside and David Wyatt (New Haven: Yale University, Southeast Asia Studies Monograph No. 24, 1982), pp. 151–73, at pp. 170–72; A. Becker, "Text-Building," pp. 218–19; and Judith Becker, "Time and Tune in Java," in *The Imagination of Reality*, ed. Becker and Yengoyan, pp. 197–210. Compare the "archaic" ideas of time discussed in Mircea Eliade, *Cosmos and History: The Myth of the Eternal Return* (New York: Harper and Row, 1959).

6. Siegel has pointed out that because *wayang* language is imagistic "the hierarchy of figures within the *wayang* stories could thus be transplanted to everyday life. And with it Javanese hierarchy could be transplanted onto the national scene. It is, however, from a Javanese point of view, more acceptable to reverse the terms of the last sentence: via *wayang* imagery the world was recognized in Javanese terms even though the language actually spoken might be Indonesian." James Siegel, "Surakartan Theater under the New Order" (unpublished ms., 1984), pp. 2–3. I myself found, when interviewing PKI cadres in 1964–65, that the Javanese among them would often ask which *wayang* figure I identified with or admired most, as a way of placing me. For the use of *wayang* exemplars in modern political action, see: Shiraishi Takashi, "The Disputes between Tjipto Mangoenkoesoemo and Soetamto Soeriokoesoemo: Satria vs. Pandita," *Indonesia*, 32 (1981), pp. 93–108; Peter Carey, "The Role of *Wayang* in the Dipanegara War," *Prisma*, 7 (1977), pp. 15–27; Ann Kumar, "The 'Suryengalagan Affair' of 1883 and its Successors. Born Leaders in Changed Times," *Bijdragen tot de taal-, land- en volkenkunde* [henceforth *BTLV*], 138:2/3 (1982), pp. 252–84; Ki Hasto, "Bung Karno dan Wayang" [Bung Karno and *Wayang*], *Warta Wayang*, 2 (1979), pp. 9–10; G. J. Resink, "From the Old Mahabharata to the New Ramayana Order," *BTLV*, 131:2/3 (1975), pp. 213–35.

7. See Benedict R. O'G. Anderson, "The Idea of Power in Javanese Culture," in *Culture and Politics in Indonesia*, ed. Claire Holt et al. (Ithaca: Cornell University Press, 1972), pp. 1–70, at pp. 13–17.

8. Jan Wisseman Christie, "Raja and Rama: The Classical State in Early Java," in *Centers, Symbols and Hierarchies: Essays on the Classical*

States of Southeast Asia, ed. Loraine Gesick (New Haven: Yale University, Southeast Asia Studies Monograph No. 26, 1983), pp. 9–44, at pp. 34–35.

9. Alton Becker, "Text-Building," p. 238; and William Ward Keeler, "Father Puppeteer" (Ph.D. thesis, University of Chicago, 1982), p. 323.

10. Clara Brakel, "Traditional Javanese Poetry and the Problem of Interpretation," *Indonesia Circle*, 26 (1981), pp. 13–24, at pp. 14 and 20; Victoria M. Clara van Groenendael, *Er zit een dalang achter de wayang* (Amsterdam: De Goudsblom, 1982), pp. 280–81.

11. The Mahabharata has been the preferred cycle in the *wayang purwa*, for it has an ancient role in legitimating Javanese kings. (See S. O. Robson, "Kakawin Reconsidered: Toward a Theory of Old Javanese Poetics," *BTLV*, 139:2/3 [1983], pp. 291–319, at p. 295.) Resink has argued that its dominance under the regime of Sukarno (who is said to have identified with Gatotkaca) was somewhat eroded under the early post-1965 New Order, since its leader Suharto identified with the Ramayana's Hanuman. (See G. J. Resink, "From the Old Mahabharata," pp. 291–319.)

12. He is in fact the highest god to appear in the *wayang*: he is the son of Sang Hyang Widi, the One God, who is never represented, and elder brother of Bhatara Guru (Siva), the highest god shown in divine form on the *wayang* screen. See J. J. Ras, "De clown-figuren in de wajang," *BTLV*, 134:4 (1978), pp. 451–65; Sri Mulyono, *Apa dan Siapa Semar* [What and Who is Semar?] (Jakarta: Gunung Agung, 1978); Anderson, *Mythology*, pp. 22–23.

13. That such a reversal is immanent in Javanese thought may be seen from Javanese peasant movements which rejected the supravillage hierarchy and proclaimed the peasant as the linchpin of the social order. The Saminist movement earlier in this century is the most celebrated of these and has been much described. (See Shiraishi Takashi, "Saminism Reinterpreted: A Study of Rakyat Radicalism in Java" [unpublished English version of "Saminisumu to Rayatto Radikarisumu," *Tokyo Daigaku Toyo Bunku Kenkyusho Kiyo*, 77 (1978), pp. 93–181]; Harry J. Benda and Lance Castles, "The Samin Movement," *BTLV*, 125:2 [1969], pp. 207–40.) Though the peasants' rejection of outside authority has generally taken the form of retreat rather than rebellion, they have often supported chiliastic expectations of change. The authorities, particularly in the colonial and New Order regimes, have tended to treat them as potentially rebellious and to arrest their leaders at the first excuse. Certain of them were strongly identified with the postrevolutionary PKI, notably the Adam Makrifat (later Pran Suh) movement, which was sometimes mockingly referred to as the "Agama PKI"; it was banned after the 1965 coup. (See Sartono Kartodirdjo, "Agrarian Radicalism in Java: Its Setting and Development," in *Culture and Politics*, ed. Holt et al., pp. 71–125, at pp. 119–22; and *Kedaulatan Rakjat*, September 4, 1962; December 31, 1965; and January 14, 1966.) Stange notes the emergence of a Javanese mystical tradition in which Semar, as the key guardian *(dahyang)* of the spirit realm, the symbol of the common people, and original ancestor of the Javanese, is supposed to return after five centuries of domination by alien cultural influences in order to restore true Javanese civilization and inaugurate an era of compassion and justice; the five centuries have just elapsed. (See Paul Stange, "Javanese Mysticism in the Revolutionary Period," *Conference on Modern Indonesian History, July 18–19, 1975* [Madison: University of Wisconsin, Center for Southeast Asian Studies, 1975], pp. 171–87, at p. 172.)

14. An extensive list of ancient and modern *wayang* forms, their characteristics, typical myth cycles, purported creators, and ideological purposes can be found in an appendix to the final report of the first national Wayang Week Conference held in 1969: see *Laporan dan Hasil Pekan Wajang Indonesia I* [Report and Results of the First *Wayang* Week] (Jakarta: Dewan Kesenian Djakarta, 1969). See also Seno Sastroamidjojo, *Renungan tentang Pertundjukan Wajang Kulit* [Reflections on *Wayang* Performance] (Jakarta: Kinta, 1964), pp. 37–54; and Sri Mulyono, *Wayang: Asal-usul, Filsafat dan Masa Depannya* [*Wayang*: Its Origins, Philosophy, and Future] (Jakarta: Gunung Agung, 1978), pp. 147–65 and 300–306. Of particular interest is the *wayang madya*, which was developed late in the nineteenth century by the Sultanate of Yogyakarta; its purposes have been extensively discussed by its Javanese originators and by foreign scholars. (See especially G. W. J. Drewes, "Ranggawarsita, the Pustaka Raja Madya and the Wayang Madya," *Oriens Extremis*, 21:2 [1974], pp. 199–215.) Long ago Hazeu had suggested that *wayang madya* reflected a changing role for *wayang*: whereas previously the art's primary function had been religious, it was now didactic, instructing the Javanese about their past

with a basically secular intent. (See G. A. J. Hazeu, *Bijdrage tot de kennis van het javaansche toneel* [Leiden: Brill, 1897], p. 99.) A look at the list of *wayang* forms provided in *Laporan* shows that the nineteenth-century introductions tended to emphasize history, showing a linkage *through time* (something new) of Java's present to its past, while in the twentieth century there emerged an emphasis on realism, contemporary affairs, and the question of right conduct in a time of change.

15. The main vehicle for conveying the message of Islam was the Menak cycle, which described the exploits of the hero Amir Hamzah. (See Kumar, "The 'Suryengalagan Affair,' " p. 266.) However, the Mahabharata cycle has also been interpreted so as to convey a Muslim message. (See Moesa, "Grepen uit de wajang, in verband met de Islam," *Djawa*, 3:2 [1923], pp. 56–62; and 'Adhiman Sudjuddin Rais, "Pandangan Islam terhadap Seni Pergelaran Wajang Kulit di Daerah Surakarta" [An Islamic Perspective on the Art of *Wayang* Performance in the Surakarta Region] [M.A. thesis, IAIN Sunan Kali Djaga, 1971].) In the nineteenth century *wayang purwa* puppets were also sometimes used to present Christian beliefs to the Javanese. (See C. Guillot, *L'affaire Sadrach: Un essai de Christianisation à Java au XIXe siècle* [Paris: Éditions de la Maison des Sciences de l'Homme, 1981], p. 74.) In 1959–60 a new type of *wayang*, the *wayang wahyu*, was introduced for performing biblical stories for the Catholic community of Central Java; a Protestant *wayang* was apparently also created (*Berita Yudha*, January 8, 1966), but does not seem to have survived. The Adam Makrifat sect (see note 13) seems to have had its own *wayang* for conveying its mystical teaching (Sri Mulyono, *Wayang*, pp. 162–63).

16. That this question was not merely the idle fretting of ideologues may be seen from Rex Mortimer, "Traditional Modes and Communist Movements: Change and Protest in Indonesia," in *Peasant Rebellions and Communist Revolution in Asia*, ed. John W. Lewis (Palo Alto: Stanford University Press, 1974), pp. 99–123.

17. M. C. Ricklefs, "Six Centuries of Islamization in Java," in *Conversion to Islam*, ed. Nehemia Levtzion (New York: Homes and Meier, 1979); and Nakamura Mitsuo, "The Crescent Arises over the Banyan Tree: A Study of the Muhammadijah Movement in a Central Javanese Town" (Ph.D. thesis, Cornell University, 1976).

18. Robert R. Jay, *Religion and Politics in Rural Central Java* (New Haven: Yale University, Southeast Asia Studies, Cultural Reports Series No. 12, 1963); Clifford Geertz, *The Religion of Java*; and his *The Social History of an Indonesian Town* (Cambridge, Mass.: M.I.T. Press, 1965). For *santri* justifications for rejecting *wayang*, see Nakamura, "The Crescent," p. 296, n. 4. Among nineteenth century Javanese Christian sects there was also ambivalence concerning *wayang*, some banning it together with other key symbols of the Agama Jawa— the *gamelan* and the *selamatan* feast (Guillot, *L'affaire Sadrach*, pp. 62 and 324). Recently, some Muslim leaders eager to overcome *abangan* resistance to a stronger Islamic orientation have abandoned the attack on *wayang* and returned to claims that it was introduced to Java by the Muslim *wali*. (See C. P. Woodcroft-Lee, "The View from the Minaret: Indonesian History as Expressed in the Writings of Some Indonesian Muslim Leaders and Intellectuals," *Kabar Seberang*, 4 [1978], pp. 29–39, at p. 32.)

19. See my "The Enchantment of the Revolution: History and Action in an Indonesian Communist Text," in *Perceptions of the Past in Southeast Asia*, ed. Anthony Reid and David Marr (Singapore: Heinemann Educational Books, 1979), pp. 340–58; and Robert Cribb, "The Indonesian Marxist Tradition," in *Marxism in Asia*, ed. Nick Knight and Colin MacKerras (London: Croom Helm, 1985), pp. 251–72.

20. Sudisman, *Analysis*, p. 24.

21. This sense of alienation, and resulting resentment, came out clearly in remarks by Aidit to the 1964 Conference on Revolutionary Art and Culture:

"Our nation consists of many ethnic groups *(sukubangsa)*. Every Communist, especially ones elected as national leaders by a congress of the party or a revolutionary mass organization, must strive to appreciate the aesthetic products of all ethnicities. Ethnic culture is the property of the entire nation. Do not, therefore, be like the Javanese comrade who, when he sees comrades from a Sumatran ethnic group watching a *wayang orang* performance, is amused because he thinks it 'odd' for them to do this. Nor should any ethnic group view the culture of another as inferior." (*Harian Rakjat Minggu*, February 7, 1965.)

It is interesting that these comments were not published for some months after the conference where they were made; we may imagine that they aroused much offense.

22. Hildred Geertz, "Indonesian Cultures and Communities," in *Indonesia*, ed. Ruth McVey (New Haven: HRAF Press, 1964), pp. 24–96, at pp. 31–41.

23. The accent mark is usually retained only in dictionary spellings, but I have kept it here to enable the reader to distinguish more easily between *modèren* and *modern*.

24. That this was a possible option can be seen from the ideology of the Gerinda Party (Selosoemardjan, *Social Change in Jogjakarta* [Ithaca: Cornell University Press, 1962], pp. 185–94). That the Gerinda was defeated by the PKI in elections in the Javanese heartland shows that mere radicalism and *abangan* orientation were not enough: the *abangan* masses themselves had now accepted the goal culture of modernity.

25. The Lekra did not announce itself as a "mass organization" of the PKI, but it was generally recognized as reflecting the Communist *aliran* (ideological stream) and as being effectively under the party's control.

26. Mukadimah (Preface) in *Lekra Menjambut Kongres Kebudajaan* [Lekra Welcomes the Cultural Congress] (Jakarta: Persatuan, 1951), p. 47.

27. Joebaar Ajoeb, "Laporan Umum Pengurus Pusat kepada Kongres Nasional ke-I Lembaga Kebudajaan Rakjat" [General Report of the Central Executive to the First National Congress of Lekra], in *Laporan Kebudajaan Rakjat, I* [People's Culture Reports, I] (Jakarta: Pembaruan, 1959), p. 25. This deprecation of *wayang* was not shared by all PKI cadres, and there was some attempt indeed to use *wayang* for conveying the party message even in that period: see, for example, the new *wayang* play proposed in the party newspaper *Harian Rakjat*, September 5, 1952. Indeed, such use by the PKI seems to have occurred as far back as the colonial period. (See Iskandar, *Vogelvrij! Uit het leven van een naar Nieuw Guinea verbannen Indonesiër* [Amsterdam: De Strijd, 1927], pp. 1–5.) However, this appears to have been done only occasionally and on an ad hoc basis.

28. Joebaar Ajoeb, "Manifesto Politik dan Kebudajaan" [The Political Manifesto and Culture], *Laporan Kebudajaan Rakjat, II* [People's Culture Reports, II] (Jakarta: Pembaruan, 1962), p. 18; "Keterangan Lekra mengenai Wajang dalam Bahasa Indonesia" [Lekra Statement on *Wayang* in the Indonesian Language], in ibid., pp. 63–69. Nonetheless, the Indonesianization project did not entirely die. In the eyes of the Communist leaders it remained necessary to translate regional literatures into Indonesian, so that they could "become the property of the entire Indonesian nation and people." Only in this way, it was asserted, could one ward off "ethnocentrism, provincialism, and regional separatism." Joebaar Ajoeb, "Mengapa dan Bagaimana Mengabdikan Kebudajaan kepada Buruh, Tani dan Pradjurit" [Why and How to Dedicate Culture to the Workers, Peasants and Soldiers], *Harian Rakjat Minggu*, April 25, 1965.

29. Becker, "Text-Building," pp. 230–34; E. L. Heins, *Wajang Kulit* (Amsterdam: Tropenmuseum, 1973), pp. 2–3. Thus the heavy use in *wayang* performances of Old Javanese, which a modern audience can scarcely understand, is explained by the fact that the performance's "essential audience" is not the visible one but the ancestors/gods. The ultimate expression of this idea is the *wayang purwa* performed on Mt. Kawi, which takes place without any human audience at all.

30. Sakirman, *Wajang Purwa: Asal-usul dan Perkembangannja* [*Wayang Purwa*: Its Origins and Development] (Jakarta: Bagian Penerbitan Lembaga Kebudajaan Rakjat, 1961), p. 45.

31. D. N. Aidit, *Tentang Sastra dan Seni* [On Literature and Art] (Jakarta: Pembaruan, 1964), pp. 33–34.

32. Ibid., p. 45.

33. Ibid., pp. 45–46.

34. E.g., Z. Afif, "Pembaruan Wajang Purwa" [Updating *Wayang Purwa*], *Harian Rakjat Minggu*, February 14, 1965. The use of a collective *dalang* was also justified, he argued, by its employment in China—that country being at the time considered an ideological model. See also *Harian Rakjat Minggu*, February 7, 1965 (lecture by Hendra Gunawan) and February 21, 1965 (article by Juliarso).

35. This was argued at a conference of the Java Instituut in 1921; see [Sutopo], "De behoefte aan intellectuele dalangs in verband met de ontwikkeling van het wajangspel," *Djawa*, 1 (1921), p. 129; [Anonymous], "Uit de javaansche cultuurbeweging," in ibid., pp. 203–4; and Groenendael, *Er zit een dalang*, pp. 52–54. An early attempt along these lines was the *wayang wahana*, created the year previ-

ously by R. Ng. Sutarto Hardjowahono of Surakarta. It was realistic in portrayal and used tales of everyday life; accompanied by either a *gamelan* or by Western instruments, a performance lasted only six hours. (See *Laporan*; and Seno Sastroamidjojo, *Renungan*, pp. 47–51.)

36. Ibid., pp. 47–48; and *Laporan*.

37. Seno Sastroamidjojo, *Renungan*, pp. 47–51. For a latter-day attempt to revive the *wayang pancasila*, see Robert H. Crawford and Ronny Adhikarya, *The Use of Traditional Media in Family Planning Programs in Rural Java* (Ithaca: Cornell University, Department of Communications Arts, 1972), p. 13.

38. *Wayang orang* is believed to have originated in the late eighteenth century on order of Mangkunegara I (see Soedarsono, "Drama Tari Ramayana Gaya Yogyakarta" [The Yogyakarta Style of Ramayana Dance Drama], in his *Beberapa Catatan tentang Seni Pertunjukan Indonesia* [Some Notes on Indonesian Performance Arts] [Yogyakarta: Konservatori Tari Indonesia, 1974], pp. 5, 8–11.). It is said that its introduction was the result of a deliberate court decision to create an art form that resembled European theater (Hazeu, *Bijdrage*, p. 95). The innovation, however, was greeted with considerable alarm by those who were sensitive to the *wayang*'s sacred aspect and/or to the precepts of Islam. The original *wayang orang* remained a seldom-performed court drama until the 1880s, when Mangkunegara V began to promote it as a popular art. See J. J. Ras, *De schending van Soebadra* (Amsterdam: Meulenhoff, 1976), p. 24; H. H. J[uynboll], "Toneel," in *Encyclopaedie van Nederlandsch-Indië*, 4 (The Hague/Leiden: Brill, 1921), pp. 395–404, at p. 402; Claire Holt, *Art in Indonesia: Continuities and Change* (Ithaca: Cornell University Press, 1967), pp. 155–67.

39. One reflection of its "up-market" orientation is the relatively high standard of dancing, singing, and acting demanded by the *wayang orang* audience. A serious and didactic aspect is retained to some extent, in line with the *wayang purwa* style, though more from a concern to appear as high art than from any sense of the performance as a rite.

40. For different versions of the *ketoprak*'s origins, see Eva Vaníčkovà, "A Study of the Javanese Ketoprak," *Archiv Orientální*, 33 (1965), pp. 397–450, at pp. 399–403; Barbara Hatley, "Ludruk and Ketoprak: Popular Theatre and Society in Java," *Review of Indonesian and Malaysian Affairs* (henceforth *RIMA*), 7:1 (1973), pp. 38–58, at p. 52; J. J. Ras, *Javanese Literature since Independence* (Verhandelingen KITLV No. 88) (The Hague: Nijhoff, 1979), p. 6; Kuslan Budiman, "Menjongsong Kongres Nasional Ketoprak-II di Solo" [Commemorating the Second National Ketoprak Congress in Solo], *Harian Rakjat Minggu*, July 19, 1964; *Bintang Timur*, December 22, 1956.

41. Hatley notes that the Dutch detected this aspect early in *ketoprak*'s development, and feared that it might become a vehicle for promoting Communism. Barbara Hatley, "Babads on Stage: Javanese History and Contemporary Popular Theatre," *Indonesia Circle*, 26 (1981), pp. 33–43, at p. 36. Her essay provides a thoughtful analysis of the relationship between history and order in Javanese thought, seeing in *ketoprak*'s development a loosening of this tie. By desacralizing Java's heroic past, *ketoprak* implicitly declares a lack of belief in the social order which uses that past for legitimation.

42. It is this escape from oppressive limitations through disorderly conduct rather than overcoming them by the self-imposition of a counter-discipline that seems to have most greatly disturbed the *santri*, for whom *ketoprak* is anathema (Nakamura, "The Crescent," pp. 303–7). Since in its early years *ketoprak* drew material from the Western and Arabic tales of the *komedi stambul*, and used a *stambul* orchestra rather than the *gamelan*, we may assume it did not restrict its appeal to the *abangan*. Later, however, it turned to the *gamelan* and an emphasis on themes from Java's myth-history (Hatley, "Ludruk," p. 53). Compare Nakamura's account of *santri* attitudes towards the disorder of *ketoprak* with Siegel's contrast between Islamic and pre-Islamic styles of cultural expression in Aceh. (James Siegel, "Prayer and Play in Atjeh: A Comment on Two Photographs," *Indonesia*, 1 [1966], pp. 1–21.) This stress on salvation through self-discipline was of course shared by the Communists and was one of the reasons why they were eager to reform the *ketoprak* and the still more disorderly *ludruk*.

43. For the PKI's ideas on elevating *ketoprak*, see *Harian Rakjat Minggu*, August 16, 1964 (address by Hr. Bandaharo to the Second National Ketoprak Congress). Aidit was able to report with satisfaction at the Conference on Revolutionary Art and Culture that the *ketoprak* congress had agreed unanimously to reform the art "so that it will be a more effi-

cacious weapon in the hands of the People" (Aidit, *Tentang Sastra*, p. 33). Kuslan ("Menjongsong") pointed out that *ketoprak*, having originated with oppressed peasants and having served in the struggle against colonialism, had a natural political character; but, unfortunately, its lowly origins also meant that it did not have a high intellectual level and it had not completely freed itself from "feudal" ideological associations. "Feudalistic story themes must be changed into tales which can be a weapon against Feudalism.... The plots, which often spread superstition, must be made scientific. Those which are erotic must be cleaned up." In order to carry out such reforms, it was decided to establish a Ketoprak Cadre School in Yogyakarta, where leaders of *ketoprak* troupes could study the principles of drama, literature, mass organization, and ideology (*Harian Rakjat Minggu*, February 7, 1965).

44. However, in the late 1970s Srimulat, a new popular comedy theater, began attracting lower-class audiences away from the hitherto popular commercial *wayang orang* and *ketoprak* houses in Surakarta. Its productions, which some saw as a new genre, employed a mixture of Indonesian and low Javanese; they used contemporary rather than archaic settings and a mixture of pop and village musical styles. Srimulat appeared to reflect a further step in the cultural conversion of a rural folk to an urban proletariat (Umar Kayam, "Tradisi Baru Teater Kita?" [A New Tradition in Our Theater?], *Basis*, 29 [1980], pp. 366–70, at pp. 366–67; Siegel, "Surakartan Theater," p. 22). We might note that the Central Javanese, particularly from the royal centers of Yogyakarta and Surakarta, have clung to the old high culture much more tenaciously than the East Javanese, particularly those of proletarian Surabaya. Until recently *ketoprak* was as far as Central Javanese were inclined to stray from tradition, and it seems likely that Srimulat represents, in terms of the evolution of popular taste, the kind of development which occurred earlier in East Java with *ludruk*.

45. Hatley, "Ludruk"; James L. Peacock, "Anti-Dutch, Anti-Muslim Drama among Surabaja Proletarians: A Description of Performances and Responses," *Indonesia*, 4 (1967), pp. 44–73; and his *Rites of Modernization. Symbolic and Social Aspects of Indonesian Proletarian Drama* (Chicago: University of Chicago Press, 1968).

46. This attachment seems to have been established at an early date; thus the celebration of May Day by an East Java plantation workers' union in 1953 centered on a *ludruk* performance (*Warta Sarbupri*, 4:6 [1953], p. 122). After the 1965 coup many *ludruk* actors were killed or imprisoned, and all troupes were disbanded. They gradually reemerged, but always under the sponsorship of army or police units, and they were kept under heavy ideological supervision (Hatley, "Ludruk," pp. 41–47).

47. Thus a meeting of the PKI-sponsored dance association, Lembaga Seni Tari Indonesia, held to celebrate the party's 1964 anniversary, discussed an *eksperimen drama ludruk* which would give an intellectual content to the art and make it follow more closely the rules of socially-conscious drama (*Harian Rakjat Minggu*, May 24, 1964).

48. A good example of this effort can be seen in the general report to the PKI-sponsored National Ketoprak Congress of 1964, which outlined a program of ideological and aesthetic improvement (see *Harian Rakjat*, August 9, 1965; Koesno Ongkowidjojo, "Lampung dan Kesenian Rakjatnja" [Lampung and its People's Arts], *Harian Rakjat Minggu*, April 25, 1965). The Conference on Revolutionary Art and Literature passed a resolution which called for purging traditional dance forms (which included *wayang orang*, *ketoprak*, and *ludruk*) of frivolity, eroticism, and formalism; it also urged that individualism be combatted—that is, individual heroes who triumphed without the support of the masses (*Harian Rakjat*, September 27, 1964). Lekra praised the then-leftist Sriwedari *wayang orang* troupe for overcoming the difficulties posed by the famous *lakon* Arjuna Wiwaha, whose "feudal" character had seemed ineradicably expressed in its erotic and mystical emphasis: "... the comrades of the Sriwedari have turned the Arjuna Wiwaha into a sharp but artistic criticism of bureaucracy, autocracy, and the gods." (Drs. Sunardi, "Melihat Wajang Orang 'Sriwedari' " [Viewing the "Sriwedari" *Wayang Orang*], *Harian Rakjat Minggu*, May 24, 1964.) PKI leaders Banda Harahap and Naibaho explained to me (interview, March 1, 1965) that *ketoprak* troupes had at least reached a stage of consciousness that made it possible to shift their focus from traditional plots and characters to modern workers and peasants. Previously it had been necessary to convey a political message through traditional tales. Now several *ketoprak lakon* of the new type had been developed, and the party had duplicated plot outlines for circulation among interested troupes.

49. In the *wayang purwa* the clowns, "using modern language, modern ideas, and modern behavior, step among the heroes and demons and gods like wide-awake men in a dream world." Becker, "Text-Building," p. 224.

50. In its postcoup anti-Communist propaganda the army did not stress the PKI's intention to overturn good order by placing the clowns in charge, no doubt because, given Semar's divine status and identification with the common man, such a change might seem to some to have its logic. Instead, the army charged that the PKI had created *lakon* in which the Kurawa were the victors.

51. A good example of the way in which the PKI-sponsored arts emphasized social/political recognition rather than class struggle may be seen in the plot of a *ludruk* play performed in 1964 by a well-known PKI-affiliated professional troupe. As described by James Brandon (*Theater in Southeast Asia* [Cambridge, Mass.: Harvard University Press, 1967], pp. 110–11) it amounted to: poor boy loves rich girl, whose father is a government official. The father prefers a rich suitor, who, however, is a criminal type; he is exposed by the boy's father, an honest laborer (the *dagelan* or clown-figure), with the cooperation of the police. At the wedding which marks the happy end, the *dagelan* makes a long speech stressing that "True happiness in life comes not from having money but from simple friendship between people, all people, rich or poor, farmer or townsman, laborer or government official. The others are impressed by the *dagelan*'s speech. They agree. The bride's father rises and officially welcomes the *dagelan* and his son into their family. Henceforth, they all will strive to improve themselves, to bring unity to the people of Indonesia, and to promote world peace. The father raises his clenched fist in the air, 'Crush Malaysia! Crush Malaysia!' "

52. *Rites*, pp. 167–82.

53. In this interpretation I differ considerably from Peacock (*Rites*), who sees the clowns as *kolot* figures of ridicule, and *ludruk* as a whole as acculturating the Javanese proletariat to modern, positive thinking. As Hatley ("Ludruk," p. 45) points out, *ludruk* heroes do not get ahead by enterprise but by attracting the attention of the rich and powerful, for it is only by such "magical" wish-fulfillment that the poor see a chance of bettering their condition. For a detailed criticism of Peacock's interpretation see Keeler, "Father Puppeteer," pp. 7–12.

54. The tension between the *dalang*'s roles as village entertainer and mediator with the gods, as purveyor of courtly values and spokesman for the people, has been noted by students of the *wayang* (see especially Groenendael, *Er zit een dalang*; Keeler, "Father Puppeteer"), and does not seem to be simply the product of recent change. It may, in fact, be quite ancient in origin.

55. I am grateful to Martin Hatch for impressing this point upon me.

56. See *Harian Rakjat Minggu*, July 11, 1965. We might compare the PKI's recommended reforms to those enforced on *ludruk* troupes by the police and army units that have sponsored them under the New Order. No regime criticism is allowed: on the contrary, near the beginning of the performance a single clown now comes on stage and sings the joys of the New Order and the achievements of the armed forces, which have brought stability and development. The clowns are thus made formally to acknowledge official reality; later, the transvestite singers resume this role (Hatley, "Ludruk," p. 42). Popular *ludruk* plays stress the difficulties of the little man in coping with the wicked and corrupt big city; no solution other than fairy-tale rescue is proffered and no systematic explanation for his plight is provided, partly to avoid offending the authorities and partly because in fact no solution is seen (ibid., pp. 46–48). We can imagine that this ideological vacuum, symptomatic both of the New Order's problem of legitimation and its concept of the *rakyat* as a "floating mass" free of political involvement, would not have been allowed by the PKI. If under the New Order *ludruk* does not give hope, it at least continues (barring *pro forma* gestures of allegiance) to portray the world as the *rakyat* experience it.

57. Brandon (*Theater in Southeast Asia*, pp. 217–19) gives a useful discussion of the troupes' finances and political affiliations in the pre-1965 period. As he points out, most companies were pragmatic in their party choice, one manager asserting that his group always joined the cultural organization of whatever party was in power in the town where they were performing.

58. For an example of the use of *wayang* stories in the anti-Malaysia campaign, see Crawford and Adhikarya (*The Use of Traditional Media*),

pp. 14–15. In 1965 Z. Afif ("Pembaruan") described some of the new *lakon*. He noted, however, that "The innovations described above do not reflect a fundamental change" because in order to achieve a real reform "there must be completely new *lakon*, which genuinely reflect present-day reality, which cannot be depicted symbolically by the classical plays." The road to fundamental renewal had not been taken, he charged, because of a "fear of destroying or vulgarizing the *wayang*"—an opinion which was fed by "dogmatism and conservatism."

59. A similar solution—saving the art by stressing a high aesthetic level, while bending its purpose to official goals—may be seen in the post-1965 President's urging that *dalang* serve as "active communicators" of the New Order's development program: "Certainly it would not be appropriate for us to change the artistic role of the *dalang* into that of a mouthpiece for development, for if we did *wayang*'s artistic coherence would be destroyed. This would harm all of us, harm the artistic culture which we should develop. But I believe that you *dalang* understand what needs to be done. The development message can be conveyed while preserving the artistic level and coherence of *wayang*." (Soeharto, *Sambutan Presiden kepada Pertemuan dengan para dalang dalam Rangka Pekan Wayang pada Tanggal 27 Juli 1978 di Jakarta* [The President's Address at a Meeting with *Dalang* in the Context of the *Wayang* Week, July 27, 1978, in Jakarta] [Jakarta: Departemen Penerangan Republik Indonesia, 1978], p. 7.) But insofar as *dalang* have tried to follow orders they have not been received favorably by audiences, which continue to expect them to express, particularly through the clowns, the feelings and values of the common man. (Cf. Ras, "De clown-figuren," pp. 456–57; Groenendael, *Er zit een dalang*, p. 302.)

60. Singgih Wibisono, "The Wayang as a Means of Communication," *Prisma*, 1:2 (1975), pp. 53–59; Becker, "Text-Building," pp. 227–28; Crawford and Adhikarya, *The Use of Traditional Media*.

61. Becker, "Text-Building," p. 225.

62. Keeler ("Father Puppeteer," pp. 328–30) notes that the sequence of scenes is adhered to even in the highly unorthodox *lakon* purveyed by the fashionable *dalang* Ki Nartosabdho. A further unifying element is the fact that the physical appearance and the character of any given puppet is fixed: the puppet-carver and puppet-master do not "interpret" *wayang* personae but attempt to realize most exactly a character which is assumed to have a real if invisible existence (Holt, *Art in Indonesia*, pp. 140–49). Their art is judged by its success in approaching that ideal reality. Thus the standard Indonesian-language account of *wayang* devotes itself not, as a translation of the title would suggest, to a history of the genre, but to detailed description of the appearance and character of the individual puppets—that is, to the unchanging images which exist in an immanent past. (Hardjowirogo, *Sedjarah Wajang Purwa* [The History of *Wayang Purwa*] [Jakarta: Balai Pustaka, 1966].) Innovation can thus take place only by introducing new puppets and new *lakon*. In modern times, however, the influence of Western theater and changing social norms have made for reevaluation of some of the major *wayang* heroes (Anderson, *Mythology*, pp. 27–28) and also for a certain leeway in presenting them.

63. Such "demystification" of *wayang* was often deliberate. When the Central Java Lekra sponsored a festival in Yogyakarta in January 1964, it purposely chose to put on the Bharatayudha—the climactic *lakon* of the Mahabharata cycle, the performance of which is traditionally held to be spiritually perilous. There was no incense-burning, no offerings, and no *selamatan* feast (the normal minimal ritual safeguards). The plays were performed on five successive nights, but for only five hours at a time. All this, it was argued, served to expose the superstitions regarding the requirements for a *wayang* performance (*Harian Rakjat Minggu*, February 9, 1964). Such a stance was intentionally ideological; but the same kinds of changes were, as we shall see below, introduced by amateurs of the *wayang* from among the new bourgeois elite, who wished to play *dalang* but felt uncomfortable with what they, too, felt to be superstitions and unnecessary ritual.

64. See Robson, "Kakawin Reconsidered," p. 294; Zoetmulder, "The Wajang," pp. 89–94. Keeler, "Father Puppeteer," p. 310, notes the popular view that it was the *dalang* who first taught the villagers *basa*—the proper use of language, the basis of communication and social order.

65. For a general discussion of the *dalang*'s role and training, see Groenendael, *Er zit een dalang*, and Keeler, "Father Puppeteer."

66. For an account of modern *dalang* training courses, organizations, and changing roles,

see Groenendael, *Er zit een dalang*, pp. 51–59, 208–24; and Sri Mulyono, *Wayang*, pp. 99–108, 258, 263–65. Sri Mulyono himself was one of the Gajah Mada University students who inaugurated the four-hour *wayang* performance (see below).

67. The PKI placed its main emphasis on *ketoprak*, perhaps because it was locked in a contest with the Nationalist Party for patronage of that art. In 1957, it founded the All-Indonesia Contact Body for Ketoprak (Bakoksi), with headquarters in Yogyakarta. By 1964, Bakoksi had, according to one official PKI source, 800 member groups (*Harian Rakjat*, February 4, 1964); according to another, 1,371 (Kuslan Budiman, "Menjongsong"). It was in any case the largest politically aligned theatrical association in the pre-1965 period (cf. Brandon, *Theater in Southeast Asia*, p. 215). *Wayang orang* and *ludruk* were accommodated, with other traditional and modern dance and theatrical forms, in Lekra's Institute of Dance Arts (Lestari). *Ludruk* was eventually given an institute of its own, the Lembaga Ludruk, with headquarters in Surabaya. At its first congress, held in 1964, it claimed 250 member troupes (*Harian Rakjat Minggu*, August 9, 1964). In connection with the *wayang* reform campaign a Lembaga Dalang Karawitan was established by the East Java Lekra in January 1965. Chaired by the well-known *dalang* Ki Gito Sewoko, it formed a "creation team" which sponsored a *wayang* festival in Kediri, at which both male and female *dalang* presented politically relevant *lakon* (*Harian Rakjat Minggu*, February 7, 1965).

68. Dharmoyo W.S., "Sampai Kapan Wayang Dapat Bertahan?" [How Long Can *Wayang* Last?], *Warta Wayang*, 1 (1979), pp. 4–5; Sri Mulyono, *Wayang*, pp. 248–62; J. C. Tukiman Taruna, "Wayang: Apa Yang Akan Terjadi?" [*Wayang*: What Will Happen to It?], *Basis*, 25 (1976), pp. 322–25, 335.

69. Sri Mulyono, *Wayang*, pp. 112–38. A second National Wayang Congress, held in July 1978, established an organization for the promotion of *wayang*, Sena Wangi, membership of which was to be 50 percent practitioners of *wayang*, 25 percent patrons *(pembina)*, and 25 percent *wayang*-lovers (the last category presumably being composed of people less powerful than those in the second). It founded a journal, *Warta Wayang*, and announced a five-year plan for the promotion and improvement of *wayang* (*Warta Wayang*, 1 [May 1979], pp. 48, 58–59). For a Central Java *wayang* association of similar ilk, see Groenendael, *Er zit een dalang*, pp. 229–38.

70. *Laporan*, pp. 13–14; Sri Mulyono, *Wayang*, pp. 126–27.

71. Sri Mulyono, *Wayang*, pp. 265–70; Singgih Wibisono, "The Wayang," p. 58.

72. For New Order efforts to control the *dalang* and utilize *wayang* for official purposes, see Groenendael, *Er zit een dalang*, pp. 224–36, and Singgih Wibisono, "The Wayang." In a sense, we may see the government's efforts as an extension of that process of eliding the boundaries between court *wayang* and popular *wayang* that began with the foundation of the court-sponsored *dalang* schools early in the century: the popular *wayang* is "upgraded" to the purposes as well as the style of the court *wayang*, and thus the cultural space controlled by the political center is expanded. Of course, the court is not located in the same place; indeed, as Groenendael notes (p. 136), *wayang* performances rarely take place at the old royal courts, and their elderly court *dalang* are little more than curators. What has happened is that the court center is now the presidential palace in Jakarta, and the high culture is that of the modern urban elite. Modern communications, education, organization, and surveillance methods extend its reach far beyond that of the older royal centers, with the result that folk and local characteristics are overwhelmed. The high-culture "national" model becomes standard not only in the sense of the standard set, but also in the sense of what is normally obtainable, and not following this standard becomes a conscious act of resistance. At the same time, modern technological capabilities and commercial openness facilitate the development of urban-based "pop" cultural resistance, which can evade the grip of government-controlled radio and television by the use of cassettes (Martin Hatch, "Popular Music in Indonesia" [paper presented to the International Conference on Popular Music, Bologna, 1983], pp. 10–11).

73. Groenendael (*Er zit een dalang*, p. 174) notes that *dalang* in the countryside are, with very rare exceptions, dependent on other forms of activity for their main income; increasingly they are not peasants or petty traders but teachers or other officials. Moreover, the village celebrations where *wayang* performances traditionally played a purifying and protective role are losing their significance: "The interruption of the traditional agricultural rhythm (evident in the fact there are now several harvests per year), the separation of the *dalang*'s activity from the traditional purification ritual (by associating it

with the Independence Day celebration), the reorientation from a local, Javanese center to the national, Indonesian center and the resultant increase in scale, all have a profound and irreversible effect upon the traditional Javanese world view and hence on Javanese society. It is a development whereby the invisible spiritual protectors and the *dalang* are likely to lose their grip on the community" (p. 195). Keeler ("Father Puppeteer," pp. 294-95) notes that recent rural prosperity has in fact meant a rise in income for *dalang*, or at least for the better-known. Fewer villages sponsor *wayang* performances at harvest time, but more families can afford to do so for their ritual purposes. In the long run, he points out, such display is likely to give way to conspicuous consumption of modern goods.

74. Anderson, *Mythology*, pp. 27-30; Sri Mulyono, *Wayang*, p. 95. In this evolution the *dalang* becomes increasingly a stage performer. Certain *dalang* become fashionable on this basis, and to sponsor a *wayang purwa* performance by a "trendy" *dalang* becomes a display of wealth and status among the urban elite (Barbara Hatley, "Indonesian Ritual, Javanese Drama: Celebrating *Tujuhbelasan*," *Indonesia*, 34 [1982], pp. 55-64, at p. 55). This model is spread widely through radio and television sponsorship of *wayang* performances and the sale of cassettes featuring favorite songs and scenes by favorite *dalang*. In the towns, *wayang* is increasingly commercialized, performances being held in halls which spectators pay to enter. At the same time, broadcasts and the availability of cassettes and printed plot outlines have encouraged many *wayang*-lovers to try their hand at the art. The result has been an explosion in the number of people claiming to be *dalang*, a loss of mystical associations, and a general shift toward the concept of the *dalang* as pure entertainer. See Singgih Wibisono, "The Wayang," p. 56; and Efix Mulyadi, "Situasi Pedalangan Kita Rawan" [The Situation of *Wayang* Performance among Us is Worrying], *Kompas*, September 1, 1978 (Interview with Drs. S. D. Humardhani, rector of the Indonesian Fine Arts Academy [ASKI] of Surakarta, in connection with Indonesia's Third Wayang Week).

75. This tendency has become obvious even in *ketoprak*, both because it has been more willing than *ludruk* to adjust to high-culture standards—Ras notes that already by the late 1930s it had eliminated the usual introductory *jogèd* dance, had begun to use females to act female roles, and had adopted more realistic costuming and scenery—and because, in turn, it has received high-culture recognition: *ketoprak* performances were broadcast on the postrevolutionary radio, and records and cassettes were made of the genre. As a result, "professional" standards were set, storylines became fixed, dialogue planned, and so on (Ras, *Javanese Literature*, pp. 6-7).

76. An interesting case was the ban on a film made from *Arjuna Mencari Cinta*, a novel by the young writer Yudhistira Ardi Noegraha. Yudhistira's Arjuna stories satirize corrupt Jakarta elite life, but the names of the unsavory characters that appear in them are those of *wayang* heroes. The film was banned not for attacking the elite but for "damaging the *wayang* world." Officials declared that it might be shown if all *wayang* names were omitted including the one in the title (Benedict R. O'G. Anderson, "Sembah-Sumpah: The Politics of Language and Javanese Culture," in *Change and Continuity in Southeast Asia*, ed. Roger A. Long and Damaris A. Kirchhofer [Honolulu: University of Hawaii Center for Asian and Pacific Studies, Southeast Asia Paper No. 23, 1984], pp. 15-57, at p. 42). Yudhistira's use of *wayang* in his very popular stories is significant: while he assumes in his audience an extensive knowledge of the *wayang purwa*, he deliberately attributes to its characters qualities the opposite (or the exaggeration) of those the *wayang* original represents. He thus takes much more liberty with the old legitimating myth cycle than does the *ketoprak*, in which Arjuna continues to appear as a hero rather than, as for Yudhistira, a spoiled Jakarta teenager. *Ketoprak* makes *wayang* heroes human; Yudhistira makes them laughable. His purpose is implicitly but clearly a denunciation of the established order (Savitri Scherer, "Yudhistira Ardi Noegraha: Social Attitudes in the Works of a Popular Writer," *Indonesia*, 31 [1981], pp. 31-52).

3

"Good Omens" versus "Worth": The Poetic Dialogue Between Ton Tho Tuong and Phan Van Tri[1]

Jeremy H. C. S. Davidson

In Viet-Nam, poetry and politics have never been very far apart. In the precolonial period, poetry was not merely the major vehicle for literary expression, it was also the principal means for the presentation of differing views on contemporary social, political, and educational questions. Furthermore, in Viet-Nam, as in other regions under heavy Chinese cultural influence, the small groups who actively participated in politics and poetry-writing heavily overlapped in membership. Following the traditions of state Confucianism and the imperial examination system borrowed from China, candidates for official positions in the state administration were required to master the subtleties and intricacies of the Chinese classics and of verse composition in the Chinese manner. Conversely, those traditional scholars who were not, or had ceased to be, officials, maintained intimate social and intellectual ties with the political elite, since together they formed the thin, powerful social stratum of literati who dominated most aspects of Vietnamese society.

Poetry's proximity to power meant not only that it was of real political importance, but also that its practitioners had opportunities and ran risks rather difficult to imagine in contemporary Western societies. For those who associated themselves closely with the prevailing powers-that-be, there were always rewards aplenty. The dangers were not less plentiful for those who, for whatever reasons, set themselves up as critics of the established order. As the national epic, *The Story of Kim, Van, and Kieu*, noted:

Have talent but don't be too sure of it,
For (the words) talent *[tai]* and calamity *[tai]* make a rhyme.[2]

In times of peace and relative social harmony, poetry and power were usually more or less aligned. There was not much to complain about, and authority felt secure enough to tolerate its periodic critics. But in times of political or social crisis, tensions inevitably arose, encouraging repression on the one hand and an artfully esoteric, allusive style of expression on the other. Few events in Viet-Nam's history have been as catastrophic as the rapid penetration of French imperialism in the second half of the nineteenth century: repeated military defeats, foreign occupation, political collapse of the ruling dynasty, Christianization, not to speak of the sudden appearance of an immensely intimidating industrial civilization on Vietnamese soil. Seldom before in

Viet-Nam's history, even during periods of Chinese occupation, were poetry and power so suddenly and drastically counterposed. Small wonder, then, that Viet-Nam's poetry-makers, faced with an unprecedented crisis, found themselves pulled in violently opposite directions, as they sought, in very different ways, to bring the two together again: some by "relocating" poetry closer to the new power, others by trying to summon the old power to the defense of poetry.

The present essay is intended as an introduction to the best known and remembered "battle of poets," a battle which was precipitated by the impact of an apparently invincible French imperialism. What I hope to show are the extraordinarily complex conflicts which occurred amongst the traditionally trained scholar-mandarins of Old Viet-Nam when they came face to face with the reality of coping with a radically altered world.

Background

The reign (1820–40) of the Emperor Minh Mang is generally taken to represent a certain high point in the consolidation of Vietnamese state institutions on the principles of neo-Confucianism.[3] Knowledge was thought to be properly acquired by reading and learning the works of the Confucian sages. Success in passing state examinations, at increasingly difficult levels, demonstrated a man's understanding of, and sometimes ability to interpret, this knowledge. Successful scholars were regarded as *quan-tu*, "superior men," who provided the manpower for the mandarinate and with whom rested the responsibility for accurate and effective judgment in all public affairs.

Yet Minh Mang's world was no longer a wholly traditional one. His father, Nguyen Anh, the founder of the Nguyen dynasty (under the reign-name Gia Long), had made extensive use of Frenchmen during his reign. In turn, the French had occasionally made their mark. Pigneau de Behaine, the Bishop of Adran, had even succeeded in converting Gia Long's son Canh to Roman Catholicism. Canh, however, died shortly before his father. On his accession to the throne, Minh Mang led a reaction against these foreign influences. To ensure that the Vietnamese people adhered to classical rather than to foreign learning, Christian missionary work was prohibited, and by 1833 violent persecution of Vietnamese converts became state policy.[4] The French response was harsh: in 1847 the fortifications at Da Nang were leveled and Vietnamese ships in the harbor were destroyed by naval gunfire. The anger and fear produced by this affair led the reigning emperor, Thieu Tri (1841–47), to decree the immediate execution of any European caught on Vietnamese territory. Under his successor, Tu Duc (1848–1883), the situation deteriorated further. The emperor was increasingly cloistered from events by those high-ranking administrators who handled dealings with the outside world. In the 1850s there was mounting dissension within the educated elite, many of whom came to despise the court for its indecisiveness and weakness; in their eyes it seemed incapable either of organizing resistance against the invaders or of helping patriots to conduct a struggle of their own. Their dissent often took the form of literary attacks and sometimes of open, armed revolt.

Subsequent French missions, like that of de Montigny in 1851, made unnecessary shows of brutal force, causing xenophobic retaliations, which then led to further French assaults. In 1858, Da Nang was captured once again. Early the next year, Admiral Rigault de Genouilly attacked and captured Saigon. Returning in full force in 1860, he greatly extended French control in Nam-ky, the southern region which the French called Cochinchina. Since this area was the rice-bowl of Viet-Nam, he was thus able to deny food supplies to the central region. In 1862, Tu Duc and his administration attempted to lessen the immediate pressure on their state by formally conceding to the

French much of the territory the latter had recently acquired through military action, i.e., the three eastern provinces of Bien Hoa, Gia Dinh and Dinh Tuong, plus Poulo Condore. The imperialists also insisted that the Vietnamese pay an enormous indemnity and agree not to cede Vietnamese territory to any other foreign power without prior French consent. What the court conceded, however, Southern Vietnamese society was by no means prepared to accept. The French found it impossible to get the mandarinate's help in administering their newly annexed territory and were thus forced to introduce direct rule from 1862.

In 1863, Tu Duc sent Phan Thanh Gian (1796–1867), who had signed the peace treaty of 1862 ceding the eastern provinces to the French, with a diplomatic mission to Paris in a vain attempt to buy back the lost provinces.[5] Subsequently, in 1864, the Vietnamese began a guerrilla war based within the three western provinces of Nam-ky, i.e., Vinh Long, An Giang and Ha Tien. In 1866, Gian was appointed *kinh luoc* (Viceroy) of this region, since it was becoming ever more obvious that the French aimed to acquire these provinces as well. In 1867 these fears were realized. Admiral de la Grandière took only the four days between the 20th and 24th of June to seize Gian's viceroyalty. Gian, who was recognized by most Vietnamese outside the Hué court as a great patriot, was so deeply ashamed of this second loss to the French that he committed a long drawn out and agonizing suicide in July. This suicide caused widespread distress[6] among the anti-colonialists and their literary supporters, as well as among the general populace. When, in 1868, he was posthumously and ignominiously deprived of all of his official titles and distinctions by the emperor, anti-dynastic feeling was greatly exacerbated.[7] It was into this depressing social and political environment that our poet antagonists came to maturity.

As the French established themselves in Nam-ky and extended their influence to the North and Center, one group of scholars, awed by the military, technological, and scientific strength of the French, and attracted by their "modernity" as well as the wealth and honors they offered, became collaborators. Another group of scholars advocated a material modernization on the Western model together with a retention of the traditional Vietnamese philosophical outlook and an avoidance of political association with the French. This group established itself mainly around the court. Yet another group, often called the abstentionists, fought the French intellectually by using literature to revile them and by acting as mentors to the military patriots whom they exhorted to expel the enemy by force. Among this third group were such leading poets as Phan Van Tri, Huynh Man Dat (1807–83), Duong Khue (1839–98), Chu Manh Trinh (1862–1905), Nguyen Khuyen (1835–1909), and Tran Te Xuong (1807–1907).

Ton Tho Tuong was an outstanding member of the first group. A native of Binh Duong district, Tan Binh prefecture, Gia Dinh province, he came from an established military mandarinal *(vo quan)* family. His grandfather and father had both helped Nguyen Anh in his successful bid to establish himself as the ruler of Viet-Nam. Since his father was a *cu-nhan*, or licentiate, who had been an official of the Nguyen administration, Tuong had gone to Hué while still quite young. There he quickly earned a reputation for his poetry and calligraphy. When his father died in 1840, he had to go back to his natal village for the funeral. Perhaps because of the loss of his father at an early age, he became a playboy. By the age of 30 in 1855, he still had not passed the village-level examination *(thi huong)*. Nevertheless, in that year he sought permission from Hué to become an official and was granted a post in the military administration because of his ancestral connections. As this post fitted neither his tastes nor his abilities, he resigned and went south once more. His impoverishment led him to write poetry for sale; worse still, he was caught in the act of writing a poem for another examinee in the examination hall at Hué. Pardoned because of his father's merit,[8] he was then sent back to Gia Dinh where he set up the Tao Dan Bach Mai Thi Xa, the poetic commune of the White Plum Literary Group, with which initially, it seems, most of the literati in the South were associated. His ambition to become a civil mandarin *(van quan)*, however, remained unfulfilled; his earlier misdeeds counted too heavily against him. By now he had become completely disaffected from the Hué court, and from the Confucian traditionalists. This point in his life could perhaps be encapsulated in the saying *tuy thoi hanh dong*, or "follow the times and act (accordingly)."

When in 1862 the French asked for Vietnamese to assist them in the administration of their newly acquired territories, many Southern Vietnamese Catholics volunteered; so did a small group of non-Catholics—among them Tuong. As we have seen, he had strong financial and personal reasons for cooperating, but his poetry suggests that he also came to perceive the solutions to Viet-Nam's problems in a way different from those of his poetic and political opponents. Being remarkably able, he was quickly appointed county-chief *(tri-phu)* of his home prefecture, Tan Binh, and was later asked by the French to negotiate the surrender of the military patriot Truong Dinh. In spite of his lack of success in the latter effort, he was appointed next year as secretary to Gian's mission to Paris. There he helped prepare the concessionary documents favoring the French. From the time of his return to Southern Viet-Nam in 1864, he became a target of derision among his former poet-colleagues and friends, whose moralizing and satirical spirit continued to be directed against both the court and those who worked for the French.

One of these critics was Phan Van Tri, a native of Thanh Hong village, Bao An district, in today's Gia Dinh province. In 1849, he became a *cu-nhan*, as result of which he is usually known as cu Tri. But he did not undertake a mandarinal career, since he was one among the many literati who thought the Hué court unworthy of support. He first withdrew to Binh Cach in Tan An, and then to Phong Dien in Can Tho, where he opened a school and taught until he died in 1910. Here he dwelt in relative poverty, enjoying the simple pleasures traditionally associated with *lettrés* and poets—fishing, singing, playing chess, and drinking[9]—and likening himself to a well-known character from the days of the Han dynasty.[10] In Nam-ky he was one of the coterie of scholar-poets and potential bureaucrats who were either "resting" or "withdrawn"; the group of his close friends included many who were abstentionists and/or active supporters of the patriotic military resistance. Among these were such impressive *lettrés* as the famous nationalists Nguyen Dinh Chieu (1822–88), Bui Huu Nghia (1807–72)[11] and Huynh Man Dat. A prolific poet who wrote largely in *nom*, Tri was connected at an early stage with Tuong's poetic circle and spent time improving his prodigious poetic talent under the critical eye of Phan Thanh Gian. Tri had visited Gian on several occasions for the latter's appraisal of his poetry and had, apparently, been severely criticized for some of his metaphorical verse; but his poetic reaction to the loss of Vinh Long in 1862 won him great respect, for the poem reflected the widespread anger at the humiliation of Hué's surrender to the French of the three eastern provinces.[12]

The Loss of Vinh Long
Nonsensically the horns blow the sounds of *nam ba* [lit., "five, three," a reference
   to the sounds of the French military bugle]—
One hears it reach the ear, (and) the stomach is sharply pained (from afar).
The winding river Rong [the Dragon River, i.e., the Mekong] sombrely smokes in
   haziness,
Flaming red-gold Phung city [the Phoenix city, i.e., Saigon] sorrowfully beckons.

> The dispersed households are deeply affected because of sentences of diverse rancor;
> Carving up of the land—people feel hurt by the substitute for peace [i.e., the treaty with the French].
> Wind and dust [i.e., battles] repeatedly uproot and fell the grass;
> Holding silently on one's mouth a smile, one finishes speaking of the deplorable plight of our mandarins.[13]

Such losses led him, and many like him, to become increasingly hostile to those fellow countrymen who had become collaborators with the French, and in particular to Ton Tho Tuong, a former friend, who had now become an associate of the aggressors. Somewhere around this time cu Tri set up the "abstentionist" Ty Dia (Avoid the Land [the enemy has taken]) movement, which many of his poetic colleagues joined. All efforts to entice him to join the French, including blandishments from people such as Tuong, were unsuccessful.

THE POETIC DIALOGUE

Such then was the context in which the Tuong-Tri "poetic war" took place. The opening shots, so to speak, were fired by the remarkably talented and deeply educated Tuong. In the poem *Tu' Thu' Quy Tao* ("Tu Thu Returns to Tao"),[14] he borrowed the life-story of an earlier Chinese patriot led for reasons of personal loyalty into serving a ruler not his own, in order to defend his own course of action. Aside from its political theme, this poem was notable for its novel and exceedingly difficult modification of a simple, standard metrical form.[15] The "Tuong" rhyming scheme was quickly copied by admirers and exploited by enemies. In particular, Tri used it to skewer his adversary. He satirized Tuong as an actor in the operatic drama, *hat boi*, then especially popular among the feckless nobility and bureaucracy at Hué. Looking out at both Tuong and the Hué court, Tri wrote in *Opera Actors*:[16]

> Some have scabies, other have scurf,
> However much their clothing, they can't hide it any more.
> The loyalist's red face has white eyes,[17]
> The flatterer's black beard a few scraggly hairs;[18]
> (Although) on the crosspieces (of the building) there is a roof, still they roof themselves with parasols.[19]
> Between their legs they have no horses, yet they raise their whips.
> No wonder people say actors are unfaithful.
> They smear their faces (with make-up) and hit one another with fists and again with punches.[20]

Tuong naturally tried to defend his position. Likening himself to the good wife who always remembers her own family but feels duty bound to side with her husband's, he wrote a plaintive reply drawing on the theme of the *Kieu*. Assuming the guise of Lady Ton, he wrote:

> On the back of a horse a sword completes the character *tong* [to follow]:[21]
> (For) a thousand years one holds high the moral integrity of the girl of Giang-dong.
> Separated far from Ngo, unable to leave because of attachments to the cluster of silver clouds [i.e., the senior members of the family],
> Returning to Han, one adorns and (decorates) refinedly a slender piece with pink cheeks [i.e., a woman].

> Make-up [i.e., the woman] would prefer to take along dense wind and dust [i.e., difficulties].
> What are the golden stones [i.e., the path of love] so that one blushes for the mountains and rivers [i.e., the motherland]?
> Whoever returns, send word with Chau Cong Can,
> I would prefer to lose your heart, elder brother, and gain the heart of my husband.

To this Tri sharply responded in turn:

> You there, Ton Quyen, do you know?
> The righteous man venerates (his) lord, the woman venerates her husband.[22]

By these lines he implied that there was no genuine comparison between Tuong and Lady Ton. She represented the classical Confucian virtues: the pieties of subject to the ruler, wife to husband, and child to parent. The Vietnamese saying goes "A boat follows its tiller, a woman follows her husband"; so Lady Ton acted fully in keeping with the proper behavior for a wife. Tuong's behavior had nothing classical or exemplary about it and his claims to that effect were mere "acting" and deception.

The real war, however, broke out with the dissemination of *Tu thuat*[23] ("Being Autobiographical"), a set of poems in which, it seems, Tuong intended to present himself yet again as a good Vietnamese who made the right, though exceedingly difficult, decision to associate with the French.[24] Precise dating of the *Tu thuat* is difficult. From internal evidence it appears to have been begun late in 1867, following the death of Phan Thanh Gian, and continued into 1868, though Tuong's first stanza (I/7) alludes to the resistance movement of Truong Cong Dinh which collapsed with its leader's death in action in 1864. The immediate stimulus for the *Tu thuat* is obvious. Tuong was the target of much poetic derision, frequently in response to poems he himself had penned, by former friends and members of the Southern Vietnamese intellectual and poetic circle. Hence he sought to explain himself, his actions, and the necessity of working with the French to his former colleagues and to the Southern Vietnamese at large. The poems tended to be copied by hand for a limited readership but were then sung in accordance with specific regional musical patterns to a local audience gathered for the occasion. It is possible, too, that his employers had asked him to popularize their presence and to try to win over more of the literati to collaboration.

A further political and literary stimulus was certainly provided by Do Chieu, who had recently composed *Respects to the Deceased Truong Cong Dinh*,[25] lamenting the latter's death while fighting the *bach quy* (white devils), and *Funeral Oration for Phan Cong Tong*, dealing with the, as then believed, battle-deaths of the two sons of cu Gian.[26] Both sets of poems were in the *the lien hoan* (linking body) style, which Do Chieu had often used for political poetry. Tuong adopted this style for his *Tu thuat*, perhaps in order to encourage a subconsciously approving image of the French by making use of a poetic form that had general popularity among the Southern Vietnamese. A more personal reason was probably that Tuong had been the negotiator both with Truong Cong Dinh and with the Phan brothers, and in both cases had failed to make them lay down their arms.[27]

The stanzas of the original *Tu thuat* are redolent with metaphors which are difficult to convey in English, and they make use of remote Chinese historical and literary figures and events as a cloak for, or a reflection of, contemporary personalities and events in Viet-Nam. The same is true of Tri's riposte, *Hoa van* ("Capping Rhymes"), though Tri's allusions are more direct and harsh. Together the pair provide a good example of

Vietnamese poetry as a method for expressing political opinions in the guise of refined literary discussion.

TU THUAT VERSUS *HOA VAN*[28]

Tuong starts the poetic exchange by stressing that Viet-Nam's geography and history continue to exist, but that its rulers have failed to prevent the present state of decadence. Heaven and Earth, traditional symbols of the Gods and the nation (the former being the source of the classical Mandate of Heaven [*thien menh*] to the ruler), seem to consider the Vietnamese elite unworthy of continued authority, yet Viet-Nam still survives:

I/1–2 The rivers and mountains of the Three Provinces, their renown is still here.
What did Heaven and Earth incite that we should reach this state?[29]

In his capping rhyme, Tri insists that the struggle for independence must continue and that to submit to the French is to be defeatist.

I/1–2 To win or lose is not yet decided, there as well as here,
It has not already obliged us to be like this.

"There as well as here" refers to the presence of the resistance movement in the western provinces, as well as in the French-controlled eastern provinces; it may also allude to struggles between the southern elite and the central court. Tuong in reply points out the industrial and military power of the more modern French:

I/3–4 With lightning speed, perfectly straight, the telegraph[30] wires stretch away;
Clouds belch out, pitch-black, the smoke of boats flies.

Tri replies, pointing out the consequences of this for the Vietnamese:

I/3–4 Ben Nghe[31] [Buffalo Calf Jetty] does not mind the hardships (of) the conflagration, of fires burning,
(Nor) Con Rong [Dragon Dune], although dust and ashes fly.

Tuong's "lightning" can be used as a metaphor for war, and this meaning is capped by Tri's "dust and ashes," which alludes to the fate of two villages razed to the ground by the French in 1859 in retaliation for the fierce resistance of the inhabitants. Since both villages were located on the Mekong, the lines pick up Tuong's allusion to engine-driven French ships. Where Tuong's talk of black clouds, belching out, invokes a massive French naval presence, clouds, Con Rong, and the Cuu Long ("Nine Dragons") River, i.e., the Mekong, provide Tri with references to the Dragon which is the mythological father of the Vietnamese people.

Impressed by French military strength and technical ability, Tuong feels the need to join them:

I/5–6 Restlessly, secretly, I feel that I should ask for a place;
I rejoice personally, having been deeply worried for days.

He argues that Vietnamese weakness is clearly shown by French power (I/7). Resistance is futile, and what is required is a leader who can show the people an effective way to peace and prosperity (I/5–7). To this Tri responds:

I/5–6   Rearing wild animals, killing rabbits, we still wait for the time (which is bound to come),
           To throw the net and hunt the deer [32] (which will also have their day).

He means that patriots should withdraw to the wilds and live a guerrilla life; success will come in due course. Here he openly contradicts the sense of Tuong's next couplet:

I/7–8   The mouth of the tiger, the jaw of the dragon does not easily pierce (it).
           I advise the young: Do not get mixed up in other people's business.

These lines refer to the failure of the armed movement led by Truong Dinh (the jaw of the dragon). Tuong counsels Vietnamese youth not to involve themselves in fighting against the French (the tiger), since they will inevitably be defeated. To this Tri mockingly replies:

I/7–8   Do not borrow the breath of the tiger to frighten the monkey for a short while.
           Our heart is iron and stone, how is it unsteady?[33]

The monkey is the cowardly Vietnamese who submits to the minimal presence ("the breath of the tiger") of the enemy. The French can only be in power for a short while, for there is always a spirit of national solidarity, strength, and resistance ("our heart is iron and stone").

In stanza II, Tuong commences by trying to make it clear that he does not want Vietnamese youth to die because of what he considers misguided action:

II/3   Foolish youth and a deep well, I do not have the heart to let them be together.

In the previous line, however, he has used *ba* for *bac*, "to reject"—"(He) who hires himself out, takes care of the job (and) rejects wrong action"; and this line gives Tri the opportunity to interpret *ba* (in *ba vo*) as "broadcast," and to reply:

II/2   Not investigating his own lot, he skillfully talks of wrong action [*noi vo*, which also means *noi ba lap*, "to talk nonsense"].

Having begun by mocking Tuong in II/1 ("Unsteady [his] heart of iron") for his indecisive and unfeeling stand, Tri himself proposes:

II/3–4   Intelligent people, busy and caring about reputation,[34] are not dazzled (by wrong action skillfully expounded).
           Foolish youths are bewildered and frightened, years do not wait (for them to become intelligent).[35]

Tuong's poem continues:

II/4–5   The road is long, (both) day and night, (yet) years do not wait.
           From the clothes one has already seen the rolled up (sleeves) of the craftsman.

"Good Omens" versus "Worth"   61

This is a very recondite reference to his trip to Paris accompanying Phan Thanh Gian, and his involvement as secretary in the preparation of the treaty ceding to the French the three eastern provinces; he also advises against resistance activity, counseling the people to come over to the French now, otherwise it may be too late ("years do not wait"). To this Tri reacts scornfully:

II/5   The peace treaty was prepared for print by the (hand of the) craftsman.

Tuong continues to defend his actions, particularly against the "chess move" of Do Chieu's *Fleeing the Bandits*:

II/6   Whatever the horse-drawn carriages,[36] I intend to recover the chess move.
          [The horse-drawn carriages refer primarily to the great mandarins who have failed in their undertaking against the French, but also to the new overlords.]

Since the young and inexperienced Vietnamese bureaucrats have even greater reason to fail, Tuong maintains that he will find a way to solve the problem, by collaboration, and that others should follow his example. Tri replies:

II/6   The business of fighting to win or lose is like a chess move.

Here he rejects Tuong's prediction of the failure of resistance and insists that dishonor strikes the coward (II/1–2), who does not dare to do his duty (II/7), but does not affect the hero (II/6) who dies defending his cause. Such a man is "a hero regardless of triumph or reverse." Tuong's pessimism, first broached at II/1–3, is now reiterated:

II/7   Lucky unlucky, unlucky lucky, where is it definite?

It leads him to castigate the resistance fighters and their intellectual mentors, likening them sarcastically to:

II/8   The mouth of the (northern) house-lizard, the tongue of the southern, let our ears ignore (them).

Angered by these references to creatures regarded as treacherous and poisonous, Tri responds:

II/7–8   Not yet avenging the tome [i.e., the treaty which desolated the nation] to pay his debt to the nation [i.e., his obligations as a citizen],
          How can he dare (to stand with) face covered and with ears ignoring?

Once again Tri alludes directly to Tuong's involvement in the shameful treaty with the French, thereby implying that he has been working with the enemy for a long time. At the same time he prepares to turn (III/2) Tuong's house-lizard metaphor against him.
    Tuong's third stanza is a lament. He sees the disgrace of the nation but feels he must try to remedy it by active involvement in a new approach to the situation, i.e., by taking the French way:

III/1–2   With ears ignoring (them) and face covered at a time when all is ruined,
          One thinks of the affairs of the world adding shame to the affairs of self.

Tri uses almost identical language to begin his destructive reply:

III/1 How can he have ignoring ears at a time when all is ruined [smashed to smithereens, i.e., not a silent ruin]?

He responds to Tuong's attack (II/6–7) by rephrasing his own earlier line (II/2)—"Not investigating his own lot, he skillfully talks of wrong action"—as:

III/2 He only knows how to reproach others, not to reproach himself.

Tuong continues (III/3–4) by stating that the Confucian principles of the scholar-bureaucrats have failed, and are collapsing under the weight of the French military presence:

III/3–4 Rising thickly, the ashes (of war) damage the path of moral principle;
Obscuringly, dust shuts the door of the nobility.

The French confuse the Confucian bureaucrats (obscuringly), defeating them in battle (ashes, dust); they retreat in all directions, shutting themselves off from their responsibilities, having already excluded Tuong from their ranks. Tri retaliates (III/3–4) by asking why Tuong still maintains that he possesses moral principles and how, as an administrator for the French, he dares to equate himself with a traditional Confucian bureaucrat:

III/4 Being like that is also called the doorway of the nobility?!

In the next stanza, a particularly sad one, Tuong attempts (III/5–8) to explain his newly accepted responsibilities to the people, and describes his position metaphorically (III/5–6):

III/5–8 On both sides the shoulders carry (on a pole) the five heavy rules;
A hundred piculs (weight), the bell hangs on one flimsy cord.
Whether buffalo or horse, whatever they call him, he puts up with it.
While this person [lit., body] is still not spoken of (realistically), what can one say of his fame?

He remains the active scholar-official, bearing responsibilities which resemble the Confucian *nam gieng* ("five constants").

Tri now exploits certain of these words to compose an erudite answer:

III/5–8 Deep grooves (on the shoulder make one) miscalculate the containing (capacity) of small boats.
A heavy bell is boldly fastened by a thin cord [*manh*].
If the body has a certain renown, the tassels must have it (too).
I counsel people: Let's treat reputation seriously.

Tri's use of "containing (capacity)" makes a deft satirical link between Tuong's *gieng* and *manh*, since *gieng* (*nom*, "law," "rule," is also written with a Chinese character *ying* for "full to overflowing") while *manh* ("cord") can also refer to "boat," since in *nom* it

"Good Omens" versus "Worth" 63

is composed of a radical for "boat" and a phonetic which means Mencius, the second major exponent of Confucianism. In this way Tri chides Tuong's understanding of the path of traditional learning, and ridicules his apparent ability, warning people not to be misled by it. Since Tuong talks of the heavy responsibility he, the only caring individual, bears ("A hundred piculs [weight], the bell hangs on one flimsy cord"), Tri counters in III/6 by suggesting that a real patriot should courageously take risks (*to gan*—"to be large of liver," hence brave). Tuong (III/7) maintains that he will patiently endure the vilification to which he is subjected, whether he is treated as a commoner (*trau*, "buffalo") or member of the elite (*ngua*, "horse"), and questions his opponent's knowledge of, and hence ability to criticize his reputation. Tri retorts (III/7) by likening his antagonist to a plant, using *tua*, which means "stamen," thus "male," as well as "short-lived" and "tassel," thereby alluding to Tuong's being dressed in French administrative regalia. The context indicates an additional reference to "head," thereby implying additional doubts as to Tuong's real ability, and advising the audience to pay closer attention to his claimed trustworthiness.

In stanza IV, Tri caps Tuong line for line. When Tuong says:

IV/1   What can one say of his [meaning "my"] fame and function when all is completely ruined?

Tri retorts with:

IV/1   Reputation is not a word used in speaking of [lit., does not talk of] truly contemptible men.

When Tuong chants:

IV/2   The ocean's vast, Heaven's high, one thinks again (there's) even more,

Tri makes a recondite dialect and calligraphic pun on the word *cang* (more) to frame his answer:

IV/2   One burns (candle-)wax to become grease [lit., "ashes"], tears are no more.[37]

Tuong develops his plaint neatly:

IV/3–4   Going up the mountains to catch tigers, it's not yet easy to be impertinent;[38]
Going into the river to catch fish,[39] isn't it obvious that one is condemned unjustly?

In the first line he has picked up II/3's reference to the forces of the Phan brothers unsuccessfully trying to fight the French (i.e., the tigers). Going up into the mountains is a rash undertaking with little chance of success, but a small intrusion into the rivers to catch fish might well prove beneficial. Why then is there such a violent reaction to his participation in the French administration of Nam-ky? Tri notes:

IV/3–4   The two doors of the nobility shove one another back and belly.
One famed and educated family, bereft, was completely destroyed.

He seems to mean that Tuong's desire for honor and power has been rewarded but he has brought about the demise of a family of Confucian scholar-bureaucrats who participated in the resistance. Thus he suggests that Tuong was largely responsible for the destruction of the family of Truong Dinh, or perhaps of Phan.

Tuong continues forcefully:

IV/7–8   Cheeping, laden, I feel sorry for the brood of chicks that have lost their mother.[40]
It is also an attempt to dare to be boastful [that is, self-assertive].

How can soldiers who have lost their leaders continue to resist the French effectively? he asks. ("Cheep" seems to refer to the noisy but useless sound that such leaderless "chicks" make.) Tuong implies that he will assume a protective role for them under the umbrella of the French.

The following lines by Tri on responsibility imply that he recognizes that Tuong has a sense of Confucian virtue, though he views him critically:

IV/7–8   Caring for a person of the same literary upbringing, so must I remind (him):
How easy it is for us [inclusive] to dare [i.e., flaunt] a name [i.e., reputation] that is boastful!

Educationally well-equipped for the task he has undertaken (V/1), Tuong states clearly that people like him, who are accused of being mere facades for the French, are actually from the same guild (in the professional sense of being part of the literati) as those who, like Tri, do nothing but talk:

V/2   (Those) selling appearance and (those) moving lips are also from one (and the same) guild.

Hence criticism by Tri and his allies is invalid. Tri immediately replies by suggesting deceit on Tuong's part:

V/1–2   If one is being boastful, the talk must be artful,
Dishonest men, honest men, how are they from one (and the same) guild?

But Tuong's next two lines are extremely powerful:

V/3–4   The silk thread rolled around the wings of the dragonfly (shows) the steadfastness (and determination) of the spider,
The wind bears the breath of the tiger, scaring the imposing-looking fox.

They suggest a criticism of the weak, pompous, Vietnamese intelligentsia, the "fox," who try to be imposing—thereby turning back on Tri the accusation of being a facade. A mere whiff from a distance of the French "tiger" is enough to scare them. Once again Tuong insists that the French will continue their expansion and will take over Viet-Nam, just as the spider ensnares the dragonfly. Naturally Tri disagrees:

V/4   The tiger sure to lose its strength [or: its position of authority] is easily defeated by the fox.

The French will certainly lose in the end to the Vietnamese, who are like a goose which has lost a few feathers but can still dominate smaller birds:

V/3   As for the wild goose, although its feathers are damaged, where is its fear of the sparrow?

Continuing his argument, Tuong suggests that:

V/5   If one is industrious and concerned [i.e., involved], does one wait for food to approach the mouth?

Within the French sphere, one is well cared for, if one does one's job; the hard working are more farsighted than the miscalculating (V/6). This "deception" is countered by Tri's allusion to the honest man Nhan—if one is like him, one does not yield to usurpers, regardless of the consequences.

V/5–6   The pupil (of the eye of the captive) Nhan,[41] how did it fear the knife approaching the tongue?
What did Khuat[42] worry about, the water rising from behind?

Tuong's urging patience (V/7–8) and his specific reference to the Ty Dia—

V/8   (To those who are) dancing along the edge [i.e., making a commotion, and living on·the periphery of activities] I request: Let's not run away and hide.

are met by Tri's call for properly timed action against the French:

V/7–8   If we see the means [lit., "machine"] and find the right moment, we shall act;[43]
Wanting it to develop like a big task, we *dare* to run away and hide.

Keeping the Ty Dia in the forefront of his argument, Tuong urges his audience:

VI/1   Let's not run away and hide from the tasks of the home [i.e., nation].

To this Tri replies:

VI/1   We run away and hide since we're busy because of home.

Tuong continues:

VI/2–4   After this, I still think of the (deplorable) events of the distant road.
Ghosts in a severe and violent outburst enrage two youths,
Heaven has worn to a shred the compassionate heart of one old man.

Here he refers to the Paris mission and cu Gian (VI/2), whose suicide incited his two sons to rebel (VI/3). He blames their father's death on Heaven (VI/4), whose Mandate has again failed to confer appropriate rule on those successful in action. Both Gian and Tuong failed in their negotiations with the French.

Tri chides him for blaming his predecessors (VI/2), welcomes the passion of the Phan brothers' revolt (VI/3) and bemoans the results of the servile bureaucratic behavior (VI/4) he ascribes to Tuong and his like:

VI/2–4 Daring to rebuke men of old is not reckoning far.
  With zeal let us have the enthusiasm of the strength of youth.
  Bowing and scraping and being obsequious (to get things done) also expended the breath of the old [i.e., cu Gian].[44]

Tuong, meanwhile, maintains that, despite difficulties, everything is under adequate control. Alluding to the powerful French presence he writes:

VI/5–6 Steering is already steady, in rough seas one glides;
  The hamlet intends to batten down when the rain falls.

Tri takes up the sea and sky analogy of this and earlier verses (Tuong IV/2, 3–4) and answers:

VI/5–6 The sweet smelling lure (and) the precious fish[45]—fishing (with a hook) is not effective [cf. Tuong IV/4].
  If the bow is weak and the bird high(-flying), one shoots but (the bird) does not fall [cf. Tri V/3].

Not all Vietnamese are duped. How can everything be under control when the administrator (Tuong) is not properly trained?

Tuong's regret for family loss (VI/4, 8) in this war-torn environment is countered by Tri's comparing him to a self-important frog who looks at the sky with a vision blinkered by the walls of his well. This line also harks back to Tuong's first allusion to the danger of wells (II/3):

VI/7–8 From the bottom of a well looking up at the sky, (what he sees) swells the eyes of the frog.
  To be a man like that is just so [i.e., a matter of form]!

Warning others, defending (even feeling sorry for?) himself, and encouraging collaboration by the talented, Tuong proclaims:

VII/1–2 Also a matter of form are people who certainly ought to take care!
  If they have ability and they endure difficulties, only then will they develop into students.

Tri replies that intelligent people who care for their nation are far removed from the French and from Tuong, and that, in order to be an effective administrator, one must first be a student (thereby defending the traditional education system in which Tuong had not been successful):

VII/1–2 Just so, intelligent men are also far away and caring.
  (To be) experienced at governing, one must (first) be a student.

Men's qualities will reveal themselves: when ink is placed on wood, the grain shows clearly whether it is straight or warped—another dig at Tuong who was caught taking an examination for another candidate.

Tuong now moves on to refer to the formidable kinds of material knowledge that the French control:

VII/3–4 Silver, vast, immense is the sea, the bridge is ready to be built;
Blue and obscure [i.e., hazy] is the sky, the ruler [meter] means to measure it.

The hint he gives that intelligent Vietnamese youngsters should become "modern" students, is treated with ridicule by Tri (VII/4). Tuong's comment that the French are better at planning military strategy than the Vietnamese thus implies a rationale for his long-term strategy of working with the French:

VII/5 On the wide table one figures through some chess moves.

This line leads Tri to delve deep into traditional morality to reply:

VII/5 What carriage of Chau waits in the capital city of Five Ministries?[46]

Similarly, when Tuong urges traditional scholars to stop their studies and wait for a French dominated-peace before resuming them—

VII/6 In high-storied buildings [i.e., classical libraries], one bundles up again the hundred volumes,

he is answered with an erudite reference to a scholar who helped the ruler win the nation and establish peace, prosperity and harmony:

VII/6 The House of Tong is just half full of books![47]

Nevertheless, Tuong's inner thoughts, poetically displayed, show considerable strength of character:

VII/7–8 This heart (of mine), although it pleads, yet it is not ashamed.
Silently I consider carefully within my mind that I also know what to tell.

In answer, Tri uses the word *cac-co*, "difficulty," to recall *cac-ke*, "gecko, chameleon" (cf. III/2; and Tuong II/8), thereby insinuating that Tuong has become merely a mouthpiece for the French:

VII/7–8 Seeking the mouth to praise people by (can) develop into difficulties.
The Way of Heaven [Providence] hates the crooked; isn't it obvious what one follows it for? [or, "isn't it obvious why one scrutinizes oneself?"]

Tuong's stanza VIII forms an introduction to the more plainly autobiographical last two stanzas and is, itself, quite personal, revealing a weakening of his forbearance, and the

68   Context, Meaning, and Power

wounding effect that Tri's "capping rhymes" have had on him. Lines 1 and 2 contain a warning to his antagonist against whom he has not yet taken action; lines 3 and 4 recall an earlier verse (III/7) and hint at some long-suffering resignation:

VIII/1–4   Have I not already told you men?
    Please do not accumulate resentment and spurn and laugh at me.
    In case that creature still bears whip burns [lit. "marks"],
    Take little notice of (the hardships of) this body, which puts up with (your) despising eyes.

Tri continues from his previous line's Confucian context to denigrate his opponent even further and to make connections with earlier stanzas (II/2, 5; III/2–4; VII/7–8):

VIII/1–4   What one follows it (the Way of Heaven) for, is that one knows that the point of attention is (a) man,
    Who does not worry about reputation but only fears smiles.
    In three regions tomorrow, although the ink is old too,
    A pair of pupils [eyes] look and already see nothing in the pupil [i.e., reflected in it].

Tuong's reputation is sullied. He has responded to the smiles of the French by helping sign the 1862 treaty which ceded the three provinces. Again Tri stresses the lack of vision, of understanding (VIII/3; cf. VII/4; VI/7) on Tuong's part.

Tuong, however, presents himself as a man of outstanding quality:

VIII/5–6   The moon between three autumns, clouds too (must) reveal it.
    Flowers, in bloom during nine summers, in the heat are still bright.[48]

Tri exploits the fact that the moon is also known as the jade palace *(cung ngoc)* to discuss "flawed jade," questioning its worth, and implying thereby that some people are bought and sold:

IV/5   As the merchant exults while not yet experiencing jade,

so,

VIII/5–6   A good jade with many stains, in what way is it regarded as of high quality?
    The clumsy worker with little color dyes, (his cloth is) not bright (colored).

In these lines he attacks Tuong the craftsman as a clumsy worker with little imagination and skill (II/4). Again he likens him to "a foolish youth" (cf. Tuong II/3–4 = Tri II/3–4):

VIII/7   The foolish youth finishes life old and still foolish.[49]

Since time is important, Tuong decides to explain some of the things he has done, referring back to Tri's earlier line (VI/3):

VIII/8   (As for my) bowing and scraping [i.e., humiliating myself] to get things done, I'll relate so many [lit., "a few tens"] (undertakings).

Perhaps thinking of the recent failures of youthful revolt, Tri pessimistically replies:

VIII/8   What's the use of years [i.e., age] when there are only one or two tens?

Tuong begins his two final autobiographical stanzas by noting that Viet-Nam was under civil, that is, Confucian scholar-official control (IX/1) for four generations (IX/3). During part of this time he was an administrator in the eastern provinces of Nam-ky (IX/4) and agreed with the decision that, since

IX/2   The snake was long, the stag large, thus it was prudent to separate them.

The snake, one must remember, is the smaller dragon, that is, Viet-Nam as a whole; the stag is Nam-ky. Thus he claims that fate has ordained that snake and stag should not be together; to achieve peace they must be separated. Men should not be compelled to follow tradition (IX/5) and try to keep the two united. But the Confucian literati *have* tried to shore up their traditions, claims Tri, perhaps with a hint of panic:

IX/3   In all earnestness we devoted ourselves to solidifying the foundations of moral principle.

Only traitors and those without the Mandate of Heaven—and no foreigner could ever be granted this mandate—would divide up the nation, and thus present a deceptive facade (cf. Tuong IX/4):

IX/2   The land that is broken off, who despises and dares to separate it?

IX/4   (And) looking busy, does one imagine *that* (to be) the task of making a living?

Tuong next says:

IX/5–6   With all their strength the people follow Heaven (but) cannot catch up;
Wasting effort, the bird tries to fill the sea without equaling it.

Here he links the Vietnamese people to Kua fu, a character in the *Lieh- tzu*[50] who tried to race with the sun, and eventually died of thirst. The Vietnamese people should, therefore, be sensible and give up their support for the court at Hué ("Heaven"), accepting their progressive new masters, the French. He describes their resistance as futile, comparing it with the action of the legendary bird that tried to fill the sea with stones.[51]

Tri regrets the instability of the imperial court—the people indeed can no longer rely on it. But he pounces on the word *bang* ("to equal") for his next line, which criticizes Tuong as crafty and deceitful:

IX/5–6   I feel sorry for the people because the nation sits not firm.
(And) I reproach the individual holding the balance [i.e., scale], (who) weighs not equally.

Tuong concedes the risks of the path he has taken:

IX/8   I close my eyes and venture into mistakes in the path of constant (virtues).

Tri, however, continues his analogy of balance:

IX/7–8   When the wind is violent, only then does one know that the trees and grass are sturdy.
         The lineage follows (earlier) men who upheld the five constant (virtues).

Tuong's concluding stanza is both aggressive and defensive. He questions Confucianism and the scholar-bureaucracy (X/1), asking why one should commit mistakes in order to obtain the support of the teacher (a direct blow at "teacher" Tri), when the right course of action, he believes, lies outside this traditional path:

X/1–2   What was the path of the constant (virtues) before being virtuous as well as honest?
         Why make mistakes [i.e., fail] in (moral) duty to be worthy of the teacher?

Tri, however, continues his defense of the pre-French educational system with:

X/1–2   The five constant (virtues) originally were truly virtuous as well as honest,
         On those occasions whoever exhorted them was skillful and busy as a teacher.

The land that the French have annexed is, Tuong claims (X/3), at peace, and its populace is beginning, though "shyly" (X/4), to accept the richness of its potentialities under French leadership (cf. Tri V/7). Then Tuong writes:

X/5–6   Literal meanings[52] teach the young; wrangles are still filled in [i.e., patched up].
         For white eyes [i.e., the blind] seeing the sky, it is difficult (to see how) wings fly.

This is an allusion to the blind poet Do Chieu's previously cited poem *Fleeing the Bandits*. It obliquely asks how a blind man can know the meaning of the things he describes. (Tuong is questioning whether tradition and the old educational system can offer solutions to the present situation.) Tri (X/5–6) maintains that this comes from an instinctive feeling of the heart. Tuong himself concludes by saying that this is also his feeling, for

X/7–8   I only want some day to get what I desire, to be satisfied.
         The rivers and mountains of the three provinces, their renown is still here.

For Tri, however, the conclusion of his poem is far from meaning the end of its topic, the state of the nation:

X/7–8   A storm-gust of wind carries over the uprooted [fallen] grass.
         To win or lose is not yet decided, there as well as here!

Conclusion

Evident throughout these poems are the opposing views held by the initiator of the poetic dialogue, Ton Tho Tuong, and his primary opponent, Phan Van Tri. Tuong maintained that traditional Confucianism as an educational, moral and administrative system was no longer appropriate to cope with the crisis Viet-Nam faced when the French imperialists began their conquest. Tri, however, strongly believed that Confucianism, if properly followed, could be effective, especially if it were seriously studied and practiced. Tuong, having been to France, and obviously impressed by the advanced development of Western technological, material, and military culture, felt that Viet-Nam must learn from the French, and that resistance was pointlessly self-destructive. Tri continued the traditional stand against the invader: provided one retained the proper spirit of resistance, the occupier would eventually be ousted, as earlier history had repeatedly shown. Apparent also throughout the poetry is an acute awareness of time: its immediacy and the duration needed to achieve success. Tri encapsulates this concern in a very searching question:

> How much time (is there to be) to bring back the opportunity to unify?[53]

Moral rectitude *(nghia)* versus crookedness; right action produced by proper education and training versus improper action resulting from inadequate instruction; true versus salaried reputation—these themes in the polemic reek of the essence of Confucian philosophy, of Viet-Nam's traditional high culture, and of patriotic belief. In my view, Tri's language is more scholarly, more refined, more exquisitely poetic than Tuong's. His command of the *the lien hoan* style is more powerfully controlled, his literary and historical allusions more erudite and clearly expressed. (However, Tuong may have had personal reasons for keeping some of his references hidden.) Finally, Tri's skill at metaphor is greater and his clarity of thought more impressive.

Yet the antagonists were evenly enough matched to make the poetic battle captivating then as well as now; it has been the subject of much literary and political controversy ever since.[54] One can certainly see from Tuong's *Tu thuat* how rich are the levels of understanding in the language and in the literary references, and how relevant the argument posed by Tuong and answered by Tri in the late 1860s was to the long-term struggle for national independence and reunification.

Ironically, however, within the context of military and literary resistance to the French invasion, one may regard Tuong's decision to work with the foreigners as revolutionary and Tri's refusal as traditionally conservative. Following the apparent failure of open armed resistance, a reassessment, and hence a revised understanding, of the situation in its social, political, ideological, national and other contexts was made, and a rekindling of Vietnamese national spirit took place.

As is to be expected, since the Second World War Vietnamese interpretation has varied according to each commentator's understanding of the context in which the poetry was written and his sympathy for the two poets and their intentions. Vietnamese literati may well feel some sympathy for Tuong in his propagation of the potential of French modernization, since this approach was furthered by those who later, in the period 1895–1913 at least, felt that military resistance was no longer possible and that one had to defeat the colonialists by their own means (an approach proposed by the Dong Kinh Nghia Thuc, for instance). On the other hand, Tuong was widely regarded as a collaborator, and this role did not meet with much favor, except perhaps among some members of the Roman Catholic community, especially in the South. In particular, his actions have been interpreted as motivated primarily by personal financial considerations. His advocates, ignoring his faults, have tended, as hagiographers do, to hold him up as more virtuous than perhaps he was. They have even advanced the view that his demeanor in the polemic—his display of a certain forbearance—was that of a *quan-tu*, "a (Confucian) superior man." The view held in Northern Viet-Nam, however, is that Tuong was always attempting to deceive the public by his poetry and in particular by the *Tu thuat*; but the deceptive nature of his poetry was unmasked at each turn by another poet who managed to "cap" it.[55] What is in any case clear is that, as his poetry suggests, he thought that helping the French was rational and useful. He certainly worked hard along these lines until his death of malaria in Hanoi in 1877. And in his poetry he sowed the seeds of later political action—always one of the poet's goals in Confucian Viet-Nam.

That cu Tri has been highly esteemed by nationalists, Communists, and their supporters is quite natural. In his *Hoa van* Tri was not simply proposing traditional Confucianism as the answer to his country's dilemma. Rather, it was that element of philosophy, of regional thought, of cultural expression, that forms the warp and weft of the national culture; in other words it was the expression of Vietnameseness, of Vietnamese resistance to imperialism that Tri clearly represented. It is in this, in his rejection of Tuong's propositions in the *Tu thuat*, and in the language of his *Hoa van* that Tri's immediate and continuing popularity reside.

For in Viet-Nam, as elsewhere, but perhaps more openly in countries within the sphere of Chinese cultural influence, the competing influences of the quests for wealth and honor have been long observed, and the dilemmas facing the moral man in unprecedented situations have long been recognized. Several centuries earlier, another Vietnamese assessment of such a situation was pithily given by Nguyen Binh Khiem (1491–1585):

That way, ethics, this way, duty, just words one hears.
One hears them stop, and clink again as cash.[56]

Phan Van Tri took his stand with hope and morality, perhaps with even a dash of self-righteousness. It has been a stand admired by all those who rejected colonialism and collaboration with a foreign power, and who supported movements for national independence. In spite of Tri's strong commitment to state Confucianism, socialist realists and many other nationalists seem very ready to accept the ending to his *Cam hoai* (X/7–8):

The nation, one tomorrow, will change its destiny to one of peace,
The South in common will enjoy reunion in peaceful equilibrium.[57]

His meaning is crystal clear; it was the context that needed to be, and now has been, changed.

---

1. A fuller version of this essay, with Vietnamese texts and more detailed annotations, especially of the translations, is to appear in the *Bulletin of the School of Oriental and African Studies* under the title "*Collaborateur* versus *Abstentioniste*: A political polemic in poetic dialogue during the French acquisition of Southern Viet-Nam."

The given names of the two protagonists are Tuong and Tri. In Chinese characters, Tuong means primarily "good omen," then "happiness"; while Tri means "worth" and also "being on the job," "on duty," hence "a responsible character engaged in a reputable task." One of the problems in arriving at accurate interpretation of written material from the pre-French and transitional periods is the lack of original manuscripts. This problem is growing as *nom* (Chinese-style script invented for Vietnamese) and *Han-Viet* (Chinese read with the Vietnamese pronunciation of the characters) materials become more scarce, and misunderstanding increases. We should note, however, that the homophony of Vietnamese and the fact that the poems would have been recited aloud to an audience, encouraged much free association of ideas, and permitted listeners a very wide range of possibly related meanings.

An alternative translation of the first five stanzas of the poems analyzed has been published as "Document 8, Ton Tho Tuong (1822–1877) and Phan Van Tri (1830–1910): Collaboration vs. Resistance (ca. 1866)" by Truong Buu Lam in his *Patterns of Vietnamese Response to Foreign Intervention: 1858–1900* (New Haven: Yale University Southeast Asia Studies Monograph Series No. 11, 1967), pp. 81–86. Lam's translation is much freer than mine and his interpretation is also different.

2. The *Truyen Kim Van Kieu* was written by Nguyen Du (1765–1820). An allegorical autobiography in which the author assumes the guise of the main character, the woman Thuy Kieu, it contains a background rich in social, political and historical information relating principally to Northern and Central Viet-Nam. See Huynh Sanh Thong, trans. and ed., *Nguyen Du: The Tale of Kieu* (New York: Yale University Press, 1983), pp. 166–67.

3. See Alexander Woodside, *Vietnam and the Chinese Model* (Cambridge, Mass.: Harvard University Press, 1970).

4. Georges Taboulet, *La geste française en Indochine* (Paris: Adrien-Maisonneuve, 1955–56), pp. 323ff.

5. Among them, Gia Dinh was especially dear to Tu Duc as it was the birthplace of his mother and of many other ancestors.

6. Nguyen Dinh Chieu (= Do Chieu) in his *Respects to the Deceased Phan Thanh Gian* concluded: "The world [i.e., Viet-Nam] from now on wears the autumn wind." Since the autumn wind is the west wind, he implies that Viet-Nam is dominated by the French and that, after Gian's death, no one in the scholar-bureaucracy is capable of effectively resisting French expansionism. See Nguyen Ba The, *Nguyen Dinh Chieu (Than-the van thi-van), 1822–1888* [Nguyen Dinh Chieu (Life and Literature) 1822–1888] (Saigon: Tan Viet, 1957), p. 144.

7. Two of Gian's sons, Phan Ton and Phan Liem, had organized renewed military action against the French soon after their father's death, in accordance with the concept of filial piety central to Confucianism.

8. See Tran Van Giap et al., eds., *Luoc truyen cac tac gia Viet-Nam* [Abridged Biographies of Vietnamese Writers], 2nd ed. (Hanoi: NXS Khoa hoc xa hoi, 1971), p. 423.

9. Ibid., pp. 432–33, Entry No. 564.

10. This was Yan Guang (37 BC–43 AD), better known to the Vietnamese as Nghiem Tu Lang. A close friend of the emperor Guangwu (reigned 25–57 AD), he helped him to refound the Han dynasty, and then returned to the countryside to fish early in the morning and till the fields late in the evening. Tri may, however, have drawn the analogy to Nghiem Lang from a reference in Do Chieu's famous *truyen* (verse-novel) *Luc Van Tien* [The Story of Luc Van Tien]. This powerful allegorical autobiography was an immediate success and created in Southern Vietnam an instant rival to the national epic, the *Truyen Kim Van Kieu*.

11. Bui Huu Nghia was a traditional Confucianist scholar-bureaucrat of Central Vietnamese origins. When the French began to take over Nam-ky, he withdrew from service as county chief of Tra Vang in Vinh Long and sought refuge in Can Tho province. In 1868, he joined the revolt of the *lettrés* in the South, becoming a member of Tri's anti-cooperation Ty Dia movement. Arrested and imprisoned in Vinh Long, he was eventually released through the intervention of former friends who were now working with the French, most particularly Ton Tho Tuong. He is especially famous for his beautiful and impressive classical play *Kim Thach ky duyen* [The Miraculous Union of Kim and Thach], which Huynh Man Dat helped edit. See Nhat Tam, *Huynh Man Dat (1808–1883). Phu hai cu thu khoa: Bui Huu Nghia—Nguyen Huu Huan* [Huynh Man Dat] *(1808–1883)* [Appendix on Two Premier Laureates: Bui Huu Nghia—Nguyen Huu Huan] (Saigon: Tan Viet, 1956), pp. 19–57; Duong Dinh Khue, *Les chefs d'oeuvres de la littérature vietnamienne* (Saigon: Kim Lai an quan, 1966), pp. 315–16; Tran Van Giau, *Tho van yeu nuoc nua sau the ky XIX (1858–1900)* [Patriotic Literature of the Second Half of the XIXth Century (1858–1900)] (Hanoi: Van hoc, 1970), pp. 90–91.

12. Tran Van Giau, *Tho*, pp. 72–73.

13. Phan Thanh Gian and his colleague Lam Duy Hiep, both of whom signed the treaty of 1862 conceding the three eastern provinces to the French.

14. Tu Thu was a loyal supporter of Luu Bi (162–223 AD), the emperor of Thuc, one of the Tam Quoc (Three Kingdoms, 220–264). Tao Thao, emperor of Nguy, the most powerful of the Three Kingdoms, based in north China, wanted his services so he kidnapped Tu Thu's mother and wrote him a deceptive letter in her style pleading with him to desert Luu Bi. When the mother saw Tu Thu appear in Tao Thao's court, she was overcome with shame, railed against him, and committed suicide.

15. Tuong used the *tam cau Duong luat* (the 7-word, 8-line Tang dynasty metrical stanza), including where essential, as the final, and therefore compulsory, rhyme five words ending in *-oi*. Since such words had a limited range of meanings in Vietnamese, except to the very skilled and erudite, he thus created a new rhyming scheme straight away, which came to be called *van Tu Thu* (Tu Thu rhyme) from the poem in which it first appeared. See Nhat Tam, *Phan Van Tri (1830–1910): phu Hoc Lac Nhieu Tam* [Phan Van Tri (1830–1910): Appendix on Hoc Lac and Nhieu Tam] (Saigon: Tan Viet, 1956), p. 15, No. 2. Among Tuong's contemporaries who responded with poems in his new rhyme scheme were Huynh Man Dat and Bui Huu Nghia (see Nhat Tam, *Huynh Man Dat*, pp. 11, 39–40, No. 7–8).

16. Tran Van Giau, *Tho*, p. 75; cf. Huynh Sanh Thong, trans. and ed., *The Heritage of Vietnamese Poetry* (New Haven: Yale University Press, 1979), p. 202, No. 444. It must be remembered that in both China and Viet-Nam actors were traditionally regarded as duplicitous; hence they were barred from obtaining the formal, conventional education required for entering the ranks of the mandarinate.

17. In traditional operatic theater, red represents loyalty, white treason; white eyes are also indicative of blindness.

18. Thin, scraggly beards, as opposed to thick ones, represent insincerity.

19. Parasols are either ceremonial apparel or symbols of political authority.

20. Collaborators forget their origins and turn against their compatriots.

21. Ton Phu Nhan was the only daughter of the Ngo ruler Ton Kien (d. 192 AD), and younger sister of his son, Ton Quyen (181–252); she married the Luu Bi mentioned in note 14. For this poem, see Tran Van Giau, *Tho*, p. 80, especially lines 3, 4, 6, and 8.

22. Ibid., p. 74.

23. The *Tu thuat* is written in a Tang dynasty prosodic style, the *tam cau Duong luat*, which, when joined into a set of poems with an interlocking set of rhymes, is known in Vietnam as *the lien hoan* ("linking body"). These poems are normally divided into ten or more stanzas of which the very first and the very last lines of the whole poem are exactly the same; the last word or last few words of the first verse become the first of the verse following, and so on. The major rhyming word, which is the last syllable of lines 1, 2, 4, 6, 7, must, if there is to be a "capping verse" (*hoa van*) be identical in that *hoa van*; similarly the tonal prosody of each line in level (*bang*) or oblique (*trac*) tone words must also be the same.

24. Whether Tuong expected or intended his *Tu thuat* to be replied to is uncertain, though earlier *hoa van* may well have made him aware of the possibility. Also, it is uncertain whether Tuong wrote the entirety of the *Tu thuat* before Tri began to reply to him or whether they wrote their stanzas seriatim. The latter seems to be the case, but there is no hard evidence to support either possibility. Nonetheless, as the latter seems more probable, I have followed it in making my interpretation of the poetry. After Tri's first "capping verse," the *Tu thuat* and Tri's replies developed into what seems to have been a poetic duel, each writer often able to make telling reference to, or creative use of, ideas in his opponent's last or earlier stanzas.

25. See Nguyen Ba The, *Nguyen Dinh Chieu*, pp. 112–18; Trinh Van Thanh, *Thanh-ngu dien-tich; danh nhan tu-dien* [Dictionary of Celebrities, Literary Allusions and Sayings] (n.p., 1966–67), pp. 407b–8b; Tran Van Giau, *Tho*, pp. 51–53.

26. Nguyen Ba The, *Nguyen Dinh Chieu*, pp. 107–12; Trinh Van Thanh, *Thanh-ngu*, pp. 998a–99a; Tran Van Giau, *Tho*, pp. 59–60.

27. Tuong was sufficiently impressed by his visit to Paris and Madrid to rewrite, as the *Tay phu nhat ky* [Diary of a Journey to the West], Phan Thanh Gian's *Su trinh nhat ky* [Diary of the Envoy's Itinerary]. Bui Giang, *Giang luan*

ve Ton-Tho-Tuong va Phan-Van-Tri va nhac goi hinh anh cac bac danh-si cu cua Viet-Nam [Dissertation on Ton Tho Tuong and Phan Van Tri and Recollections of the Images of All Old Famous Scholars of Viet-Nam] (Saigon: Tan Viet, 1960), pp. 164–89; and Tran Xuan Toan, trans., "L'embassade de Phan-Thanh Gian (1863–1864)," *Bulletin des amis de vieux Hué*, 6 (1919), pp. 161–216, 8/3 (1921), pp. 147–87, and 8/4 (1921), pp. 243–81. The latter is a descriptive text in which Gian records how he was impressed by such aspects of French material culture as trains and artificial street lighting. These were also the aspects of modernization that Tuong wished to introduce to Nam-ky, as I/3–4 demonstrates.

28. The Vietnamese texts on which my translations are based are found in Tran Van Giau, *Tho*. The sources for other versions, or poems, if not found there, are referred to specifically.

29. "Heaven and Earth brought about the state of war," says Tri in his *Cam hoai* [Heartfelt Recollections], another set of ten poems in the *the lien hoan* pattern which, although obviously inspired by Tuong's *Tu thuat*, and therefore a continued consideration of the problem, was a personal poetic expression of his ideas on the topic. See Nhat Tam, *Phan Van Tri*, pp. 38–43; and Tran Van Giau, *Tho*, pp. 86–89. These poems, and particularly lines such as these, have led certain Vietnamese writers to advance the dubious argument that Tri had, by this time, actually changed his earlier stand, and partly come round to Tuong's point of view. (See, e.g., Bui Giang, *Giang*, p. 278.) Of course, given the subtlety and complexity of the two poets' positions, it is possible to see that they sometimes shared values, though disagreeing upon how to achieve them under prevailing conditions.

30. The first telegraph lines were installed in Saigon in 1862.

31. French military atrocities at Ben Nghe, an old name for the area around Saigon including Gia Dinh province, were first written about in a famous, moving poem by Do Chieu, with its sarcastic final line:

Fleeing the Bandits
The market melts away as soon as it hears the sound of western [i.e., French] guns;
A chess board, so in an instant it falls from the hand.
Fleeing from homes hordes of children run aimlessly here and there.
Losing their nests flocks of birds fly swooping hither and thither.
Ben Nghe's riches melt like foam,
Dong Nai's roof thatches and tiles form dye the color of clouds [i.e., become ashes].
I ask you, quellers of rebellion [i.e., Vietnamese imperial troops], this time where have you gone?
Be brave enough to let the black (common) people be caught in this calamity!

On this poem, see Tran Van Giau, *Tho*, p. 46; Nguyen Ba The, *Nguyen Dinh Chieu*, p. 105; and Huynh Sanh Thong, *The Heritage*, p. 197, No. 433.

32. "Hunt the deer" takes the informed member of the audience straight back to Do Chieu's poem and to a specific regional reference, Dong Nai (Deer Field), i.e., Southern Viet-Nam.

33. Listening to the polemic of stanza I between Tuong and Tri, Bui Huu Nghia wrote a poem responding to Tuong's argument (Nhat Tam, *Huynh Man Dat*, pp. 37–38). Though it follows Tri's rhymes, it expresses Nhgia's personal views very clearly (the following text is taken from Tran Van Giau's *Tho*, pp. 90–91).

Answering the "Tu thuat" of Ton Tho Tuong
In heroes, the Six Provinces lack what here?
How (did they) allow the rivers and mountains [the country] to reach this state?
The flames of Tam Tan rise strongly and the earth burns,
The cloud clusters of the Ngu quy fill the sky flying.
Tigers depend on thickly wooded mountains for shelter and support, meaning to wait for the (right) day.
Foxes disorder the abandoned gardens, reclaiming them will have its day.
In one corner [the three Eastern provinces] I feel sorry for the people of water and fire.
(Who says that) in the Temple of the South all the main pillars are easy to make unsteady!

"The people of water and fire" means "the country at war," and also continues the image of water under burning oil, of devastating French attack. "The main pillars" is an allusion to the highest ranking dignitaries in the imperial court, while the Temple of the South is a reference to the Temple of Confucius. Here Nghia suggests that true nationalists are like these central pillars: no one can shake them.

34. Cf. Tuong II/2; Tri IV/5–6, VIII/4–6, and below. The view that if you make a good reputation you should preserve it whatever the

circumstances, represents a strongly traditional Confucian and Vietnamese cultural stance.

35. Much later in the poem he reminds his audience of the arrogance that a limited view may engender by recalling a popular folk tale:

VI/7 From the bottom of the well looking up at the sky, (what he sees) swells the eyes of a frog.

In obvious reference to Tuong, he further observes:

VIII/7 The foolish youth finishes life old and still foolish.

36. Trinh Van Thanh has suggested that Tuong is taking up the principle "if the carriage in front breaks (down), the carriage behind it must avoid it," in order to mock the defeated literati of traditional Confucian persuasion. See his *Thanh-ngu*, p. 1247a. The horse *(ma = ngua)* and the chariot *(xa = xe)* are extremely important pieces in Chinese and Vietnamese chess. See Terence Donnelly, *Hsiang Ch'i, The Chinese Game of Chess* (Goring-by-Sea: Wargames Research Group Production, 1974), pp. 15–16, 20–22.

37. The dialect opportunity is the Southern Vietnamese pronunciation of *cang* as *can*; since in prosody both are treated as *bang* rhymes, Tuong's *cang* may be read as *can*, written in *nom* with the character for "to be dry." Furthermore, Tri uses an allusion to a line in an untitled poem by the Tang dynasty poet Li Shang-yin (812–56 AD): "[During the time it takes for] wax to burn to become grease [lit., 'cinders'], tears begin to dry," although the Chinese text actually begins "Candle guttering becomes ashes. . . ." See *Quan Tangshi* [Complete Tang Dynasty Poems] (a punctuated reprint of the Kangxi collection) (Peking: Zhonghua shuju, 1960), 539, p. 6168, line 16/4.

38. *Chua de lao* may also be translated: "it is not yet easy to be deceitful"; the original text in *nom* should resolve any misunderstanding.

39. *Danh ca* normally means "to fish by using a narcotic and then beating the fish," but it may also mean "to wager."

40. Some Vietnamese writers who are pro-Tuong maintain that this line shows he loved his sovereign (mother hen) but that he cared for his people (chicks) more, accepting responsibility for them (i.e., becoming their "mother hen") in an attempt to bring peace and prosperity through working with the French. See, for example, Dinh Xuan Nguyen, *Apports français dans la littérature vietnamienne (1651–1945)* (Saigon: Xa hoi, 1961), p. 10.

41. Nhan Cao Khanh (Han-Viet form of Yan Gaoqing), who lived from 692 to 756 AD, was a Tang district governor in Changshan during the An Lushan rebellion. The story has it that when forced to surrender to the rebels he refused to change his allegiance and fearlessly denounced his captors. They then cut out his tongue.

42. Khuat Nguyen (Vietnamese form of Qu Yuan), who lived from 343 to 277 BC, was a great Chinese poet-statesman of the Kingdom of Chu during the period of the Warring States. He drowned himself after being vilified by an enemy. See David Hawkes, trans., *Ch'u Tz'u: The Songs of the South* (London: Oxford University Press, 1959), pp. 11–15.

43. Tri V/7 is based on the proverb: *kien co nhi tac*, "see the opportunity, then act."

44. A later comment on this behavior and on Tuong VIII/8 is Tran Te Xuong's poem, *Lots of Mandarins*, which includes the following lines:

In Big Rattan Guild Street, my! there are lots of mandarins.
"City Security" [a name] is pitch-black, "Schools" [name] is spotty!
Inextricably mixed with (lots of) husbands, the wife over there is Mrs. "Finance"!
To succeed at exams, bowing and scraping, the mandarin begs (from) uncle academicians far removed.

See Duong Dinh Khue, *Les chefs d'oeuvres*, p. 396.

45. The sweet-scented, tasty lure or bait *(moi)* cannot entice the noble, precious (or crafty) fish, despite the possible outcome implied by the figurative meaning of the traditional procedure *mac moi cau ca* (catch the bait to hook the fish) which is "a lure to make people covetous." On another level, *moi* may conjure up the idea of the "turtle" which is a national symbol; while "precious fish" *(ca quy)*, usually referring to the carp which, traveling up river to mate, leaps the waterfall and is transformed into a dragon, is a symbol for success in the traditional examination system—something which Tuong was unable to achieve.

46. Here Tri recalls the action taken by the emperor Wenwang of the Zhou dynasty (?1050–256 BC), who sent his personal carriage to pick up a certain person and bring him back to court to become his general; the idea is that a king can act informally to choose the right person at the right time. He implies that Tuong is pretentious and mistaken about his position.

47. Tri is here alluding to the story of Zhao Pu (921–991) of the ephemeral Tong dynasty who, it is said, kept a set of Confucius's *Analects*, one half to help the first emperor to create the state, the other to help the second emperor establish the dynasty and profess peace.

48. Tuong equates himself with a moon so bright that not even the clouds over three continuous autumns can obscure it; and with brilliant flowers that bloom in the midsummer heat over nine continuous summers. Thus his character and achievements shine through all attempts to blacken his reputation.

49. Several associations occur here: *trot dai*, "to make a mistake (doing something)": *trot doi*, "to live one's life"; and, most importantly, *(gia chang) trot doi*, "to commit a serious blunder in old age." All are aimed at undermining Tuong.

50. See Angus Charles Graham, *The Book of Lieh-tzu* (London: Murray, 1960), p. 101.

51. There is a Chinese legend that the daughter of an emperor drowned in the Eastern Sea and then turned into a bird-star. Because she was so angry with the sea for depriving her of human life, she spent the whole of her existence as a bird-star dropping stones into the sea in an attempt to fill it up and "kill" it. Naturally she was unsuccessful as the sea is infinitely vast—a point which Tuong had made twice earlier (IV/2, VII/3).

52. Cf. note 40. *Nghia den*, "literal meaning" (lit., "black meaning"), in the context of learning, may be contrasted with *nghia bong*, "figurative, metaphorical meaning" (lit., "shadow meaning"), in that the first, implying as it does a word-for-word meaning, conjures up the traditional Chinese and Vietnamese dictionary formats and definitions—written or printed in clear black characters. On the other hand, *nghia bong* suggests the lack of clarity, of definition, that speech or theater or shadow puppetry may engender. The first suggests a point of reference, the second needs the first to build on; then it can be very creative and appealing to the nimble, artistic minds of people like Tri and Tuong.

53. See his *Cam hoai* I/7, reproduced in Tran Van Giau, *Tho*, p. 86.

54. Cf. ibid., pp. 71–72, and Bui Giang, *Giang*, p. 280.

55. Tran Van Giap, *Luoc*, pp. 423–24, No. 549.

56. P. Schneider, "Nguyen Binh Khiem, Porte-parole de la sagesse populaire: le 'Bach-van am quoc-ngu thi-tap' (Receuil de poèmes en langue nationale de la retraite du nuage blanc)," *Bulletin de la Société des Études Indochinoises* (New Series), 49 (1974), p. 640.

57. Tran Van Giau, *Tho*, p. 89.

4

BURMESE CONCEPTS OF REVOLUTION

Robert H. Taylor

The idea of revolution has generated a flood of polemical and philosophical writing during the past two hundred or more years. Complex and debatable as any definition of political or social revolution may be, whether for Americans, Russians, Frenchmen or others, the term "revolution" itself is a powerful symbol both of the founding purpose and of the continuing rationale of many modern states and the societies which they govern. For the Burmese, too, since the 1940s the idea of revolution has come to be a key concept in the state's political symbolism but because of the absence of an established and widely recognized single word for it in the earlier evolution of the Burmese language, two words implying two quite different concepts of revolution have emerged. Both in writing and in speech, the use of one or the other of these words, *ayēi-daw-bon* or *taw-hlan-yēi*, tells where a Burmese stands politically in relation to the two most significant events in Burma's recent political history, the simultaneous regaining of independence and outbreak of civil war in 1948, and the military coup of 1962.

The introduction of Marxism into Burmese political thought in the 1930s fostered a debate about the nature of government and social change, but as the political context of this debate was altered by new political, economic and military experiences, the Burmese term for revolution emphasized by the national elite has changed. The choice of word for revolution has come to indicate the conscious purpose enunciated by state leaders to justify their actions. This essay analyzes the development and use of the two Burmese concepts of revolution in order to indicate the interaction between the historical context of political action and the meaning of political terms favored by political leaders.

In the classical, precolonial Theravada Buddhist-derived political thought of Burma, the concept of political and social revolution did not exist. Political change meant primarily the substitution of one ruler by another of the same kind. Since 1948, however, the concept of revolution has become the metaphor which leaders who intend not only to control but to transform radically the nature of the polity use to convey to their followers the essence of political purpose. Both the leaders of the first postindependence government in 1948 and the formateurs of the Revolutionary Council government in 1962 justified their accession to and use of power in the name of the revolution. In both instances the ideal of revolution meant a progressive moral and social change that would result in the establishment of a new and just social and political order. Upon the attainment of power by erstwhile revolutionaries, however, the idea of revolution became the justification for state policy and the basis for the legitimacy of all those who claimed the authority of the state.

The gaining of Burma's independence from Britain in 1948 was accompanied by the introduction of a form of democratic socialism justified by an ideology similar to mainstream 1930s British socialist thought. The political party that provided the intellectual justification for the state's early form and policies took the name Ayēi-daw-bon Party and the efforts of the government to survive the civil war that followed immediately upon independence was described as Prime Minister U Nu's *ayēi-daw-bon*.[1] But on March 2, 1962 the leaders of Burma's army, accusing the civilian politicans who had led the state since 1948 of having abandoned the goals of Burma's revolution, took power under the name of the Taw-hlan-yēi, or Revolutionary, Council. Since then they have restructured the state and economy and installed a one-party political system.

Why did the leaders of the 1948 and 1962 revolutions use different words to encapsulate the spirit of their political actions and purposes? One might have thought that by the late 1940s the idea of revolution would have become clearly fixed in the leaders' minds, but such a conclusion would be erroneous. Rather, the continuing existence of alternative Burmese concepts of revolution highlighted the unresolved struggle between rival attitudes toward government, history and social change that lay behind the Burmese civil war and led to the military elite replacing the civilian government in 1962.

I do not mean to suggest here that either rival elite has actually been consistent in its usage of the concepts. As Edelman wrote, "Accuracy is not the important characteristic of political language, but the appraisals common to members of a group [are]."[2] I do think, however, that a discussion of the two political attitudes indicated by the two alternative concepts of revolution may provide an insight into the nature of political thinking as it has shaped political action. By analyzing the Burmese words *ayēi-daw-bon* and *taw-hlan-yēi* it is possible to understand better the ideational roots of state action following the "revolution of 1948" and the "revolution of 1962." First, however, it may be helpful to note the general nature of political language change in modern Burma.

During this century many words conveying new or originally foreign political concepts have evolved and become somewhat regularized in Burmese usage. As editorialists and ideologists debated among themselves and with the wider public about the nature of modern political life, the language of political discourse came to be used more and more self-consciously and carefully, since controversial ideas needed to be expressed consistently.[3] For example, the problem of conveying the idea of socialism in Burmese generated in the mid-1930s a plethora of terms, some rooted in Burmese tradition, some growing out of contact with English intellectual and political traditions that were part of the colonial experience.

The first shapers of Burmese Marxist thought, Thakin Soe and Thakin Than Tun, attempted to deal with these issues consistently and thus set the linguistic parameters for their successors, both Communists and (later anti-Communist) socialists. Accordingly, in 1938 when introducing Soe's pioneer ideological tract *Hsoshelit Wada* ("Socialism"), Than Tun was forced to concede that although it was undesirable to use an English word to convey political ideas to the Burmese public, there was in this case no alternative, in view of the political connotations attached to other indigenous terms then in use.[4]

Than Tun identified five expressions commonly used in the 1930s to signify socialism. The first, *alut-thamā wada*, literally "workers-ism," conveyed the idea of trade unionism which to the ideologists of Burmese Marxism was not genuine socialism. The English term "Fabianism" was also in use, but to Than Tun it was unsatisfactory not only because it was a foreign word, but also because it really meant another capitalist form; he described it as meaning an upper-class movement doing things for the workers, rather than the workers doing things for themselves.

Two other terms growing directly out of Burmese culture were more appropriate, but had to be rejected because of their identification with allegedly nonsocialist political movements. *Hsīnyēithā wadą*, "poor man's policy" or "proletarianism," although in itself an appropriate term, was rejected because it had become identified with the political cause of Dr. Ba Maw and his Hsīnyēithā Party and was therefore attached to the capitalists and imperialists with whom Dr. Ba Maw worked when Premier. It had become the kind of "socialism" that, according to Than Tun, stood in opposition to genuine socialism. *Dọbama wadą*, or "we Burmanism," had also become identified by some as a kind of socialism, but it too had to be discarded because the Dọbama Asīayōn of the Thakins[5] was basically a Burman and Buddhist organization; it did not incorporate all the poor of Burma because it excluded non-Buddhists and non-Burmans and thus confused political matters with religion.

The fifth phrase in use, *bon wadą*, or "common-ism," came nearest to expressing Marxist socialism and indeed Thakin Soe in *Hsoshelit Wadą* used the term interchangeably with *hsoshelit*. Yet because of its cultural antecedents it was not in the long run acceptable. For although in this century *bon* has come to indicate "common" or "joint," in the nineteenth century it meant, among other things, a palatial abode, a plane of existence in Buddhist philosophy, or a company of traders. Thus Than Tun concluded that the English word socialism had to be used, at least temporarily, until a new term could be coined in Burmese. Of course, *hsoshelit* is still in use today by all Burmese political groups—as in the title of the current ruling party, the Myanmạ Hsoshelit Lānsin Pati (Burma Socialist Programme Party)—for no satisfactory indigenous term has been agreed upon.

Other ideologically loaded political terms have presented fewer problems for publicists. There has been near universal accord for many years that *ayīn-shin sa-nit*, "owner of wealth system," means capitalism. For some time socialism and communism were thought of as the same concept, but gradually a contrast between these ideas developed. Nowadays communism is sometimes identified by the term *bon* that Thakins Soe and Than Tun used in the 1930s, but in the writings of some ideological theorists it is also rendered by the culturally attractive Buddhist term *pa-dei-tha pin*, a Burmese version of the cornucopia.[6] But the government and the Burma Communist Party have both had to accept the same solution as for socialism, and merely transcribe communist into Burmese as *kon-myu-nit*.

With regard to other innovations in the language of politics, it has been possible to agree in practice on specific indigenous words for general, less controversial concepts. Burmese words to express the notions of "history" and of "politics" as used in English have become standardized, so that there is little disagreement over their meanings. Even in these cases, however, uniform usage has only been achieved quite recently. When the ideas of "politics" and "history" first came to be used in their European sense, editors felt it necessary to print the English words with their new Burmese equivalents in the titles of essays. One of the earliest articles on modern politics in Burmese, published in *Thuriyạ Maggạzīn* ("Sun Magazine") in December 1919, was entitled "History and Politics, *Yazạwin Pạnya hnit Tāingpyi Okchok hmụ Hsainya Pạnya Akyāung*."[7] The Burmese part of the title can be translated literally as "About the Study of Chronicles and Knowledge Concerning Country Control." In his important pioneering essay setting forth the materialist conception of history in 1938, Thakin Than Tun also used *yazạwin*, or chronicle, to signify "history."[8] However, this usage, like the 1919

Thuriya usage for "politics," has now been abandoned. The generally accepted term for history is now *thamāing*, which originally meant the chronicle of a monastery or of a village.[9]

The concept of "politics" was analyzed and dissected in a Marxist mode in two essays by Thakin Aung San in 1940.[10] These essays, which follow closely the ideas of Thakin Soe, stand, alongside Than Tun's on the idea of history, as seminal articles in the evolution of Burmese Marxist thought. Called "Naingnganyēi Amyōmyō" ("Kinds of Politics"), Aung San's uncompleted series was an effort to develop a term that approximated an English Marxist concept of politics common during the 1930s. When he looked back over precolonial Burmese literature to try to find an indigenous expression for politics instead of the new (now standard) term *naingnganyēi*, literally "the conquered area's affairs" or "the kingdom's affairs," he found only a long phrase that can be rendered as follows: "internal affairs; the ruler's affairs are as broad as a cumulus cloud—the colour of a chicken egg, the *pauk* tree with a parakeet."[11] While conveying the constantly changing and nebulous nature of political reality, this precolonial concept centered on the affairs of the ruler, neglecting the masses, and was too unwieldy to use in popular politics or political analysis. Aung San regretfully concluded that the modern word *naingnganyēi* would have to be used.

The first Burmese Marxists were less self-conscious of the implications for politics of the words they used to signify revolution. The use of *ayēi-daw-bon* or *taw-hlan-yēi* did not seem to pose the terminological dilemma for political activists that other words did, perhaps because it seemed obvious to them what the two terms meant. But in retrospect it becomes apparent that the subsequent violent conflicts that developed among Burmese Marxists stem in large part from the fact that while they agreed that Burma required a revolution, they did not share a common conception of what this meant.

Ayēi-daw-bon, the name attached to the revolution of 1948, is the older of the two terms and the first frequently used to denote the concept of revolution. The School of Oriental and African Studies' Burmese-English dictionary gives these meanings for *ayēi-daw-bon:* "affair, cause, campaign, struggle, revolution; fortune, prospects, position; historical account of a campaign of struggle for power."[12] Amongst politically involved people in Burma today, it is the first of these sets of definitions that is most important, although the latter are also well known.

The root of *ayēi-daw-bon* is *ayēi*, meaning a business or affair, to which is appended *taw (daw)*—the suffix denoting royalty, a deity, or (now) the state—and *bon (pun)*, a narrative or sequence of events, giving literally "story of royal or state affairs." Judson, in a dictionary he prepared in the early nineteenth century, noted that *ayēi-daw*, while literally meaning royal affairs, was a term applied especially to wars waged by kings, but also rebellions, etc., while *ayēi-bon-sa* (*sa* meaning paper) was a journal of military occurrences.[13] In current daily parlance the term is generally taken to mean the style or nature of a movement or matter concerning royalty or the state; it indicates a political movement in a similar but more forceful sense than the alternative but neutral term *hlok-sha-hmu*. An *ayēi-daw-bon* is also a body of literature, being the five or six historical accounts of the struggle for power by Kings Danyawadi, Yazadarit, Hanthawadi Hsinbyushin, Nyaungyan Min, and Alaungpaya.[14]

In 1940 *ayēi-daw-bon* was taken as the Burmese name for the secret party formed by Aung San and others to overthrow the British, which is normally called in English the People's Revolution Party. The same name was taken in 1945 by the Socialist group, later party, within the Anti-Fascist People's Freedom League (AFPFL) and thus came in the 1950s to indicate the idea of revolution identified with the AFPFL-Socialist-led government, referring to the attainment of independence along with the party's social democratic ideology. By that time, however, it was often thought of in terms of a people's cause or a people's movement rather than as a revolution to overthrow established authority and to redistribute values and power.

Such was not the case when the word first came into common political usage in the 1930s through Marxist Thakins in the Dọbama Asī-ayōn and student movement and through the founders of the Communist Party (Burma). Then it stood for a European idea of revolution and was used to describe, for example, the French Revolution or the contemporary Burmese students' revolutionary movement.[15] It became the rallying-call of radical nationalists; publications by polemicists such as Thakin Soe and Thakin Aung San typically included at the beginning or the end of their treatises the slogan *"ayēi-daw-bon aung-pase"* (Victory to the Revolution).[16] Thakin Soe used *ayēi-daw-bon kyī* (*kyī* meaning great) to denote the Marxist concept of the eventual world revolution.[17] The first publication of the Communist Party (Burma) in 1940 was entitled *Ayēi-daw-bon*.

In the 1930s Burmese Marxists were less confident about the use of *taw-hlan-yēi* to express the idea of revolution. This newer word was less firmly fixed in the language of political action and Burmese history, and its roots are more complex than those of *ayēi-daw-bon*. It apparently stems from the old concept of the redemption of slaves or of indentured labor.[18] The initial element, *taw*, is the same as *daw* in *ayēi-daw-bon*: that is, a thing belonging to a deity or a sovereign. The next unit, *hlan*, is more interesting. In the nineteenth century *hlan*, in conjunction with *taw*, meant to treat a superior with disrespect or insolence, or to be in rebellion. Its cognate, *lan*, used with *taw*, then meant to be liberated from slavery, to obtain freedom or become a free man. (The *yēi* at the end merely means matter or affair, like the *ayēi* in *ayēi-daw-bon*). Modern dictionaries, however, indicate quite clearly that *taw-hlan-yēi* has come to mean revolution or, in some contexts, resistance, such as the movement against the Japanese military regime during the Second World War. The cognate and original meanings of "to treat with disrespect" and "to rebel" have not been forgotten, however, and it is not unreasonable to see the term as meaning almost literally to turn back (or to repel) the sovereign.

One of the earliest uses of a variant of *taw-hlan-yēi* to imply the concept of revolution occurs in Thakin Soe's second major tract, *Bamạ Taw-hlan-hmụ* ("Burma's Revolution"), published in 1939. *Hmụ* means virtually the same thing as *yēi*.[19] Soe had the previous year in *Hsoshelit Wadạ* used the phrase *taw-hlan pun-kan-hmụ* to connote revolution when discussing what would happen in a society in which there was a severe economic depression and the workers had come to understand the laws of economics.[20] This usage added to *taw-hlan* the phrase *pun-kan*, which itself is sometimes now translated as revolution, and which in the nineteenth century, and still often today, meant to rebel or to mutiny. According to Judson, *taw-hlan-pun-sa* (*pun-sa* being the same as *pun-kan*) meant an act of rebellion or of treason. Since the 1940s the term has been in common use for rebellion.[21]

Unsurprisingly, confusion in usage has continued. For example, a 1937 article reprinted as an appendix to Soe's *Hsoshelit Wadạ* described the 1848 revolution in France as a *thu-pun-hta* (a variation of *pun-kan*), the 1905 revolution in Russia as a *taw-hlan* and the 1917 Bolshevik revolution as a *pun-kan*.[22] In its roneoed *Ayēi-daw-bon* (1940) the Communist Party reversed the two terms (i.e., used *pun-kan taw-hlan-yēi*) in calling on Burmese to rebel against the imperialist system. The same reverse order formulation was used by the essayist and journalist Nyo Myạ in 1981 to describe the rebellion of the Wun-tho Sawbwa against the British in the 1880s,[23] just as AFPFL Secretary-General Thakin Than Tun had done in 1945 to describe Franco's insurgence against the republican government of Spain in the 1930s.[24] *Taw-hlan* was used also in conjunction with *hpyat chạ* (to cut and bring down) when in 1937 the All-Burma Students' Union described what the proletariat would do to the capitalist system.[25]

A 1970 semi-official publication of the governing Burma Socialist Programme Party written by its then chief ideologist, U Chit Hlaing, provides a glossary of terms now in official use in Marxist and party writings in Burma.[26] Curiously enough, in giving an equivalent for revolution, Chit Hlaing provides a direct transcription of the English word, as he does for evolution. For cognate terms, however, he reverts to variations of *taw-hlan-yēi*; *ayēi-daw-bon* does not occur in his list. For social revolution Chit Hlaing provides *hkit pyāung taw-hlan-yēi*, literally, era-changing revolution (the title that Thakin Soe used in *Hsoshelit Wadạ* for his three chapters on the materialist conception of history, the capitalist laws of motion, and dialectical materialism). For revolutionary construction, Chit Hlaing offers *taw-hlan thōw ti-hsauk-hmụ*, a literal paraphrase of the English term.

This discussion of the origins and development of the two Burmese words for revolution has as yet revealed little about the development of Burma's politics. What it has suggested, however, is that in practice the two words have come to stand in the minds of politicians for different concepts of political action. The following discussion will attempt to set forth in somewhat schematic terms these contrasting concepts of the idea of revolution before attempting to delineate what these have meant in the changing political thought of Burma. After examining these idealized concepts it may be possible to demonstrate how in actual practice the articulation of these ideal systems has shaped Burma's two post-independence political orders.

Ayēi-daw-bon has come to stand for a form of revolution that is less radical and less complete than that implied by *taw-hlan-yēi*. Being almost literally a term to denote the form of the state's or sovereign's affairs, *ayēi-daw-bon* has been used by those leaders inclined to use the inherited colonial state as the main mechanism for promoting social change. This bureaucratic perspective suggested that the revolution was to be achieved by building on the existing state structure and that revolutionaries should attempt merely to extend its scope. Indeed, the constitutional order inaugurated in 1948 amounted to no more than an enlargement on the principles of rule inherent in the 1935 Government of Burma Act of the British Parliament.

In terms of political and historical theory, the *ayēi-daw-bon* concept of revolution views the state as an institution that exists to reflect the interests of society as presently formed. Hence the principles of western democracy, especially of the British type, could be, and easily were, incorporated into the 1947 constitution as the central document of the *ayēi-daw-bon* thereby achieved. Furthermore, the idea of representative democracy as a means to carry out radical social change was thought to be a viable notion because the *ayēi-daw-bon* concept of revolution held that the nature of man is basically good and therefore man is naturally interested in social change and radical reform. The masses, being good, could not stand in the way of the social reconstruction the leaders wanted to introduce. Indeed, because the masses were amenable to social revolution, there was actually a fear that they would demand change too rapidly; thus a major problem for the government elite was to find means by which to channel and control instinctive mass radical action to meet the practical exigencies of everyday governance. In this way the *ayēi-daw-bon* view of the nature of the masses was linked to the idea of the administrative state; what the rulers had ultimately to do was to balance the radical demands by the masses for a redistribution of values against the continual need for social order and stable relations with the outside world.

The *ayēi-daw-bon* concept implies a belief that historical forces will ultimately determine the nature and positive accomplishment of the revolution and therefore rulers have only to preside over social change for good results to emerge. The revolution is really a problem of managing the historical forces which inevitably push in a positive direction because of the masses' natural pressure for goodness and justice. In recognizing the historical inevitableness of the proper revolutionary outcome, the *ayēi-daw-bon* concept includes as a corollary that it is essential in making policy to use "objective" standards for determining and justifying policies. Whether in regard to Burma's history or to the historical experience of European or other Asian socialist movements, the *ayēi-daw-bon* concept is based on the belief that there is always an external referent to present action which provides a valid basis for judgment at any time.

Because it assumes that the Burmese revolution follows the same trajectory as all other historically determined processes of social change in a larger world revolution which by definition is progressive, the *ayēi-daw-bon* concept contains the belief that events are inevitably going in the preferred progressive direction, and because its proponents have seen the outside world as further advanced than Burma along this historical path, external referents are most appropriate. Ironically, however, a notion of the historical inevitability of revolution implies a highly ambivalent view of the nature of time. There is no need to hurry the revolutionary process, for the correct solution must emerge in the end and it is not possible to speed up its natural evolution. In sum, the *ayēi-daw-bon* concept is one which sees revolution as an inevitable movement for good propelled by the progressive masses who, nonetheless, must be carefully managed to prevent them from going faster than objective circumstances will allow.

If the ideal of *ayēi-daw-bon* is based on a natural movement toward the good, the ideal of the *taw-hlan-yēi*, by contrast, stresses the importance of endeavors to resist evil. Where *ayēi-daw-bon* emphasizes the role of the state as a continuing institution guiding the revolution through the channels of history, *taw-hlan-yēi* insists upon the need to force the participation of the masses in social change, and views the state's structures as impediments to the revolution. This profound difference is a consequence of contrasting assumptions about the nature of history and of man.

In the *taw-hlan-yēi* view, the state and other political organizations are mere instruments which are to be shaped at will by political leaders for motivating the social action needed to create radical change. Radical change is not inevitable but must be compelled. The paramount reason for this necessity is the nature of man in the mass. The masses are basically good, but they are erratic. Unlike the revolutionary leaders, they are not politically aware and thus are easily misled by the enemies of progress who pursue their own selfish interests. An activist elite of cadres is thus required to lead the masses on the correct path toward socialism. The mission of this elite is to mobilize and sustain a radical will even at the expense of historical or external definitions of "common sense" and political or economic rationality as seen by others.

Following from the original root of *taw-hlan-yēi*, this concept of revolution thus conveys the idea of righteously uprooting the existing structures of authority and the interests which benefit from them in order to create a new distribution of social values. If the masses cannot see this truth for themselves, they can and must be led onto the correct path. It is of interest to note that while the coup-makers of 1962 have extolled the role of the peasantry in the making of Burma's modern history and have in particular highlighted the Saya San rebellion of 1930 as a crucial event in Burma's revolutionary inheritance, they have called the insurrection not a *taw-hlan-yēi*, but an *ayēi-daw-bon*—indicating thereby the inability of the peasantry alone to create a progressive and successful movement.[27]

In contrast to the *ayēi-daw-bon* concept of revolution, the *taw-hlan-yēi* idea accepts a modern but undeterministic concept of time derived from Buddhist philosophy. History is not necessarily progressive and therefore it is mandatory to guide the revolution. While all matter and all of man's work, including the revolution itself, must eventually succumb to impermanence, in this life men must act quickly to shape the historical moment. Since time is short, leaders, having only so many years in which to shape history before they succumb to impermanence, must act to speed up the processes of social change. Otherwise the historically propitious revolutionary moment will be lost and evil men with reactionary interests will manage to turn history in a negative, retrograde direction.

The *taw-hlan-yēi* concept of revolution thus contains a strong belief in the necessity for leadership, to change history for the good and to combat the reactionary forces of evil. For this reason, and because all precedents are the result of previous conflicts between good and evil historical forces, action and policy must be determined *sui generis* and external criticism spurned, because it represents either outmoded or evil interests.

A review of a few salient periods in the development of Burma's modern politics may help to illustrate the nature of the two concepts of revolution in practice. An individual's position with regard to these two concepts and to political action has (understandably) often been a function of where he stood vis-à-vis power and state authority. A common experience for revolutionaries once they become members of the governing elite and actually confront the burdens of power is that they find it necessary to moderate their earlier revolutionary views. What is crucial, however, for understanding modern Burma's politics is that contrary to this usual pattern, the process of learning about government that the national elite underwent after independence led the army leadership not to moderate their views about revolution but to move from the *ayēi-dawbon* to the *taw-hlan-yēi* concept before they took power and to operate within the latter frame of reference for the next decade or more.

One can push this analysis further back in recent history to gain insights into the nature of the conflicts that developed amongst the political elite in the crucial first decade after the idea of revolution became current, but still before independence. Such an analysis may reveal a coherence in the framework of political action and history heretofore lacking in the study of modern Burma's politics.

The political behavior of individual leaders during the late 1930s and 1940s demonstrates the manner in which some elite members switched from one concept of revolution to another as their own positions in the nationalist movement changed. Take, for example, the contrasting positions of Thakins Aung San and Than Tun during this period. Both men in their youth were generally identified as revolutionaries and both were early polemicists for the Marxist view of politics. But during the course of the decade between 1938 and independence, their reputations as revolutionaries diverged.

Aung San openly spurned the political order created by the British and accepted by the older generation of nationalists. Once he had taken control of the Dọbama Asīayōn, he carried on a variety of activities that indicated a complete acceptance of the *taw-hlan-yēi* world view. This acceptance can be seen most clearly in his taking office in 1939 as the first General Secretary of the Communist Party (Burma) and in his quixotic trip to Amoy to seek Chinese Communist assistance in expelling the British, no less than in the series of articles he published in 1940 on the nature of politics. When it proved impossible to make contact with the Chinese Communist Party, there was nothing in Aung San's *taw-hlan-yēi* concept of revolution to prevent a tactical alliance with the Japanese militarists in order to gain independence.

By contrast, the later leader of the postwar Burma Communist Party, Than Tun, was at this time pursuing a much more cautious policy, in keeping with the *ayēi-daw-*

bon view of revolution. Revolutionary mass action, with or without foreign assistance, did not then seem to him to be a viable option. When he looked for a standard for judgment in political affairs, he did not cast caution and precedent aside as did Aung San, but rather followed the political line of Nehru and the Indian National Congress, much as conservative Burmese nationalists had done in the 1920s.

By 1945, however, Aung San and Than Tun were in essential agreement and pursued policies of negotiations with Lord Mountbatten and the returning British military administration which can only be described as fitting the *ayēi-daw-bon* concept of revolution. They accepted the line of argument advanced by the Indian Communist Party through Thein Pe Myint, that it was essential for revolutionaries to come to terms with the inevitably progressive trends in world history.[28] Thakin Soe, however, the man who had refused to cooperate in any way with the Japanese as Aung San (and eventually Than Tun) had done, eventually spurned the advice of the Indian Communist Party, and took an independent position based upon the assumptions about the nature of politics underlying the *taw-hlan-yēi* view. Well before this line was internationally sanctioned, he denied consistently that nationalists and revolutionaries could trust the imperialists in negotiations, and held that it was absolutely essential to lead the masses in a revolution against both the Japanese and the British simultaneously with an attack upon indigenous landlords and capitalists.[29]

Following the September 1946 strike by civil servants, police and students, described by Burmese participants as the 1946 *ayēi-daw-bon*, the British were forced to change their policy on Burma's independence, but by 1947 the positions of the revolutionary leaders had changed as the independence the British promised seemed to include strings that limited Burma's freedom. By then Than Tun had come to accept a position nearer that of Soe, while Aung San's position remained consistent with the *ayēi-daw-bon* frame of reference, as did the positions of all the leaders of the Ayēi-daw-bon (Socialist) Party. As independence approached and after Aung San's assassination, the dominant leaders of the governing AFPFL, guided ideologically by the Ayēi-daw-bon Party, accepted that the independence granted by the British was indeed genuine and that they must now proceed to build socialism in Burma slowly, since it was impossible to ignore the constraints that power, international conditions and historical circumstances imposed upon rulers. Soe, Than Tun and their *taw-hlan-yēi*-minded followers, like many members of the armed forces, contested this stance, arguing that the military and financial agreements that the government had accepted as conditions for independence made the prospects for change illusory. Continued ties with the British were unnecessary and the continuity of governing institutions accepted in 1947 was a denial of the new Burma in the new world promised by the AFPFL in 1945.[30]

This analysis of the major conflict between the *ayēi-daw-bon* and *taw-hlan-yēi* concepts of revolution in 1947–48 may seem straightforward at first, since these positions corresponded respectively with the positions of the Socialist and Communist leaderships. However, the use of these party labels has actually tended to confuse rather than to clarify analysis. What is usually forgotten is that at this time the Communists and Socialists publicly held very similar ultimate goals, analyzed politics in comparable ways, and used fundamentally identical political symbols. An analysis of party statements and manifestos makes this clear.[31] But they disagreed over the theory of the state and the nature of history that would allow for the full achievement of Burma's revolution. The Communist position was that the state had to lead the masses whereas the Socialists held that it must represent existing interests. The Socialists felt that the state should be limited by society and Burmese culture in building socialism, whereas the

Communists wanted to alter the nature of society and the state (as the Marxists of the 1930s had done). The Communists spurned ties with the capitalist world, its management and its technology, while the Socialists held these to be crucial for Burma's future.

The Socialists and Communists also disagreed radically over the nature of leadership and its relationship to society. The Socialists acted as if they felt that leaders had to control the spontaneous and basically erratic behavior of the masses while the Communists emphasized the need to organize the masses in order to build continuing demands for radical change. These perspectives followed logically from their conflicting ideas about the role of the state. Their alternative views can be seen, for example, in the way in which the Communists before independence encouraged spontaneous attacks on landlords in Lower Burma and traditional leaders in the frontier areas, while the Socialists and their allies used armed force to put down these movements, even though both groups shared the same rhetoric of opposition to landlords and feudalism.

Had the coup of 1962 not taken place, analysis could halt at this point with the conclusion that since the Communists lost the civil war that followed independence, the *taw-hlan-yēi* view of revolution has become irrelevant to Burma's politics. Throughout the 1950s, the AFPFL, dominated intellectually by the Ayēi-daw-bon Party, managed Burma's official revolutionary inheritance. The entire direction of its policy coincided with the self-motivating and non-forced ideas of change implicit in the *ayēi-daw-bon* concept. Policymakers kept a close eye on foreign models and sources. The holding of the 1954 Asian Socialist Conference in Rangoon was an act of legitimation and confirmation of their ideas. When major industries were nationalized, the effect was merely to change the ownership of 51 percent of stock, while joint stock ventures ensured that management and external contacts remained in the hands of foreign interests. Not only were foreign economic aid and social and political advice welcomed, but American economic and planning consultant firms as well as former British colonial officials were hired. The careful attention that Ministers gave to cabinet government and the federal provisions of the constitution reflected the legalistic bias that naturally followed from the *ayēi-daw-bon* view of what is possible. But behind the scenes, the idea of a *taw-hlan-yēi*-style revolution remained alive in the ranks of the National United Front, the illegal Communist parties, and, most importantly, in parts of the army and civil service which maintained tenuous contacts with various opposition factions and groups.

Nonetheless, by the late 1950s it seemed to outside observers that what could be described as *taw-hlan-yēi* ideas had almost vanished from Burma's internal political debate. The military Caretaker Government which governed from 1958 to 1960 pursued economic and political policies which in style, if not always in content, were in the *ayēi-daw-bon* mold. These policies included the anti-Communist psychological warfare campaigns and the formation under army auspices of the National Solidarity Association to guide the public in support of the constitution. The return to power of U Nu in the 1960 elections and the consequent loss of all power by the Ayēi-daw-bon Party seemed to indicate that even the *ayēi-daw-bon* concept of revolution was no longer politically important. The revolution now seemed embalmed in dead rhetoric under the independence monument replicas that dot the central squares of Burma's major towns and cities.

However, the accession to power of the Taw-hlan-yēi Council government by military coup on March 2, 1962, heralded a radical change in the dominant notions of Burma's politics. Whereas the civilian government had sought in recent years to ignore questions of revolutionary change, the military government now sought to emphasize the idea of revolution itself as the key to the solution of the country's problems of unity, stability, and equity. Implicit in the analysis of Burma's political problems made by the leaders of the Taw-hlan-yēi Council was the view that the root of the country's malaise lay in the recent denial of the promise of revolution. The Revolutionary Council's policies for the next four or five years were almost all predicated on the view of man, state, and history contained in the *taw-hlan-yēi* concept of revolution.

The Taw-hlan-yēi Council did not bind itself with the legal trappings of formal legitimacy as had previous civilian and military governments since the 1940s. Rather than inventing a legal justification for their seizure of power, the Council ignored the constitution, viewing it as a fetter that did not even deserve the respect that would be conceded by its formal abrogation. By their willingness to promote underground Communists and leaders of the aboveground National United Front to positions of authority and influence in social and economic planning, the Taw-hlan-yēi Council also spurned earlier definitions of acceptability for personnel and policies. From nomenclature[32] to administrative practice, the Taw-hlan-yēi Council sought to make Burma over.[33]

The most striking indications of the government's *taw-hlan-yēi* view of policy were its actions in regard to foreign relations and the domestic economy. The nationalization of all foreign-owned (mainly British, Indian and American) firms and businesses, as well as indigenous ones down to the level of local tea-shops, indicated a denial of the legitimacy of foreign standards of behavior, something a government working from the *ayēi-daw-bon* view could never have done. The overnight demonetization of 50 and 100 *kyat* notes was another draconian measure which a government more concerned with the advice of conventional economists would not have carried out. The fact that Burma accepted advisers and aid from the Soviet Union and Eastern Europe during the 1960s would seem to suggest that foreign standards of judgment and advice were still welcomed, but in fact very little aid was forthcoming and even less advice accepted. Burma's virtual isolation from the world economy and international affairs after 1962 was a direct consequence of the *taw-hlan-yēi* view.

The views of the Taw-hlan-yēi Council government were first expressed programmatically in "The Burmese Way to Socialism" and theoretically in *The System of Correlation of Man and His Environment*. These two statements have provided the ideological guidance for the government of Burma since 1963 and no effort to understand the *taw-hlan-yēi* concept of revolution can ignore them. While there are places in these documents where statements occur which do not completely coincide with the description of the *taw-hlan-yēi* ideal set forth above, the differences are minor, involving primarily rhetoric about the use of history and foreign models as standards of judgment; practice suggests that these have in fact been very unimportant in the decision-making process between 1962 and the mid-1970s, when the revolutionary process culminated in the introduction of the 1974 constitution of the Socialist Republic of the Union of Burma.

The initial doctrinal statements of the Taw-hlan-yēi Council reveal an attitude towards the state, man, and society consistent with the *taw-hlan-yēi* view. In its discussion of the previous period of parliamentary democracy in Burma, "The Burmese Way to Socialism" dismisses multiparty government as an impossible means for achieving socialism, because antisocialist forces use it to mislead the masses. Not only was the 1947 constitution inappropriate for the achievement of socialism—the aim of all Burmese revolutionaries—but, "The Burmese Way to Socialism" emphasized, it was essential to abolish the bureaucracy inherited from the colonial state. At the same time, the authors of both documents stressed the necessity for a stable, centralized state in order to avoid the anarchy which would otherwise result, given the existence of interests antithetical to the revolution.[34]

In *The System of Correlation of Man and His Environment*, man is described as marked by two primary characteristics. He is essentially egotistic, but also "an altruistic social animal."[35] The contradiction between man's natural egotism and his need to live in society requires the guidance of revolutionary socialists in order to build, and then avoid the destruction of, socialism. Man's tendency to go astray means that the revolutionary state and its institutions, primarily the revolutionary political party, must constantly guide him in the correct direction. Until the views of man can be changed by education and moral improvement, the party will have to recruit good cadres to lead the masses in the correct socialist direction.[36] While noting the importance of history in shaping the conditions of man's and society's present circumstances, the leaders of the Taw-hlan-yēi Council stressed that they were "just Burmese revolutionaries and socialists who are keeping pace with the life of history."[37] Yet they were not bound by its precedents, for each new period of history has its own conditions, which man has to alter by his own will. As stated on the first page of *The System of Correlation of Man and His Environment*, their "philosophy and programme should seek to extinguish the bad and cultivate the good traits in man's moral character." The leaders of the revolution had to bend the state to this end—to conduct a revolution that was a movement for good against evil.

With the consolidation of the Burma Socialist Programme Party, the ending of its transitional phase and inauguration as a mass party, and the introduction of the 1974 constitution, the revolution of the Taw-hlan-yēi Council was complete. Nonetheless, residues of the *taw-hlan-yēi* concept of revolution continue to provide the basis for government legitimacy and the framework of political thought. The second embalming of the concept of revolution in Burma's political symbolism has set the limits of government action; Burma's future will be shaped by the revolutionary inheritance of the post-1962 period. The continuing importance of the *taw-hlan-yēi* idea lies in the emotional content that it symbolizes for its adherents. Their success in getting its acceptance by a sizeable proportion of the larger population was surely helped by the clear complementarity of the *taw-hlan-yēi* concept with nationalism. The inability of the *ayēi-daw-bon* view to sustain itself as a viable option reflects its believers' inability to tap a deeper emotion in the political public.

---

1. Pu Kalēi, *Thahkin Nu Ayēi-daw-bon* [Thakin Nu's Revolution] (Rangoon: Thudammawati, 1949).

2. Murray Edelman, *The Symbolic Uses of Politics* (Urbana: University of Illinois Press, 1964), p. 115.

3. For a broader, linguistics-based discussion of the evolution of modern Burmese, see Minn Latt Yekaun, *Modernization of Burmese* (Prague: Oriental Institute, 1966).

4. Than Htun, "Hsoshelit Wada hnit Bama Yazawin" [Socialism and Burma's History], *Dagun Maggazīn* [Dagon Magazine], 217 (1938), pp. 7–15. This essay was reprinted in *Bon Wada hnit Do Bama* [Communism and Our Burma], ed. Thein Hpei Myin (Rangoon: Bawsetow Sapei, 1967).

5. Thakin was the title taken by radical Burmese nationalist youth to indicate that they rather than the British were the "masters" of Burma. The organization of the Thakin movement, the Dobama Asī-ayōn, was initially much influenced by the philosophy of Nietzsche and the nationalism of Mazzini and the Sinn Fein movement. Its founder, Thakin Ba Thaung, was also attracted to the ideas of National Socialism. See Tin Htun Aung, *Myanma Nainnganyēi hnit Thahkin Ba Thaung* [Burma's Politics and Thakin Ba Thaung] (North Okkalapa: Aung Se Saok Taik, 1980). The movement eventually split into socialist and conservative nationalist factions after former student politicians and Marxists entered it in force in 1938–39.

6. As in the title of Thakin Tin Mya's memoirs, *Bon Bawa Hma Hpyint* [From the Communist World] (North Akkalapa: Tathetta Sapei, 1974). See also the glossary to Chit Hlaing, *Puhtusin ei Lāwka Amyin* [The World View of the Common People] (Rangoon: Inkyintow Sapei, 1970), pp. 273–91.

7. *Thuriya Maggazīn* [Sun Magazine], 3 (1919), pp. 1–3.

8. Than Htun, "Hsoshelit Wada." For a discussion of Burmese terms for kinds of history, see Tin Ohn, "Modern Historical Writing in Burmese," in *Historians of Southeast Asia*, ed. D. G. E. Hall (London: Oxford University Press, 1961), pp. 85–93.

9. In 1963 the use of *thamāing*, rather than *yazawin*, was given an official ideological imprimatur by the government's party. See Myanma Hsoshelit Lānsin Pati, *Lu Hnit Patwūnkyindo ei Anyanmanya Thabāwtayā* [The System of Correlation of Man and His Environment] (Rangoon: Sapei Biman, 1963), p. 44.

10. Aung Hsān, "Naingnganyēi Amyōmyō" [Kinds of Politics], *Dagun Maggazīn*, 234 (1940), pp. 61–70; 236 (1940), pp. 17–26.

11. Similar to the expression "Internal affairs; like the *pauk* tree [a particularly colorful flowering tree] and the parakeet [i.e., difficult to see the bird in the tree]; plans always changing; can not know [what will happen]" found in Kantewmin Kyāung Hsayadaw's work *Lāwka Thaya Pyou*, Paragraph 26, Rahkaing Thumyat yei Thehulei Hsothe, as cited in Taik So, *Sa ko Saka ko* [A Guide to Burmese Quotations] (Rangoon: Chin Twin Taik, 1974), p. 12. Kantewmin Kyāung Hsayadaw lived c. 1438–1513 A.D.

12. Hla Pe et al., *A Burmese-English Dictionary*, VI (London: School of Oriental and African Studies, 1981).

13. A. Judson, *Burmese-English Dictionary*, rev. ed. (Rangoon: Baptist Board of Publications, 1966).

14. Maung Maung Kyi, *Ayēi-daw-bon 6 Saungtwei Thamahut Myanma Minmyā Ayēi-daw-bon* [Six Records of the Burmese Kings' Revolutions] (Rangoon: Nanmyin Sapei, 1970; original imprint 1923); Yi Yi, "Ayēi-daw-bon Kyanmyā Pyathana," in *Kanthā Seile Satanmyā* (Rangoon: Min Hla, 1969).

15. Kyaw Ho, "Nagani Saok Athin Hlut Sasusayin" [Publications of the Red Dragon Book Club] (Rangoon: Rangoon Arts and Sciences University, Library Department thesis, 1979), pp. 22, 28, and 37.

16. So, *Hsoshelit Wada* [Socialism] (Rangoon: Saok Hpyan Chiyēi, 1939); Aung Hsān, "Naingnganyēi Amyōmyō."

17. Sō, *Hsoshelit Wada*, p. 1.

18. Michael Aung-Thwin, "Kingship, the Sangha, and Society in Pagan," in *Explorations in Early Southeast Asian History: The Origins of Southeast Asian Statecraft*, ed. Kenneth R. Hall and John K. Whitmore (Ann Arbor: Michigan Papers on South and Southeast Asia No. 11, 1976), p. 209.

19. Sō, *Bama Taw-hlan-hmu* [Burma's Revolution] (Rangoon: Hpyan Chiyēi Dana, 1939).

20. Sō, *Hsoshelit Wada*, p. 146.

21. See, for example, Anonymous, *Kayin-Bama Thwei Seyēi* [Karen-Burmese Blood Bond] (Rangoon: Pyithu Sapei Hpyan Chiyēi Dana, 1945), p. 4, and the essay (pp. 15–29) in the same volume by Maung Maung Sein, head of the Burma Communist Party Central Committee office in Rangoon, written in November 1944.

22. "Hsīnyēithā Min Hsīnyēithā Chin [Proletarian King, Proletarian Kind]," reprinted from *Myo Nyun Maggazīn* (September 1937) as appendix 3 in Sō, *Hsoshelit Wada*.

23. Thidaga Yayatha, *Maung Lu Kyin* (Rangoon: Pankyamun Sapei, 1981).

24. Anonymous, *Neithuyein Hmattān* [Record of the Neithuyein Meeting] (Rangoon: Tantowhsin Thatīnsa, 1946), p. 32.

25. Sō, *Hsoshelit Wada*, p. 203.

26. Chit Hlaing, *Puhtusin*, pp. 273–91.

27. See Pyi-htaung-su Myanma Naingngan Taw-hlan-yēi Aso-ya Pyankya-yēi Dana [Revolutionary Government of the Union of Burma], *1292—Taung-thu-le-thama Ayēi-daw-bon* [1930—The Peasants' Revolution] (Rangoon: Sapei Biman, 1965).

28. This line followed the well-known analysis of the American Communist leader Earl Browder.

29. Robert H. Taylor, "Introduction: Marxism and Resistance in Wartime Burma," in *Marxism and Resistance in Burma, 1942–1945: Thein Pe Myint's 'Wartime Traveller'* (Athens: Ohio University Press, 1984).

30. By the time of the formal transfer of sovereignty, Soe and Than Tun had been expelled from the AFPFL and had formed two rival Communist parties. It is worth noting

that General Ne Win and others in the army leadership felt much the same way about the final Anglo-Burmese agreements, though for rather different reasons.

31. See Ba Swe, *Guide to Socialism in Burma* (Rangoon: Government Printing and Stationery, 1956), for an example available in English. This report was originally presented to the December 1946 conference of the Ayēidaw-bon Party. For an equivalent Communist document, see Bama Pyi Kon-myu-nit Pati, *Sīlūnswa Htuhtaung Kyaso* [Burma Communist Party, Let Us Establish Greater Unity] (Rangoon: August 20, 1945) which contains the resolutions passed by the Second Party Conference held in July 1945.

32. Hla Pe, "Officials' Titles in Burmese," in Hla Pe, *Burma* (Singapore: Institute of Southeast Asian Studies, forthcoming).

33. The only possible historical parallel to these radical acts were the plans drawn up in 1948 for a program of "Leftist Unity" to end the civil war. Foreign pressure caused these plans to be stillborn.

34. Myanma Hsoshelit Lānsin Pati, *Lu Hnit Patwŭnkyindo*, pp. 46–48, and 31. Quotations and page numbers are taken from the official English translation.

35. Ibid., pp. 6–7.

36. Ibid., pp. 28–29.

37. Ibid., p. 35.

5

KĀNPATTHANĀ: THAI VIEWS OF DEVELOPMENT

Harvey Demaine

The term "development" must now be one of the most widely used in the English language. In a world often described as divided between North and South, these terms are used to distinguish between groups of countries which are thought of as "developed" and others which are variously known as "developing," "underdeveloped" or "less-developed" countries. Yet it has been notoriously difficult even for social scientists to agree on just which countries are "developed" or "developing" and what the process of "development" actually implies. Numerous so-called "development" indicators have been put forward, from monetary measures such as Gross Domestic Product *per capita* to nonmonetary variables, such as relative access to health and education services. But the choice of measure actually depends very much on the definition of the term "development" itself.

The relative ambiguity as to the precise meaning of the term "development" may relate to the relative novelty of its use in economics, the discipline with which above all others it is associated. It would appear that the term only emerged in common usage after World War II, entering the economist's phrasebook via two quite distinct channels. Up to that time, it seems to have been employed mainly by those economic historians primarily concerned with the opening up of the resources of the British empire, which were said to be being "developed" by settlers and colonial governments. On the other hand there existed another tradition, which emerged from Marx's *Capital*, but which originated with Hegel, whereby "development" was understood as a series of stages in the process of man's attempt to realize his potential. Thus while the former usage emphasized resources, the latter laid stress on the progress of man and society.

When the term became more widely used in the postwar period, the first of the two views of development was dominant in the West. It was relatively easy to extend the colonial "resource development" view to the idea that "development" meant an increase in national aggregate productive capacity, and hence to equate "development" with economic growth. Typical of the view are definitions suggested by Todaro:

> the capacity of a national economy, whose condition has been more or less static for a long time, to *generate* and *sustain* an annual increase of its gross national product at rates of perhaps 5 to 7 per cent or more.[1]

and one of Thailand's senior economists:

the broad meaning of economic development encompasses the increase of national aggregate production (gross domestic product) through the growth of goods and services provided.[2]

It is instructive that in the latter definition "development" is qualified by the adjective "economic," thereby emphasizing the process as a specifically economic phenomenon. There is no overt recognition that development might include other elements of human welfare, although there is perhaps an implicit assumption that economic growth will allow improvements in social facilities. To some extent the emphasis of this view of development has changed over time as gross domestic production *per capita* has tended to replace the aggregate measure as the basic criterion. One could argue, however, that the change primarily marks a recognition of the depressive effect of rapid population growth in the first two postwar decades on the overall impact of increases in gross domestic product and does not necessarily imply any significant attention to distributional questions. The assumption was that the rapid gains in overall growth of GDP would somehow automatically "trickle down" to the mass of the population or create conditions allowing for wider distribution of economic and social benefits.[3]

It has been mainly the persistent failure of even substantial rates of economic growth to produce such improvements in living conditions for large sections of the populations of the developing countries, particularly in rural areas, which has tended to provoke a reaction against the view of "development" outlined above. This reaction has largely had its origins in the second of the two historical views of the term and has led to the conception of "development" as:

> a multidimensional process involving major changes in social structures, popular attitudes and national institutions, as well as the acceleration of economic growth, the reduction of inequality and the eradication of absolute poverty.[4]

For some proponents this view has implied the need for sweeping political changes, while for others the necessary changes in social structures and attitudes can take place within the existing politico-economic framework, but require a reordering of state priorities. The emphasis has thus shifted away from resource development to human development. For thinkers such as Goulet the shift has led to a further widening of the meaning of "development" to give it a "spiritual" or "inner" meaning, involving not only fulfillment of basic needs, but human self-esteem and freedom from servitude.[5]

THE SOUTHEAST ASIAN CONTEXT

Given the continuing debate on the meaning of the term among specialists and practitioners, it is scarcely surprising that there continues to be uncertainty and controversy in the developing countries over what exactly they are trying to achieve by "development" and how they can bring it about. Very often the experiences of national leaders under colonial rule have had a marked impact, leading to the formulation of ideologies which positively embrace or reject a particular view of development which is believed to have been beneficial or inimical in the past.

Such tendencies can be seen clearly in Southeast Asia. In the aftermath of the colonial period, there have been sharply contrasting reactions to that historical experience ranging from outright rejection of the old resource-development framework on the part of Vietnam and to a lesser extent Burma, to an apparently willing adherence in the Philippines. Yet the modern history of the region also illustrates clearly that dramatic changes in view may take place in a particular state. The case of Indonesia is especially instructive: in its first fifteen years of independence, Indonesia, under the leadership of Sukarno, rejected the Dutch colonial framework of development for a development path originally based on traditional Javanese views of self-help and mutual assistance, but later increasingly influenced by Maoist ideas. (Both of these "philosophies" of development are clearly more population-oriented than resource-based.) Subsequently, the economic chaos of the late Sukarno period provoked a profound reaction and the development philosophy followed by the New Order government since 1967 is characterized by an explicit emphasis on economic growth as the prime development target.

Elsewhere in the region there have been comparable changes in view over time which, if not as dramatic as those in Indonesia, nevertheless remain interesting. An especially interesting case is Thailand, precisely because of the lack of any formal colonization by the European powers in the nineteenth and twentieth centuries.

KĀNPATTHANĀ: THE HISTORICAL CONTEXT

The term *kānpatthanā* (development) is a relatively recent coinage. It seems to have emerged only after 1957, as a key element in the politico-economic philosophy of Field Marshal Sarit Thanarat, the country's political leader from 1957 to 1963. However, a similar word, *watthanā*, had been used by Field Marshal Plaek Phibunsongkhram, who dominated Thai politics after the coup of 1932 and was Prime Minister from 1938 to 1944 and again from 1947 to 1957. It is interesting to note that the standard Thai-English dictionary definitions for both these terms emphasize "progress, advancement," the sort of terms commonly used for human development by those colonial economic historians for whom development itself was seen mainly in the terms of resource exploitation. The appearance of *patthanā* or *watthanā* in Thai after 1932 suggests that something more was implied than was connoted by the word previously in vogue, namely *būrana*, for which the dictionary definition is "reconstruct, rehabilitate, repair or restore."[6] (In the Thai countryside one still often comes across temple signs saying *rātsadǫn būrana*, meaning that the buildings have been restored or rehabilitated by the local population.) This usage, equating development with the improvement of public works, is rather narrow in scope, but it is consistent with the historical traditions of Thai society in which the monarchy promoted and supervised public construction, while the population was obliged to provide the necessary labor. Right up to the early reigns of the present Chakri dynasty, the organization of facilities for irrigation, drainage and transportation was typical of this sort of development.

Despite the change of vocabulary after 1932, it is not clear that this traditional idea of development changed substantially, at least until very recently. While Phibun's concept of *watthanā* was aimed mainly at creating the outward appearances of modernization and (Western) civilization in Thai society, notably by the encouragement of European dress and social habits, and lip-service to European-style democratic institutions, his *ratthaniyom* philosophy called for a loyalty to the state quite similar to the old tradition of loyalty to the monarchy, in order to bring about national progress.[7] Under Sarit the stress on formal Western values was reversed; in his view of the country as a large family and of himself as its father, he was returning, as he saw it, to the Sukhothai tradition of government in which the paternal ruler looked after the interests of his people according to various principles of kingly virtue. This *phǫkhun* model assumed that the government was able to interpret and understand the wishes of the people, relying on a flow of information from the bureaucracy which in turn served the population by carrying out necessary (benevolent) policies. Government, bureaucracy and the people were three distinct strata in a stable sociopolitical structure, which would only be undermined by Western-style democracy.[8]

Sarit's interpretation of the "needs" of the population indicates the substance of the philosophy. For example, he attempted to help the urban poor by decreeing lower electricity rates, railway fares and school tuition fees, as well as requiring the Bangkok municipal authorities to abolish a whole series of taxes, fees and charges for official services. Development of new markets and restrictions on the prices of essential foods were part of the same policy. Sarit's frequent visits to the country's peripheral regions increased his standing conviction that roads and water were their top priority needs. He noted that "in provinces where there is an abundance of water, the people in those provinces have bright faces, fresh and clean skins, plants and food flourish, resulting in prosperity. . . ."[9]

Sarit's pronouncements on *patthanā* tended to emphasize social and moral considerations, and thus seem in harmony with the human-oriented view of development discussed earlier. Yet it was under Sarit that Thailand's first formal national development plan was formulated, the beginning of a series of plans which have come to be the most detailed expression of the official Thai view of development and of the strategies to be followed in its achievement. That Sarit himself was interested from the start in drawing up such an overall planning framework is revealed by his correspondence with his advisor, Luang Wichit Wathakan in 1958,[10] but the machinery for creating it had already been set up with the foundation of the National Economic Development Board (NEDB) in 1957. This body subsequently drew up the National Economic Development Plan (published in 1961) which set out the objectives for the next six years. This "First Plan" has subsequently been followed by a succession of five-year plans (1967–71, 1972–76, 1977–81, 1981–86).

The First Plan, which began almost contemporaneously with the United Nations' "First Development Decade," was based on research conducted into the state of the Thai economy by the International Bank for Reconstruction and Development (the World Bank) at the request of the Thai government. This review[11] was necessitated by the difficulties which had begun to emerge in the country's economy in the aftermath of the Korean War boom. These difficulties had been caused in part by the poor economic performance of the government, particularly its expanded role in the industrial sector in the early 1950s. Although this expansion represented an attempt to compensate for the absence of local Thai (as opposed to Sino-Thai) entrepreneurs, most of the state enterprises established were inefficient and, instead of generating revenues, became a drain on resources. In addition, they acted as a disincentive to foreign investment.[12] The World Bank mission therefore recommended that the government channel its investments into the development of social overhead capital in the fields of power generation facilities, irrigation and transportation, in short create the conditions under which *private* enterprise would be able to undertake the development of the country's resources for national development. In addition it urged the government to withdraw from its participation in industry and encourage private investment through a variety of incentives.[13]

The World Bank's recommendations were broadly adopted by the NEDB in drawing up the National Economic Development Plan. The main emphases of the Plan were two. Public investment would be concentrated on developing the country's land and water resources via a major program of road construction and the building of a number of large dams for irrigation and hydroelectric power. Industrial investment by private enterprise, both domestic and foreign, would be stimulated by generous tax incentives.

One could argue that this strategy meant a return to policies traditional at least from the time of the Bowring treaty in 1855 up to the coup of 1932. These policies have been described by the economist Robert Muscat as "autonomous, satellitic and expansionist": "expansionist" in increasing national income largely through stepped-up resource exploitation, "satellitic" in relying heavily on foreign capital, and "autonomous" in limiting government intervention in the process of development to the provision of basic economic infrastructures.[14]

Yet it is doubtful whether the Thai leadership viewed the strategy followed in the Plan in these terms. The professional economists of the NEDB, many of them trained in the West, may have seen investment in economic infrastructures as a means of stimulating development, but it is unlikely that such macroeconomic considerations were paramount for Sarit. Although his stress upon roads and water coincided with that of the Plan, the Prime Minister probably viewed such projects as fulfilling what he perceived as the felt needs of the population. This orientation was clearly reflected in the foundation during the Plan period of the Department of Community Development (Krom Kān Patthanā Chumchon). The local infrastructures to be created by this Department were not viewed as stimulants to development, but were seen as development itself. A famous short story of the period shows this attitude very well:

> I never recall the official name because everyone calls it the "Progress Road" (*thanon patthanā*), just as the villages along the sides of the road are "Progress Villages" (*mūbān patthanā*).[15]

Whatever the philosophy behind the First Plan—and the Second Plan (1967–71) continued the emphasis upon infrastructural facilities and private sector industrial development—it appears to have had only limited success in achieving its goals. The two plans' stated overall objective was to increase output and arrange an equitable distribution of the resulting economic benefits. However, there was little concrete in either plan to ensure such an outcome. As Phisit notes, the First Plan in particular had several technical weaknesses, so that the government was probably in no position to make certain that the entire program would actually be implemented; but even with the improvements incorporated in the Second Plan, specific policies aimed at distribution of benefits were limited.[16] The implicit macroeconomic philosophy behind the concentration on infrastructural facilities seems to have been that such investments would lead to a "trickle-down" of benefits to all sectors of the population and areas of the country.[17]

In fact it seems clear that this optimistic view was sorely misplaced in the Thai context. The social and economic changes which had occurred in Thailand over the previous century had been accompanied by an extreme centralization of economic and politico-administrative power. In particular, the administrative reforms of King Chulalongkorn after 1892 helped bring the once largely independent outlying regions of the country under the firm control of Bangkok. Thus while the development of roads—a major goal of the early plans—did open up new lands, it also siphoned much of the resulting produce to Bangkok. The prime focus of irrigation developments in the 1960s was the Central Plain, and the export surplus of this area continued to be channeled through the capital. Indeed the country's tax structure assisted in a direct transfer of wealth from the countryside to the city, since a significant part of government revenues came from the so-called "Rice Premium," which was ostensibly a tax on exports designed to ensure an adequate supply of the country's staple food to mainly urban, domestic consumers, but which in reality depressed abnormally the farm gate prices offered to the farming population.[18]

That the benefits of the development process were not reaching large numbers of people in the rural areas, particularly in the peripheral regions of the country, the Northeast, the North and the Peninsular South, began to be recognized in the latter part of the 1960s as more reliable national income statistics began to be gathered and disaggregated on a regional basis. The data indicated that the share of Gross Domestic Product contributed by the country's peripheral regions was gradually declining while that of the center (and of Bangkok in particular) was increasing. Of particular concern was the Northeast region, long recognized as the country's poorest, which had fallen behind most rapidly, despite the establishment of a special commission for the Northeast in 1961 and the drawing up of a specific Northeast development plan in 1962.[19]

Sarit's concern for the Northeast region in the early 1960s was in part a reflection of his personal connections with the region, but it also reflected a noticeable shift in the orientation of his development policies. The maintenance of national security had all along been one of his major preoccupations. Especially after the Laotian crisis of 1960, security problems in Thailand's eastern border regions began to influence his attitude to development, even at the village level. The army was directly enlisted in the formation of Mobile Development Units (MDUs), while the civilian administration's efforts were stepped up with the creation of the Accelerated Rural Development (ARD) program. The MDUs and ARD carried out crash programs of highway construction and village development projects largely with the aim of ensuring political support in the zones regarded as susceptible to communist infiltration from Indochina.

It is notable, moreover, that these two programs were largely financed by the United States via its Operations Mission in Thailand. Thak indeed has suggested that America, Thailand's main aid donor, had long been more concerned with the security question than had the Thai government itself; thus in terms of the balance of loan and counterpart funds in US-supported projects, American spending was always more concentrated on the strategic element of road construction, whereas Thai funds, reflecting Sarit's original view of development, were used more widely on irrigation and community development.[20] But as the Thai leaders themselves became more concerned with security, so the *overall* emphasis of the infrastructural development program began to shift towards security maintenance.

Not surprisingly, the economic impact of much of the early infrastructural programs, especially in the Northeast region, was quite limited. Some benefits may have been gained from short-term construction activities, and communities alongside the new roads may have benefited from improved access; on the other hand, the programs were undertaken without discussion with the rural population as to their specific needs, and were often ill-maintained and poorly coordinated with other development efforts. In some cases farmers suffered loss of land for road construction without any compensation from the authorities. At best the benefits were localized. The same was also true of the artificial boost given to the region's construction sector and service economy through the establishment of a number of large American air force bases. In some respects the investments may even have been counterproductive in that the disparities resulting from the programs created resentment, providing a fertile breeding ground for the communist insurgency they were designed to combat. Although the Thai Communist Party (CPT) was funded and to some extent organized from the outside, it appears to have developed real appeal from the mid-1960s onwards (when an estimated 10,000 village sympathizers were recorded).[21] One element in this appeal was probably the party's view of development, which emphasized social justice and equality, things in short supply in the politico-economic climate of that period in the Northeast region.

It was not, however, just the CPT and its sympathizers who regarded what the Thai government was attempting to accomplish in the 1960s as something other than development. In the Thai universities, where critical discussion had been severely restricted in the Sarit era, debates began after the dictator's death in 1963 which were also critical of the progress that had been made. One of the country's senior economists, Dr. Puey Ungpakorn, for example, clearly voiced the need for a new view of development:

> Development is not just a matter of production. We should seek to produce in a just manner . . . and apart from justice, there are other things which need to be included in a social system to make the life of the population of a higher quality. We shouldn't forget these. This is what I mean by real development. . . . We have to overcome various difficulties, and the most important one amongst them is to help the countryside . . . or to enable the people with low incomes to help themselves.[22]

Chinawut Sunthornsima observed that "Development cannot be concentrated just in Bangkok. We have to bring development to the countryside, to the provinces as well. Our aim should be the development of all areas."[23] This view was echoed by another younger economist, Chatthip Nartsupha, who wrote that "Development of the Thai economy doesn't mean just increasing production . . . we have to build a system which satisfies our ideals. . . . What are those ideals? . . . Freedom and equality."[24]

Nor was the criticism confined to the Thai academics. One thoughtful foreign commentator argued strongly that what had taken place in the 1960s had not been "development" (defined as "the maximization of the potential of a society") but merely "modernization."[25] He believed that acceptance of the trappings of a modern state accounted for the government's stress on the upgrading of infrastructure—but only so long as such upgrading did not alter the structure of society. The desire for economic improvement in Thailand was being limited by a variety of noneconomic desires which, he suggested, could be summed up as the desire to maintain a "patrimonial" society. In the traditional form of such a society land was not heritable by private kinship or lineage groups, but was granted as a prerogative of office; power derived solely from membership in a bureaucratic structure owing allegiance to the sovereign responsible for granting offices. Jacobs argued that this structure had been maintained in Thailand despite the changes in the administrative system effected by King Chulalongkorn and the removal of the absolute monarch in the coup of 1932; and that its continued operation was a major constraint on real development.

The development strategies followed in the 1960s were pursued "not as a response to the felt needs of the population, but of the patrimonial leadership and its administrative staff" which were eager to increase respect for Thailand in the eyes of foreign powers and to maintain national security.[26] In the agricultural sector, he felt, the aim was to increase the traditional patrimonial services of the government in order to gain it popular confidence. The widespread reliance upon foreign advisers under the first two plans represented an attempt by the authorities to enjoy the fruits of development without paying the cost of institutional reform. The financial aid implicit in the presence of such advisers was seen simply as a bonus to the overall fruits of office enjoyed by the bureaucracy.

To some extent Jacobs' analysis was implicitly adopted by the Thai academics quoted above. But such views were slow to gain wider currency in Thai society, which with its uncolonized history and thus certain language limitations, proved relatively resistant to westernization. Thus, despite the criticisms of the academics, the evidence at the macroregional level presented by national income statistics, and the growing indications that, even in its own terms, the goal of maintaining public confidence and national security was not being fully achieved, there were few changes in the overall view of development within the Thai government and among its planning elite by the end of the first decade of formal development planning. Insofar as there had been change at the national level, it had been to the advantage of the orthodox macroeconomic view of the Westernized planning elite, since Sarit's successors in power, Marshals Thanom Kittikachorn and Praphas Charusathien, enunciated no alternative development view of their own.

It is true that the late 1960s saw a further attempt to introduce a specific regional component into the planning process with the establishment of the National Development Committee in 1968 and the subsequent enlisting of an American consultant team, funded by the United States Agency for International Development, to draw up a development strategy for the Northeast which might fit into the Third National Economic and Social Development Plan (1972–76). However, as Phisit suggests, the efforts of the so-called Northeast Economic Development Planning Advisory Group appeared "to be only a regionalization of the national plan to serve as a guide for national planning. . . . Their regional analysis and planning methodologies were based on the conventional sectoral approach, and tended to ignore the spatial dimension in their analysis and programming for the North East."[27] Thus this and the subsequent planning exercise for the Northeast region came to little and the Third Plan differed only in one major respect from its predecessors. This change was indicated by the Plan's title, which for the first time included the word "social," and was reflected in a shift in budget allocations from building up economic infrastructure to provision of better educational and health facilities. Educational expenditures in particular rose to a massive 32.8 percent of total government spending under the Plan, compared to only 7.6 percent in the First Plan and 21.4 percent in the Second.

The growing importance of expenditure on social development projects under the Third Plan to some extent indicates a recognition by the government and the planning hierarchy that significant groups in society had still not participated in the development process. However, the nature of the problem was conceived by the planners largely as the inability of large sections of society to take advantage of offered opportunities because of their lack of educational attainments. Hence the key concept of the new Plan was "human resource development":

> This target for national economic and social development has been established with the major objectives of developing the human resources simultaneously with natural resources. It is felt that human resources play a leading role in the effort to increase the national productive capacity. . . . The Government feels that human resources in the rural areas of the country are great natural assets which cannot afford to be neglected. . . . The increase in efficiency of the rural labour force is very closely related to raising incomes and living standards of rural people.[28]

Despite this emphasis, the development of social infrastructure under the Third Plan remained oriented towards the offsetting of the growing security problem, and thus represented a continuation of the patrimonial framework. On paper at least, the construction of schools and medical facilities aimed particularly at those backward areas where the Communist insurgency fostered by the steady leftward tide of events in Indochina was particularly severe.

Whatever the rhetoric of the Third Plan, it was clear that there continued to be substantial drawbacks to its development policy. Krit summed up the overall problem as arising from the fact that "the objectives of social development were not clearly defined."[29] The expansion of education facilities, for example, was undertaken without any clear perception as to how the type of curriculum characteristic of the standard primary and secondary education system would be of assistance in rural areas. As Dr. Puey commented:

> We have to mobilize resources for education as much as possible, especially in the countryside ... but not the sort of education that we have at the present time, which is focused particularly on assisting only those who live in the towns and cities, in the provincial centres. This is not enough; we must make education appropriate to the people in the countryside.[30]

The data available also suggest that the attempt to improve the provision of social services in the more backward parts of the country was far from being realized towards the end of the Plan. Thus, by 1975, enrollment ratios in the Upper Primary Sector in the northeast and northern regions of the country were still significantly lower than in the rest of the country (even if private educational services, which tended to be most developed in the central and southern regions, are excluded) and there were also significant disparities in the effectiveness of education and the quality of services provided. Average test scores on both Thai and arithmetic were lower in the Northeast and North than in the country as a whole, and lower primary schools in the Northeast had a relatively high percentage of untrained teachers, relatively crowded classrooms, the highest pupil/teacher ratios and the least materials per pupil.[31] Comparable imbalances existed with regard to health care, with the provision of personnel to staff the new facilities created in the peripheral regions a continuing problem.[32] The World Bank concluded that:

> Such a situation is not surprising, however, when the method of allocating current and capital grants to the changwat [provincial] administrative organisations is examined. Grants for recurrent expenditure based as they are on enrollment numbers [for education] and salary bills ... result in less support being given to the more disadvantaged provinces. What is more disturbing is *the indication that no attempt has been made to reduce the gap* by allocating more capital expenditure to the less well off provinces. Indeed *the exact opposite has taken place.* ...[33]

In his overall assessment of the Third Plan, Krit suggested that the general performance was less satisfactory than under its predecessors.[34] He noted, for example, that the agricultural sector in particular did not perform according to expectations, partly because of drought conditions, but mainly because the political upheavals of the period led to the neglect of the overall development strategy. Moreover, despite its somewhat different rhetorical emphasis, the Plan continued the old development strategy which Kosit epitomized by the terms "production and investment." The planners clung to the idea that prosperity would be created first in the most favored areas and then would spread to the remaining zones—most of them with low development potential—via labor migration, welfare spending and public services.[35]

Even in Thai patrimonial terms, problems were accumulating. In providing what it saw as traditional services to the population, the Thai government had inadvertently created aspirations and demands which it had great difficulty in satisfying. Outside the elite groups in the capital other interests in society were growing more conscious of their potential political power. In 1973 these dissatisfied interests, in alliance with more radical, Westernized elements among the student population, succeeded in toppling the military regime, which, meantime, had lost the backing of the monarch. A series of civilian governments followed, claiming legitimacy from the Western concept of democracy. But like their predecessors, they failed to provide the conditions for that other aspect of the traditional patrimonial system, national security (particularly after the final Communist victories in Indochina), which powerful conservative forces thought essential.

It was against this background that the Fourth National Economic and Social Development Plan began to be formulated. Originally drawn up during the tenure of the civilian government of Seni Pramoj, by the time it came to be implemented in October 1976 (the start of fiscal year 1977) a coup had restored military rule. Domestic political instability was compounded by the international economic instability stemming from the rapid increase in oil prices of 1973–74. For these reasons, it was felt necessary that the strategy for the Fourth Plan should be changed from an allocative conception, specifying the various projects to be undertaken and their order of priority, to an indicative framework which merely set out the broad social and economic policies which the government intended to follow.

It was not, however, merely in relation to the nature of the planning framework that the Fourth Plan differed from its predecessors. A number of aspects of the Plan revealed major new directions in the thinking of the Thai planning elite. For example, there was a shift in industrial policy to emphasize the development of new natural resources, such as natural gas and offshore tin deposits, the former in particular being regarded as a way of solving the country's growing energy problems. There was also a new emphasis on export-oriented industries and tourism, for which the development of new deep-water ports and the expansion of airport facilities were essential. On the other hand, the Plan laid new stress on the conservation of the nation's resources and the wider natural environment which, it was now realized, had suffered severely during the period of the previous plans—a trend which, if unchecked, promised to prejudice future development. Finally, there was a call for much more coordinated planning, both for rural areas and in the integrated development of town and country through the expansion of the role of secondary cities. All projects were expected to adhere to the principles incorporated within these major policies.

To some extent the new directions suggested by the Fourth Plan were responses to the needs of the moment, particularly the country's serious energy shortage and the growing import bills occasioned by higher oil prices. On the other hand, the attention to resource availability and conservation and to the particular problems of areas such as the Weeping Plain (Kulā Rǭng Hai) of Srisaket and Roi-et and the northern hill-tribe areas, did offer a new spatial perspective, paving the way for even more novel developments. In fact, in the latter part of the Fourth Plan period there was intense discussion of what came to be termed *nāeokhwāmkhit mai nai kānpatthanā prathēt* (the new conception of national development), which then was embodied in the Fifth National Economic and Social Development Plan which began to be implemented in October 1981.

By the late 1970s it was increasingly recognized that "the results of the development process up to that time had not been very satisfactory."[36] Several major problems were increasingly being identified, chief among them the growing disparity in income levels and standards of living, whether measured on a regional or on a provincial basis or between urban areas and the countryside. Estimates from the mid-1970s, around the end of the Third Plan, indicated that even in the advantaged Central Plain (including Bangkok) the numbers of people living below the poverty level probably increased over the period 1968–76.[37] Moreover, the facts began to point to the conclusion that the ongoing development strategy had failed to provide large sections of the population with any benefits whatever. Kosit argued that many groups might well have received benefits from improved provision of health and education services or from specific foreign aid projects, but that they had not been put in a position where they could be assured of even an adequate basic livelihood from their own resources.[38] He drew attention to several studies indicating that for many households twenty years of development had brought benefits only by migration (which may have made real development in the rural areas all the more difficult through the reduction of needed capable manpower). He warned that the nonagricultural sectors would find it increasingly hard to absorb the flood of migrants. Meantime, the natural environment was being destroyed by the clearing of forests for agriculture, and traditional supplementary occupations such as charcoal manufacture, basketry and wood-carving were facing extinction. Finally, competition for the use of scarce resources, whether between a government seeking to preserve watershed forests and people in search of more land, or between various interests in society (such as those eager to use the waters of the Chao Phraya river basin for electricity generation or irrigation or metropolitan water supply) was growing fiercer.

The failure of significant sections of society to benefit from the development process was not the only problem believed to stem from the strategies followed. Some experts emphasized the slowing down of economic growth itself; others the negative effects of economic growth on social stability; yet others the economic exploitation developing within society. Yet most critiques emphasized the basic point that the development process in Thailand, at least up to the late 1970s, had resulted in the concentration of benefits among certain groups in society and in specific environmentally favored areas, to the neglect of and in some ways at the expense of other groups and regions.

Recognition of this has brought about a substantial change in the Thai view of development as expressed by the national planning hierarchy in the Fifth Plan. This Plan, while designed to relieve the immediate financial problems affecting the country and maintain economic and financial stability through budget austerity, makes its prime targets the reduction of absolute poverty and the acceleration of rural development in backward areas by enhancing the rural population's capacity to help themselves in the longer term. In addition, there is an emphasis on restructuring the production process in both agriculture and industry, not only to promote exports but also to create additional employment and to make possible the decentralization of economic activities to various target areas and regions. Mention is made of the need to utilize "culturally appropriate technology" and to adjust social structures to make Thai society:

> more stable and disciplined, fair and safe as well as to provide more educational and employment opportunities for the poor. To this end improvements in public development administration, human resource development and the dispersion of basic public services to rural areas, with particular emphasis on depressed areas having less potential for development, are considered vital.[39]

Without doubt, it is the stress upon the promotion of people's capacities to help themselves, to *participate* in the whole process of development which is the outstanding innovation in the Plan and the biggest departure from the previous philosophy of national development. But its practical application promises to be very difficult, involving as it does basic changes in attitude at all levels of society, not merely amongst the technocrats of the National Economic and Social Development Board.

CONTRASTING VIEWS OF DEVELOPMENT IN THAI SOCIETY

It will be apparent that many of the views now being put forward in the Fifth National Development Plan are precisely those which were being discussed in the academic debate a decade earlier. The lengthy gestation period of such ideas indicates that the acceptance of such a development ideal by the higher echelons of the planning hierarchy or even by certain leaders within the government, including Prime Minister Prem Tinsulanon, does not guarantee that these objectives will be immediately adopted by all those involved in the development process. Indeed whatever the development philosophy adopted, its implementation depends upon the activities and attitudes of a wide range of groups in society. In the partial democracy which now characterizes the Thai political system, the government remains dependent on the support of political interest groups, including the military, to see its policies through. Even with the support of such groups, it is still vital that the civil service charged with the implementation of the policies be willing and able to translate paper policies into effective action. Furthermore there are real limitations to the degree to which even a committed and capable bureaucracy can influence economic and social affairs in a relatively open economy such as that of Thailand. It has been private capital which has been the vehicle for economic growth in Thailand over the past two decades; any change in development philosophy such as proposed under the Fifth Plan must obtain at least the tacit acceptance of this sector to be realized. Finally, the people themselves must be mobilized to adopt the new principles.

Although it cannot be denied that Thailand's political system has changed significantly since the fall of the Thanom-Praphas regime in 1973, and that military and civilian leaders seem more willing than before to seek a stable political accommodation, the political system is still dominated by groups concerned mainly with the protection of their own interests, not with those of less powerful sectors of society. A decade ago Puey Ungpakorn stated:

> Certainly in the short-term it is vitally necessary that, instead of having, as we have every day at the moment, an assembly which tries to discuss only its own affairs, or those of interest to its own party, we should have it discussing matters of national importance so that the members can sort out the country's interests in a united way.[40]

But his companions in a discussion in 1971, Professor Saneh Chammarik and Dr. Kasem Sirisamphan, were both pessimistic about the possibility of such a development. Kasem in particular expressed doubt that the country's leaders had an adequate vision to bring about the necessary change.[41] The coalition that backs the Prem Tinsulanon government today seems more stable and united than those behind the governments of the 1970s. Nevertheless it may be asked whether the coalition is bound together only by the lowest common denominator of a desire for power and whether such unlikely bedfellows as Kukrit Pramoj's Social Action Party and Samak Suntharavet's Thai People's Party can really agree on the sort of reforms proposed by the Fifth Plan. Already certain compromises have been accepted by the present coalition which call into question its overall strength of purpose.

The interests of politicians are to a great extent those of the business community, whose resources underwrite the building of the main political parties. To date this business community has not shown much inclination to accept the wider aims of government planners. The Thai government has long followed a policy of offering generous incentives to both foreign and domestic interests to encourage investment in specific industries. Latterly, an attempt has been made to use such incentives to encourage manufacturers to locate their enterprises away from the Bangkok metropolitan area (which till now has attracted as much as 80 percent of total Thai industrial capacity). However, little has come of these policies. As the World Bank notes, "The incentives available to industries located *anywhere* in the country were sufficiently generous . . . that these additional incentives appear to have had little impact on the location of industries."[42] Certainly there is little evidence for the optimistic view expressed by Chatthip that the wider distribution of income within society might be seen by the business community as a form of investment in production.[43] It appears much more likely that only fiscal policies would make possible any serious redistribution. Until recently, however, the tax system in Thailand has been marked by inequity and inefficiency; here too substantial reforms would be needed if taxation were to contribute to the redistribution process.[44]

Under these circumstances the onus for the reorientation of development policies lies with the government; and, given lukewarm support in the business community and among some politicians, it is the public sector which is crucial to the effort to bring the new view of development to practical reality. The government's official commitment is clear in the establishment, as the Fifth Plan's central component, of the so-called Rural Poverty Eradication Program which, however, is scheduled to receive only 8,593 billion baht in the course of the Plan, a mere 0.7 percent of the total estimated budget! The program includes three major components, namely:

(a) the promotion of village activities, which in the first year of the program in 1982 included village fisheries, village water resource development, small livestock production, cattle and buffalo banks, and a special village development project funded by Japan;
(b) the provision of basic services, which initially included district hospitals, health facilities, improved nutrition, legal advice to poor rural areas, basic school textbooks, and clean drinking water; and
(c) production activities, involving food production for improved nutrition, highland rice production, accelerated land development through fertilizer inputs, and development of saline soils in the Northeast.

The program is less novel in itself than in the new emphases in its implementation, in particular the need for the population to participate as much as possible. Thus the principles to be used in carrying out the program include:

(a) implementation should be fashioned according to the wishes of the village population;
(b) the village should participate in every stage of the operation of the project;
(c) the project should not involve the people in great financial risk which might leave them short of funds, but should promote methods of overcoming problems which are as simple as possible, which involve minimal expenditure and which the people can tackle for themselves;
(d) the projects should help to reduce the people's expenditure at the same time as increasing their income;

(e) after the completion of each project, the people should join together to assist in its maintenance and continued operation.

The program activities are to be concentrated specially in needy areas—covering in the first instance some 246 districts and subdistricts.

The emphasis on people's participation and the solution of the problems of particular areas will require a much more secure data base on the government's part, and this implies a flow of information *upwards* through the administration in a manner which has so far been rare in Thailand. In addition, an unprecedented degree of cooperation at all administrative levels between the ministries of the Interior, Agriculture and Cooperatives, Education and Health will be essential. All these elements are foreign to the traditions of the Thai bureaucracy. Although there have been efforts at data collection in the context of specific projects, statistical materials have not been gathered on a systematic, geographic basis. What data has been amassed has been utilized only to a limited extent in the allocation of resources and in the design of projects. We have already noted that the earlier attempts at regional planning were sadly deficient; it is an indication of the neglect of the spatial context of change that the NESDB regards the idea that each rural area differs basically from the others as "new."[45] There has in fact been a strong tendency in Thai development planning to believe that a project framework successful in one area can be translated across space without modification, frequently with disastrous results in the new area of implementation. This tendency in turn is related to the extreme centralization of the administrative process in Thailand. Given the volume of work which has to be handled by the highest echelons of the bureaucracy, any data collected is invariably diluted for the consumption of the decision-makers and thus decisions are made on a limited factual basis.

The centralization of decision-making, however, has still wider implications. First the discretionary powers of local governments at all levels are very limited. Regulations and administrative rules governing the authorization of budget expenditures and the procurement of goods have traditionally been particularly tightly controlled from the center, even minor changes requiring reference to the Bureau of the Budget. Thus local governments have little experience in assuming a wide administrative role and accordingly they have little prestige in the eyes of those making a career in the civil service. Secondly, centralized decision-making is indicative of residual patrimonializing in the government of the country. There is a reluctance to take decisions at the lower echelons of the administration for fear of disturbing the strong patron-client ties which pervade the bureaucracy. An official's advancement within that bureaucracy continues to depend in many ways on the advancement of his patron. Achievement is still often seen as carrying out the policies of the patron to the latter's satisfaction. The bureaucratic use of the term *hen chǭp* may be suggestive. The two words, which mean "see-like," imply the superior likes what he sees rather than that a general policy line is being carried out.

The patron-client relationship is, of course, a vertical relationship; and since it is this type of relationship which is characteristic of the bureaucracy, there are few solid horizontal linkages between the various ministries and departments. Departments enjoy a substantial amount of independence in their internal affairs, with their Director-Generals in practice the highest decision-making authorities. Very often the Director-General sees himself as a patron looking after the interests of the hierarchy of officials below him, interests which may not coincide with those of the ministries to which these people are nominally subordinate or of the government as a whole.

In a recent major study, Tin Prachyapruit has compared attitudes towards a more liberal administrative policy with the socioeconomic characteristics of civil servants at different levels.[46] His sample covered such agencies as the National Economic and Social Development Board, the Department of Technical and Economic Cooperation, Chulalongkorn University, the Department of Local Administration, the Community Development Department, and the Labor Department. His conclusion is that the general level of development-orientedness in the civil service is exceedingly low, with only 10.7 percent of his sample classified as "highly development-oriented" and as many as 33.9 percent included in the "low development-orientedness" category. Tin defines development-orientedness as support for such values as citizen participation, tolerance, equality, economic development, concern for the nation, commitment to work, selflessness, and result-orientation, most of which are clearly relevant to the principles of rural development incorporated into the Fifth Plan. If Tin's measures are realistic gauges of bureaucrats' views, then they are obviously a cause for pessimism.

The independence of the various departments in the Thai bureaucracy also means that the national planning agency, the NESDB (the originator of the "new view" of development expressed in the Fifth Plan), has very limited influence over the line agencies charged with implementation of planning strategies. As a World Bank study recently concluded:

> There is little evidence that Thailand's development plans systematically guide or govern the actions of departments ... in the day-to-day conduct of government affairs. Although national development plans should never be treated in mixed economies as binding and inflexible statements of government intentions, the frequency and extent to which development plans appear to be disregarded in the allocation of financial and administrative resources and in the introduction of new policies, programs and projects is indicative of a lack of full commitment to the concept of development planning.[47]

The same study also notes the problems caused by the separation of the NESDB's responsibilities for general economic analysis and long-term policy formulation and those of the Bureau of Budget for annual budgeting and control of expenditure, as well as the NESDB's relative isolation from the mainstream of the civil service.[48]

Finally, the independence of the various government departments in the Thai bureaucracy has meant that each has developed its activities on its own, resulting in widespread duplication of institutions and overlap of responsibilities. This tendency is particularly obvious in the area of rural development where there are as many as ten agencies involved in the construction of rural roads, six agencies providing rural water supply facilities, and six agencies responsible for various aspects of land development and settlement.[49] In such circumstances it is clearly difficult to ensure that services are distributed equitably and that they meet the needs of the priority rural areas. In some large departments, indeed, the problem of coordination may even extend down to individual divisions and offices, the work programs of which may conflict over access to resources and manpower.

These characteristics of the Thai bureaucratic system pose significant obstacles to the implementation of the new principles of development, and in particular to the rural poverty eradication program. To be sure, the Thai government has demonstrated its awareness of some of the problems and has attempted to effect a decentralization of planning and resource allocation down to the provincial level. In the Rural Poverty Eradication Program an attempt has been made to establish mechanisms which will help to overcome the problems of coordination between government agencies and to assist in the bottom-up transfer of information and proposals. To this end a series of committees has been established at all levels of government with the specific task of coordinating the development effort according to the principles laid down in the Plan. At the national level a National Rural Development Committee (NRDC) is charged with formulating overall policy, assigning duties to the various ministries and departments, setting the various programs and targets, and considering budgetary needs. At the provincial level, Provincial Development Committees (PDC) (which have Rural Development Subcommittees attached to them) help in the consideration of the various projects proposed by the lower levels of the administration. Further down still, District Development Committees (DDC) have been set up for the analysis and coordination of projects put forward by the lowest level of the system, the Tambol Council, which is responsible for local coordination and for presentation to its DDC of the various projects proposed by the villages. Alongside the Tambol Council, however, is another body, the Tambol Working Party for Assisting Rural Development Works, consisting of Tambol-level representatives of various departments, who provide technical and material assistance to the Tambol Council and assess the feasibility of the projects proposed. In addition, two research institutions have been established, a National Center for Rural Development Coordination with the NESDB to assist the NRDC, and an Institute for Data Gathering for Education and Development at Thammasat University as a data bank and monitoring and evaluation center for the various projects.

These new institutions are expected to operate according to a "bottom-up" framework of planning and administration. Village councils put their problems to the Tambol Council so that the latter can propose projects consistent with their needs to the various local representatives of the development agencies. At the same time the ministries allocate the technical and financial resources to each province. The Provincial Development Committee thus coordinates the requests from the lower level with the resources available, and assigns priorities among the projects. The ministries then consider the provincial proposals and in advance of the budget year set out their work plans. At each level the plans of the various departments are coordinated. Budget funds are allocated according to the plan agreed upon by the ministries and provincial administrations and are administered by the provinces. There should then be full cooperation at all levels during the implementation of the projects, as well as constant data-gathering for maintaining and evaluating the completed projects.

It remains to be seen whether this complicated structure will operate in the manner described and whether it can overcome the problems of the traditional framework of development administration. The history of the attempts to try out the new concepts in certain agencies during the latter part of the Fourth Plan and of the operation of the Rural Poverty Eradication Program in the first year of the Fifth suggests that more will be needed than the establishment of new institutions. Despite the various committees established at all levels of the administration, quite often, at the provincial level, "those responsible for each project have continued to report directly to their own department of affiliation in the manner of every man for himself!"[50] Similar problems have cropped up also at amphur (district) and tambol (subdistrict) levels. Clearly the traditional independence of the various line agencies has continued to be an obstacle to the new system. As far as the integration of projects is concerned, the problems can be seen clearly even from the list of projects undertaken in 1982. Several projects obviously overlapped. For example, a program to improve village nutrition was being tackled by three separate projects, a nutrition improvement project of the Ministry of Public Health, a nutritional foods production project of the Department of Agricultural Extension, and a small livestock production project of the Livestock Department.

In this context, it is notable that certain NESDB studies have concluded that there is a real problem of comprehension for many government officials involved in development work. The concept of integrated rural development seems particularly difficult to grasp, even though it has been a government catch phrase for a number of years. In one case known to me the concept that subprojects should be interdependent, rather than just existing in the same spatial context, seemed to be so alien that even the Thai translation of the project's title was garbled. Thus what should have been *khrōngkān pasom pasān* (integrated project) had become *khrōngkān sombūn baēp* (perfect, i.e., model project). That such a misconception was held by an otherwise forward-looking division chief known for his conceptual sophistication suggests a widely prevalent problem amongst officialdom.

Problems arising from patrimonial residues in the bureaucracy are evident in still another context. The NESDB's analysis of the 1982 operations of the Rural Poverty Eradication Program points to a frequent tendency for subprojects to be located away from the villages in greatest need. One key reason has been that often the poorest communities are the least ready to organize themselves and the most difficult to galvanize into participation. Accordingly, the representatives of the various line agencies at the local level have tended to recommend to the tambol and district authorities that projects be carried out in villages with greater organizational resources—inevitably the better-off communities. This tendency represents a continuation of "numerical target" evaluation of development which has long been common in Thailand and reflects the desire of local officials to impress those in higher authority with their achievements. In the past such attitudes have led to the falsification of data and (perhaps even worse) the cajoling into participation in a project of those who would perhaps have been better off without it. In one recent instance in Northeast Thailand, the search for fulfillment of a numerical target for an ailing sericulture project led to the incorporation of several farmers whose land was totally unsuitable for the cultivation of the necessary mulberry trees. By the time this unsuitability had been established, the mulberry trees had died, leaving the participants in substantial debt for silkworm-rearing facilities already constructed. I do not mean to suggest that most subprojects under the new poverty eradication program have led to such disasters. Most are in fact low-cost and community-oriented. Nevertheless cases like the one above do illustrate a continuing lack of perception among the local officials as to the real meaning of development in the new framework.

In the same way, officialdom continues to have a very limited appreciation of the principle of popular participation. Subprojects for the establishment of more district hospitals, the provision of primary school textbooks, basic health facilities and clean drinking water are largely designed to fill in "gaps" in basic needs facilities *as identified by the bureaucracy,* not by the villagers. The very fact that the program is composed of specific subprojects is, in itself, something of a negation of the ideal of popular participation, for it thereby clearly lays out solutions to the "problems" of the backward communities in Thailand prior to any opinions expressed by the people. A policy which truly followed the principle of popular participation would be less rigid in conception, and involve a much wider range of projects than those incorporated in the 1982 program.

To some extent this problem has now been recognized. There was a considerable expansion in the number and scope of the projects scheduled for 1983, the second year of the Rural Poverty Eradication Program. The new subprojects, mainly in the area of production and basic services, were intended to be much more area- and problem-specific; as such they covered rain-fed rice production; saline and acid soils development in the South; large livestock improvement, with special reference to eradication of epidemics; fisheries development in the South; small-scale irrigated agriculture; and prevention of soil erosion in the northern hills. These projects appear to be steps in the right direction, but even so they continue to be "generalist" projects which derive from above. They offer no assurance that officials are adhering to or fully understand the principle of popular participation. The experience of the Rural Poverty Eradication Program has shown that the local officers of the line agencies have tended to take the lead in the formulation of projects via their position within the Tambol Working Party for Assisting Rural Development. In some cases, farmer leaders have denied being given any voice in the formulation of projects. In others, a degree of consultation with the Tambol Council may have taken place, but this does not necessarily mean any real participation by the local population. Rather, it often amounts simply to a non-participatory extension of the bureaucratic structure in a way which has been long characteristic of the operations of that traditional focus of "popular participation" in Thailand, the agricultural cooperative, which is more correctly termed the pseudo-cooperative. Although most district cooperatives now have a management committee elected from amongst the farmers, all too often the district official of the Department of Cooperation Promotion actually dominates the business meetings of the committee.

The truth is that there is a continued perception by many officials that they are "the developers" and the rural population "the developed," a segmentation which at its worst leads many local officials, however junior, to perceive themselves as infinitely superior to the "uneducated," and therefore "ignorant," villagers. A simple but delightful novelette of a decade ago sums up this attitude as perceived by the villagers:

> These people who came to us, whom in general we called "town people," counted on and respected only educated or rich persons, or somebody of high rank; no matter how young, how stupid, how ignorant they were, age meant nothing to them. . . . But we knew that they expected us to respect them because they were educated and they were government people too.[51]

On the other hand, it is also clear that many villagers themselves accept their subordinate position and feel constrained in putting forward their views in the presence of particular officials. As Prajuab put it:

> So we did as they wanted by acting humble. But it would also [have] hurt them awfully if they ever knew that we counted them as what we thought they really were. . . . Sometimes we even called some of them stupid asses.[52]

An experience of my own, involving drawing up a development plan for an area in Udorn Thani province, is rather instructive. After days of interviews and discussion with villagers, proposals were finally prepared. Along with the group of officials involved I was then asked to return to the area to discuss these proposals with villagers—in the name of "participation." On the initial visit, when the team was accompanied by the Director of the Division concerned, the local representatives sat and listened for an hour, making no substantial comment. It seemed that the proposals met with their full approval. Two weeks later, however, when the team returned minus the Division Director, the meeting lasted five hours and the villagers were both critical and constructive in their extensive discussion of the proposals.

It is notable that the NESDB sees the major problem as being the villagers' low level of understanding. The frequent failure of village organizations to be the instigators of local projects is seen as arising from:

the lack of establishment of understanding of the essential nature of the projects and the method of selecting them among the various sectors, especially on the part of the villagers, who are unable to analyze their own problems and to choose projects consistent with their solution.[53]

Characteristically, NESDB officials believe that these obstacles can be fairly rapidly overcome through radio broadcasts, through simple pamphlets and through the mobile units of the Department of Public Relations and the Department of Extramural Education. Yet it is highly doubtful whether such efforts can really dispel the deep-rooted attitudes. Having long been the mere recipients of the government's paternalistic largesse, many communities have become more and more dependent upon such help, and less and less able to work out their own solutions to their problems. Thus they may well see the new framework with its self-help emphasis as simply a reduction in that assistance. By the same token, although specific measures such as the designation of coordinating officers for each department at the provincial level and the assignment of separate locations for overlapping projects may help to overcome some specific administrative difficulties, the problem of set attitudes still remains as far as the bureaucracy is concerned. Meetings and seminars to promote wider understanding of the "new concept of development" will help to a degree, but as long as the bureaucracy continues to operate on patrimonial lines there are surely narrow limits to their likely effectiveness.

Conclusion

As in the international discussion, the understanding of the meaning of "development" has changed considerably over the past two decades in Thailand. From a view which clearly equated development with the aggregate growth of the national product and gave priority to infrastructural projects and resource exploration, there has been a slow but steady change to the present view of development as a much more complex process involving the equitable distribution of wealth and the realization of human potentials through the participation of the mass of the population in the planning and implementation of an integrated program. This latter view, enunciated in the Fifth National Social and Economic Development Plan, represents a significant departure from the country's patrimonial traditions. This "new concept of development" has become the central government's official policy, propagated not only by the National Economic and Social Development Board, but also by the Prime Minister and the cabinet. But it is certainly not the only view accepted in the country. It arouses little enthusiasm among various interest groups in business and politics who view "development" as the promotion of their own particularistic interests. More important, however, is the evidence from the first year of operation of the Rural Poverty Eradication Program—a crucial part of the "new concept" under the Fifth Plan—and from other projects of similar orientation, that the necessary changes in attitude required of the bureaucracy and of the rural population have yet to take place.

The patrimonial aspects of the Thai bureaucracy so sharply described by Jacobs in 1971, still persist a decade later. The importance of patron-client relations for advancement in the bureaucracy continues to encourage self-serving independence on the part of individual line agencies. The national planning agency still lacks the real political clout needed to achieve adequate coordination between departments and integration of mutually supportive subprojects. The strong tradition of centralization assures the continuation of a vertical reporting system and reduces the possibility of the province serving as an effective locus for coordinating the desires of the people with the available resources. Preferment in the bureaucracy is still highly dependent on adherence to paper targets; the eagerness of "patron" supervisors to see tangible, i.e., quantifiable, results militates against efforts to tackle the real problem areas and to collect the complex data required for real monitoring and evaluation of progress. Attitudes of superiority to the rural population among officialdom continue to block the serious participation of ordinary people in development. Meanwhile the rural population itself, long used to passive dependency on government services, finds it difficult to fulfill the new participatory role assigned to it.

Government planners apparently see these problems as the teething troubles of the new approach. The view expressed here is much more pessimistic. For all the apparent change of emphasis contained in the Fifth Plan, the views of development adhered to by the main actors in the process, government officials on the one hand and the rural population on the other, have yet to undergo any basic transformation. Indeed, it may be suggested that, despite the shift in terminology from *būrana* through *watthanā* to *patthanā*, the basic Thai view of "development" has not transcended the old patrimonial framework. Development continues to be seen in terms of patrons (the government or its officials) offering services to clients (the population) in return for loyal support. Within the hierarchy of officialdom similar patron-client relationships persist, with officials virtually expected to exploit their offices and the resources made available in the "development" effort. Such attitudes are not easily changed by the efforts of government information agencies so long regarded by villagers as irrelevant to their needs, or by brief training courses or seminars where any real exchange of views remains quite restricted. In the West it has taken many years for perceptions of "development" to shift away from assumptions that the process was merely a matter of introducing technical innovation to a view emphasizing fulfillment of human capabilities. And this change is still very far from complete. In Thailand, however, it has only just begun. A long interval will have to pass before deep-rooted views of "development" based on indigenous traditions are eroded.

---

1. Michael P. Todaro, *Economic Development in the Third World: An Introduction to Problems and Policies in a Global Perspective* (London: Longman, 1977), p. 60.

2. Krit Sombatsiri, "Kānborihānngān wāngphāēn patthanā setthakit lae sangkhom khǒng Thai" [The Administration of Economic and Social Development Planning in Thailand], *Wārasān Sangkhomsat* [Journal of Social Science], 18:3 (1981), pp. 66–74, at p. 66.

3. Albert O. Hirschman, *The Strategy of Economic Development* (New Haven: Yale University Press, 1958).

4. Todaro, *Economic Development*, p. 62.

5. Denis Goulet, *The Cruel Choice: A New Concept in the Theory of Development* (New York: Atheneum, 1971).

6. Mary R. Haas, *Thai-English Student's Dictionary* (Kuala Lumpur: Oxford University Press, 1964), pp. 293, 367, 500.

7. Thak Chaloemtiarana, *Thailand: The Politics of Despotic Paternalism* (Bangkok: Thai Khadi Institute, 1979), pp. 142–43.

8. Ibid., pp. 152 ff.

9. Ibid., p. 231, quoting from a Sarit speech of 1960.

10. Ibid., p. 182.

11. International Bank for Reconstruction and Development [henceforth IBRD], *A Public Development Plan for Thailand* (Baltimore: The Johns Hopkins University Press, 1959).

12. James C. Ingram, *Economic Change in Thailand, 1850–1970* (Stanford: Stanford University Press, 1971), p. 231.

13. IBRD, *A Public Development Plan*, pp. 90 ff.

14. Robert J. Muscat, *Development Strategy in Thailand* (New York: Praeger, 1966), p. 19.

15. Khamsing Srinawk, *The Politician and Other Stories*, translated by Damnern Garden (Kuala Lumpur: Oxford University Press, 1973), p. 35.

16. Phisit Pakkasem, "Development Planning and Implementation in Thailand," in *Finance, Trade and Economic Development in Thailand*, ed. Prateep Sondysuwan (Bangkok: Sompong Press, 1975), pp. 223–24.

17. This idea was prominent in the work of the influential regional economist Albert Hirschman (see above at note 3). It was, however, strongly disputed in the almost comtemporaneous writings of Gunnar Myrdal: see his *Economic Theory and Underdeveloped Regions* (London: Duckworth, 1957).

18. See, e.g., Thomas H. Silcock, "The Rice Premium and Agricultural Diversification," in *Thailand: Social and Economic Studies in Development*, ed. Thomas H. Silcock, (Canberra: Australian National University Press, 1967), pp. 231–57; and Sura Sanittanont, *Thailand's Rice Export Tax: Its Effects on the Rice Economy* (Bangkok: National Institute of Development Administration, 1967).

19. National Economic Development Board, *The Northeast Development Plan* (Bangkok: NEDB, 1962).

20. Thak, *Thailand*, pp. 257 ff.

21. R. Sean Randolph and W. Scott Thompson, *Thai Insurgency: Contemporary Developments* (Washington, D.C.: Center for Strategic and International Policy Studies, Georgetown University, 1981), p. 18.

22. Puey Ungpakorn's contributions to a debate entitled "Panhā setthakit lae sangkhom" [Economic and Social Problems], in Samnak Banthit Āsā Samak [Graduate Volunteers' Office], *Nāeokhwāmkhit mai nai kānpatthanā prathēt* [New Concepts of National Development] (Bangkok: Thammasat University, 1979), pp. 42–43.

23. See his contribution to the debate entitled "Nāeo thāng patthanā setthakit" [Trends in Economic Development], in *Setthakit Thai: khrōngsāng, panhā lae nayōbāi* [The Thai Economy: Structure, Problems and Policies], ed. Chatthip Nartsupha (Bangkok: Chulalongkorn University, Economics Association, 1972), p. 147.

24. See his contribution to the volume cited above, p. 156.

25. Norman Jacobs, *Modernization without Development: Thailand as an Asian Case Study* (New York: Praeger, 1971), p. 9.

26. Ibid., p. 126.

27. Phisit Pakkasem, "Regional Planning within a National Framework: The Case of Thailand's Northeast," in *Finance*, ed. Prateep, pp. 235–44, at p. 237.

28. National Economic and Social Development Board [henceforth NESDB], *The Third National Economic and Social Development Plan, 1972–76* (Bangkok: NESDB, 1972), p. vi.

29. Krit, "Kānborihānngān," p. 72.

30. Puey, in *Nāeokhwāmkhit*, pp. 13–14.

31. IBRD/World Bank, *Thailand: Selected Issues in Rural Development* (Washington, D.C.: Working Paper No. 4, Thailand Basic Economic Report, 1978), p. 115.

32. Ibid., p. 119.

33. Ibid., p. 116, italics added.

34. Krit, "Kānborihānngān," p. 72.

35. Kosit Panpiamrat, "Prasopkān lae kānroem nāeokhwāmkhit mai nai kānwāngphāen patthanā prathēt Thai" [Experience and the Beginning of a New Conception of Thai National Development Planning], *Wārasān setthasāt* [Thai Economic Journal], 12:2 (1979), reprinted in Samnak Banthit Āsā Samak, *Nāeokhwāmkhit*, pp. 71–104, at pp. 84–85.

36. Ibid., p. 72.

37. IBRD/World Bank, *Thailand: Toward a Development Strategy of Full Participation* (Washington, D.C.: IBRD, 1980), pp. 62–63.

38. Kosit, "Prasopkān," pp. 85–86.

39. Board of Investment, *Thailand's Growth Strategy* (Bangkok: Office of the Board of Investment, 1980), p. 3.

40. See Puey's contribution to the 1971 debate on "Economic and Social Problems" cited in note 22 above, at pp. 11–12.

41. Ibid., p. 31.

42. IBRD/World Bank, *Thailand: Toward a Development Strategy*, p. 15.

43. Chatthip Nartsupha, ed., *Setthakit Thai*, pp. 160 ff.

44. IBRD/World Bank, *Thailand: Toward a Development Strategy*, pp. 19 ff.

45. NESDB, "The Rural Poverty Eradication Program" (Bangkok: mimeo., 1981), p. 8.

46. Tin Prachyapruit, "Thai Civil Servants and Their Development-Orientedness," *Wārasān sangkhomsat* [The Journal of Social Sciences], 18:3 (1981).

47. IBRD/World Bank, *Thailand: Toward a Development Strategy*, p. 28.

48. Ibid., p. 29.

49. Ibid., p. 87.

50. NESDB, "Rabob borihān kānpatthanā chonnabot nāēo mai: hētphon lae khwām-jampen" [The System of Administration of the New Framework of Rural Development: Reason and Necessity], *Wārasān setthakit lae sangkhom* [Journal of Economics and Social Science], 19:5 (1982), p. 20.

51. Prajuab Thirabutana, *Little Things* (London: Collins, 1971), pp. 114–15.

52. Ibid., p. 115.

53. NESDB, "Phāēn patthanā chonnabot phǔnthī yākjon 2526" [Development Plan of 1983 for Areas of Rural Poverty], *Wārasān setthakit lae sangkhom*, 19:4 (1982), p. 20.

6

THE DELIBERATE USE OF FOREIGN VOCABULARY BY THE KHMER: CHANGING FASHIONS, METHODS AND SOURCES

Judith M. Jacob

In writing their own language Khmer sometimes choose for effect vocabulary which not only is foreign but is consciously felt to be foreign. For example, Thai terms for everyday objects are found in early Khmer poetry, and French words occur here and there in modern novels. In neither case is the use due to a lack of appropriate vocabulary in Khmer; the foreign vocabulary is deliberately chosen. This essay represents an attempt to gather the evidence of such conscious use of foreign words in the various genres of Khmer literature, and to consider the reasons for it. The relevant "contexts" range through the centuries, from 611 AD to modern times, wherever linguistic documentation in Cambodian is available (though emphasis is given to the modern period). Throughout, an interpretation of "meaning" is applied which refers less to the literal translation value of a term than to the effect which the deliberate use of a foreign term may have or have had, as Khmer attitudes to foreign language sources and to foreign powers have changed through the centuries.

The Khmer lexicon includes a large body of fully integrated loan words, principally from the Sanskrit and Pali languages of India, but also from Chinese, Thai and Vietnamese and from European languages (chiefly French but also Portuguese and English). Most of these borrowings, however, were probably absorbed into the language unconsciously, and over time, being gradually naturalized to fit as far as possible the native phonological system. They thereby acquired currency in both the spoken and written languages and were used by Khmer speakers without a thought for their origin. Such borrowings, to be referred to as "established loans," are not the primary concern of this essay. Here I am concerned with the question of why, at various points of history, words of one foreign language rather than another were cited or consciously borrowed. Such borrowings were often so short-lived that almost no attempt was made to modify the words to suit the Khmer phonological system. In other cases consciously borrowed vocabulary was used so much that it was Khmerified, yet its use was still deliberately reserved for a particular style of writing.

In the search for illustrative material the net has been cast quite widely; yet for reasons of space only a small selection of the examples found could be presented here. When consulting texts from the past, it was not always easy to be sure when a foreign form was used as a deliberate affectation (i.e., merely because it was a word from a particular high-prestige foreign language) and when it was used of necessity (i.e., because no Khmer term would have been satisfactory). Whatever the case, unless or until a word became an "established loan," a conscious use of a foreign word was involved. Certain features of usage can help in general to distinguish self-conscious borrowing. I found that: (a) in deliberate borrowing, a whole phrase of the foreign language was often used rather than individual loan words arranged in Khmer syntactical order; (b) foreign terms used for effect often appeared only for a short historical period; and (c) in modern times, after the standardization of Khmer spelling, newly adopted foreign words were conspicuous by the variety of their "Khmer" spellings.

The results of my study are set out below in five sections, each of which deals with a distinct epoch.[1] These sections are subdivided according to genre. For the sake of clarity the following table lays out the categories of analysis.

TABLE I

Period	Genre	Language Source
The Pre-Angkor and Angkor Periods (7th to 14th centuries AD)	Inscriptions on stone	Sanskrit Pali
The Middle Period (16th to 19th centuries AD)	Inscriptions on stone	Pali
	Verse-novels	Sanskrit + Pali, the High Language, including the Royal Vocabulary Pali Thai
	Cbap	Pali
The Early Modern Period (19th and early 20th centuries)	Prose* and Poetry**	Sanskrit + Pali, the High Language, including the Royal Vocabulary Pali French
The Modern Period (Mid-20th century)	Journals, conversation	French
	Journals and official circles	Sanskrit + Pali, the New Vocabulary
	Fiction	Sanskrit + Pali, the High Language Sanskrit + Pali, the New Vocabulary French Thai English
All periods	All genres	(Chinese) (Vietnamese)

* Works specially consulted: Chronicles, Folktales, *Gatilok*, *Kambujasuriyā* articles.

**Works specially consulted: 19th century lyric poetry, *Dum Dāv*, *Nirās Aṅgar Vatt*, *Bimbābilāp*.

The Pre-Angkor and Angkor Periods (7th to 14th Centuries ad)

These centuries saw the establishment of Sanskrit as the supplier of new vocabulary in many fields, being the language of social prestige and of literature. Loan words relating to law, religion, and politics, and abstract ideas in general, were absorbed into Khmer and were naturalized both phonologically and grammatically.[2] Most of them were destined to remain as part of the Khmer lexicon, though sometimes with changed meaning, until modern times.[3] At the same time, it became the practice to use Sanskrit for all elevated linguistic activities. The educated elite of Cambodia read and wrote Sanskrit; and it is clear that there must have been much self-conscious use of the language in their conversation and private writing. Our evidence of deliberate borrowing is, however, quite limited. It is certain that paeans to the gods and kings were composed entirely in Sanskrit poetry, whereas native Khmer was reserved for practical matters. At a more everyday level, Sanskrit was frequently adopted in composing personal names, where Khmer would have done just as well. For examples of the latter practice we may go back as far as the seventh century (though the tradition continued for at least six more centuries), when dancers, singers, musicians and officials were given Sanskritic names to specify their calling. Artists typically obtained pretty names, such as "Spring Jasmine" (*Vasantamallikā*) for a dancer, "Slender-limbed" (*Taṅvaṅgī*) for a singer and "Beloved lady-friend" (*Sakhipriya*) for a musician. Officials, on the other hand, received more dignified appellations, such as "Protector of the Law" (*Dharmarakṣa*).[4]

With the establishment of Mahāyāna Buddhism in the 11th century, the Khmer language gained a new source of loans in Pali. Our early evidence of borrowing is slight, but there are a few extant inscriptions of the Angkor kingdom in which conspicuous Pali terms occur. One of these, K.144, an inscription of the 12th to 13th centuries, is lexically so much more Pali than Khmer that one has to grope for the Khmer syntax in the confusion of words. The inscription illustrates deliberate borrowing especially well, since much of the Pali occurs in whole phrases, such as *lokuttara dhamma* (the Law, which is transcendent).

The Middle Period (16th to 19th Centuries ad)

The stone inscriptions of this period have a totally different character from those of the ancient kingdom. As in the Angkorean epoch, most such inscriptions were created to record some act of merit: the freeing of slaves, the repairing of statues, or the offering of material goods to the local community of monks. But where the inscribers of Angkor distinguished sharply between texts in elaborate Sanskrit poetry and texts in terse Khmer prose, their Middle Period successors wrote in a uniform literary Khmer prose style which combined the expression of religious zeal with the provision of mundane information.[5] Some of these later inscriptions were written in person by members of the royal family, some by less eminent officials; not a few contain details of the personal lives of the writer or of the historical events of his time.

In the language of these Middle Period inscriptions it is the Pali loan words, misspelled but clearly identifiable, which serve to underscore the religious fervor of the authors.[6] Much of this Pali terminology, such as *upāsak* (layman) and *sāsanā* ([Buddhist] teaching), was probably already entrenched in the everyday language of the household, and the misspellings in themselves indicate most interestingly the degree to which the borrowed words had been naturalized. In addition to this quotidian Buddhist vocabulary, however, the authors of the inscriptions seem to make deliberate use of religious vocabulary of an elevated and specialized kind, again often in whole phrases. Thus we read in *Inscriptions Modernes d'Angkor (IMA)* 2 of the Queen Mother's "righteous faith, threefold" (*tribidh sucarit saddhā*); of her "participating in a work of merit *(anumodanā)*"; of her meditation on "impermanence" *(aniccā).*[7] She prays that the "benefit [arising out of] her merits" *(phalānisaṅ)* may achieve for her in a future life the greatest of all boons: to be born as a great man *(mahāpuris)* during the time when the Buddha will return to earth, and to hear him preach the "thirty-seven elements of supreme enlightenment" *(sattatiṃsavarabodhipakkhiyā[dhammā]).* Sometimes a Pali phrase familiar to the faithful is quoted; a reference to the ceremony at which a novice is ordained as a monk contains the words "with the *ehi bikkhu*" (which begins with the words "Come, monk").

The contemporary names also show the influence of the dominant source language of the period. For example, eminent dignitaries of the Buddhist community are given appellations like Pavaradhammā (The Noble Law) and Mahāpalī (Great Pali [Scholar]).[8] A servant offered for the care of statues is referred to as Mrs. Suddh (Pure) and a layman, who with his wife carries out an act of merit, as young Mr. Jet [for *jeṭṭhā*] (Best).[9]

It should be noted, however, that in general the language of the IMA, though very much influenced by Pali, is characterized by many features of native Khmer origin. The devices of reduplication, repetition and assonance now appear in the writing, giving the impression that the Khmer language is being consciously used as a means of elegant expression in prose.

It is in the Middle Period that we find the earliest extant non-inscriptional literature: long "verse-novels," retelling the religious tales of India. This genre includes the one composition which may, because of the extent to which it became a Khmer story and because of the profound influence it has had on Khmer culture, be termed an epic,[10] namely the *Reamker [Rāmakerti]*, the Khmer version of the Rāmāyaṇa. Otherwise the bulk of these long works consists of Jātaka stories. The ancient kingdom of Angkor had established the tradition that Sanskrit was the preeminent language for literature. But after the 15th century texts were no longer composed wholly in Sanskrit; rather the literary style of Khmer poetry was "elevated" by the deliberate insertion of Sanskrit terminology. At the same time, the close connection of the Jātaka tales with Buddhism caused the deliberate inclusion of Pali as well. The conscious borrowings of the early poets were copied by their successors and gradually a body of Sanskrit and Pali vocabulary was formed which helped to crystallize a distinct literary style. Analysis of the deliberately chosen and consciously used loans which form this "high language" reveals that the words most frequently occurring are in fact the Sanskrit or Pali translations for very ordinary phenomena, such as the following:

(a) Features of the mundane world:

earth	*dharaṇī* or *basudhā*	sun	*ādity*	mountain	*girī*
sky, air	*ākās* or *vehā[s]*	moon	*cand*	river	*nadī*
water	*gaṅgā*	night	*ādhrāt* [Skt. "midnight"]	forest	*briks* [Skt. "tree"]
fire	*aggī*	day	*dinakar*	path	*adhvā*
wind	*bāy*	world	*bibhab-lok*	flower	*puspā, pupphā*
rain	*biruṇ*			bird	*paksī, paksā*
				animal	*tiracchān*

(b) Certain possessions of the ruling class (not necessarily of royalty):

clothing	*bastr, bharaṇa:*	home	*sthān*
jewels	*ratn*	garden	*udyān*
perfume	*gandh*	horse	*ajineyy* or *assa*

(c) Attributes (adjectives, epithets and similes) of the main characters:[11]

Hero		King		Heroine	
master of men	*narapati*	serene[12]	*ksem ksānt*	beautiful	*kalyān*
handsome	*subhăn*	educated	*munī*	golden	*subaṇṇ*
mighty	*mahimā*	upholder of the earth	*bhūdhar*	unblemished	*nirmal*
victorious	*[jāñ] jăy*	[like] a roaring lion	*sihanād*	divine	*deb*
[like] the sun	*ādity*			goddess	*debī*
				jewel	*ratn*
				pure	*parisuddha*
				[like] the moon	*cănd*

(d) Parts of the body, movements or actions of the body, and kinship terms (for gods and royalty):[13]

hand	*hast*	give	*pradān*	elder sibling	*jeṭṭhā*
face	*bhaktr*	die	*sugat*	mother	*jananī*

(e) Certain numerals, some associated with religious or mythical objects:

1	[alone, sole, lonely]	*ek*	16	[heavens]	*soḷas*
2	[ ]	*do, dve*	33	[heaven of the 33]	*trăytriṅs*
3	[e.g., worlds or jewels]	*trai*	1000	[goddesses]	*sahass*
4	[e.g., pillars or ministers]	*catu*			
5	[e.g., senses]	*pañca*			
6	[levels of heaven of desire]	*cha*			
9	[degrees of purity in gold]	*nabv*			
10	[directions]	*das*			

A parallel "secularization" is noticeable in the way in which the High Language now began to be manipulated to fit the demands of poetic meters with regard to numbers of syllables and required rhymes. One finds the Indian inflexions ā, ī and o added to the truncated forms of naturalized loan words to supply optional extra syllables and expand the choice of rhymes; these inflexions are often casually used without any reference to the meaning they conveyed in the original language.

The Middle Period is also notable for the practice of citing passages of Pali (mentioned above in connection with Middle Khmer inscriptions [IMA]) in the verse-novels which retell the Jātaka tales. Quite often one finds an introductory page or two in Pali, intended to mark the dedication of the work to the Buddha. Deliberate borrowing of Thai vocabulary also occurred from the beginning of this era. In the *Reamker [Rāmakerti]*, for example, there are a score of such usages, many appearing in the older parts of the work, written in the 16th century.[14] The list includes several "everyday" words obviously chosen for literary effect—e.g., *khāv* (news), *tāṃ* (black), and *ṭaeṅ* (red)—as well as some military terms like *huoṇā* (chief) and *hmuot* (unit, company).[15] Other borrowings look like straightforward substitutions for Khmer words, but may in fact represent objects which are not identical with the objects referred to by the Thai originals (e.g., *kliṅ* [sunshade] or *kuñcae* [lock]). Even *mīoeṅ* (city), occurring in a context where roads and fortifications are described, may indicate a foreign kind of city. Other borrowings include the names of entertainments and of certain trappings of animals. Thai numerals, other than those which formed established loans in Khmer, were sometimes used for effect, e.g., /paet/ (eight) and /si:/ (four) in the opening passage of the verse-novel *Rīoeṅ Saṅkh Silp Jǎy*.[16] Imitation of the Thai became especially prevalent in the 19th century. By that time many Thai loans, such as *ṭuoṅ* (round [of moon or face]), *bhilīeṅ* (tutor, nanny), *sāvjai* (elderly court lady) and *nuon* (tender, sweet) were part of the regular stock of poetic vocabulary. Khmer poets had also by then acquired the habit of imitating and experimenting with Thai meters.

In the *cbap* (as in other poetry of which the themes were not of Indian origin) the typical borrowings are rather different. This group of didactic moral poems, much loved and quoted, is both homely and Buddhist in character. Practical advice to laymen of all social strata concerning proper moral and social conduct is given by means of examples and comparisons drawn from nature and from peasant life. The poets who composed *cbap* used an appropriately simple style. The High Language was still used to a certain extent: kinship terms employed to refer to readers treated them as if they were royal (e.g., *janak* and *janānī* for "father" and "mother"), while poetic phrases like *puspagandh* (fragrance of flowers) also appear. But on the whole the vocabulary is much more influenced by Pali.

The deliberate use of Pali vocabulary was a constant reminder of the Buddhist faith, the source of the morality which the *cbap* gently advocated. "Oneself" is often *ātmā;* "untruth" is *musāvād;* "kindness" is *mettā*, "understanding" *ñāṇ*. A person must not fall into erring *(bālā)* ways, becoming greedy *(lobho)* or pleasure-loving. Otherwise, he will forget all about the sacred precepts *(sīl)*, alms-giving *(dān)*, and increase of understanding *(ñāṇavuddhī)* and will fail to have the virtue *(pāramī)* needed to lead others. As in the Middle Khmer inscriptions, Pali phrases are sometimes quoted, as though to emphasize that it is the voice of the Buddhist brotherhood which is speaking to the layman through this poetry. Not surprisingly, certain metaphors encountered in the Middle Khmer inscriptions—e.g., "crossing the ocean *(samudr)* of life" and "proceeding along the hard way *(kantār)*" occur in the *cbap* and in later poetry.

Early Modern Period (19th to Early 20th Centuries)

Although Western influences started to be felt in general and were to increase greatly with the establishment of the French Protectorate, their effect on Khmer literature throughout the period was slight. The style of the prose works of this period is straightforward and unselfconscious. The use of the Royal Vocabulary is generally restricted to cases of necessity. It occurs throughout the (royal) Chronicles, but only in those folktales or *Gatilok* stories where royal personages are involved.

In the poetry of the period, however, the kinship terms of the Royal Vocabulary are sometimes used, as in the *cbap*, whether or not they refer to royalty, and the High Language is often employed for stereotyped themes such as sunsets and sunrises. Basically, however, the poets of this period do not concern themselves with elevating their style by means of borrowed vocabulary. Instead, they use the Khmer descriptive and phonaesthetic vocabulary to great effect, particularly in alliterative sequences such as *seb sam saṅ sār* (chat pleasantly in company), or *dīeṅ daṃ drīev droḥ* (the calling [of birds] as they go to rest).

The conscious use of Pali continues to be in evidence. In the folktales we find it in the form of Pali-like gibberish which a trickster chants in order to demonstrate, to the people whom he is about to cheat, that he is a man of learning. In the *Gatilok*, a more formal collection of retold Indian tales, the concluding moral is given by a Pali word, never an established loan, denoting the fault of character or the emotion illustrated by each story. Among such words are *vippatisār* (remorse), *lobhacetanā* (covetous thought) and *mahicchatā* (ambition).

A little self-conscious Pali also appears in lyric poetry when the subject is religion rather than love. Poets, explaining their intention to turn from the travails of passion to their Buddhist faith, often say what the authors of some of the Middle Khmer inscriptions had expressed in prose: a wish to be born again at the time of the Buddha's return.

The short "verse-novel" *Bimbābilāp* (which includes a short Jātaka story but is chiefly about the grief of the Buddha's wife when he leaves her and the court for a life of contemplation) is worth mentioning in connection with Pali since a considerable amount of difficult Pali religious vocabulary is used, evidently on purpose, despite the fact that the ordinary reader would not be likely to understand it: e.g., *satipaṭṭhānupatthambhak* (encouraging contemplation), *dhammabhisamay* (understanding of the Truth), and so on. Familiar Sanskrit loans are sometimes given their Pali spelling, e.g., *baṇṇ* instead of *barṇ* (color).

Nonetheless, from the last decades of the 19th century onwards, a steady influx of French words were absorbed and naturalized as loans. Sometimes the spelling of French loans indicated their origin even though their form no longer did so, e.g., /so:vɔ̀ə/ (*chauffeur*) spelled with final r, or /poh/ (*poste*) spelled with st and syllabary /e/ after the vowel. In other cases neither the spelling nor the pronunciation would remind Khmers of their origin, e.g., /kɔmple:/ (*complet* [suit]) was not given its final t and had the form of a Khmer minor disyllable.

Alongside these established loans there were words which were very familiar and which were to stay in the language until the postwar period, but which had untranslatable meanings. Such were /msiə(r)/ (*Monsieur*)—/lò:k/ did not convey all that was to be conveyed about the foreignness of the person thus alluded to; /re:sī: dɔŋ/ (*résident*)—only the French term could bear the full implications of the position of this representative of colonial power; and /rò:mɔŋ/ (*roman*), indicating prose fiction, a hitherto unknown genre. Sometimes a complete French phrase was cited, e.g., /kù:vè:rnaə(r) dɤ: la: ko:saŋsì:n/ (*gouverneur de la Cochinchine*).[17] When such relatively unfamiliar French words were used, the Khmer form, indicating the pronunciation as above, was usually followed by the French word in roman letters. This habit of adding what was in fact a key to the meaning was to persist and be much in evidence in later journalese; it indicated an appeal to those readers whose education in French had a formal character.

THE MODERN PERIOD (MID-20TH CENTURY)

In the post–World War II period, when a substantial number of young people were being educated at French universities, the language of journals and of conversation among members of the ruling class was interlarded with consciously cited French terms concerning politics, philosophy, literature, etc. Quite apart from the abstract nouns which French could usefully supply, young intellectuals familiar with French also appreciated the democratic simplicity of French pronouns in contrast with the status-indicating Khmer system. In the 1950s I remember hearing a group of educated Phnom Penh Cambodians of various ages and social levels using *vous* to each other in a political discussion, apparently because they appreciated the equality which *vous* suggested. How conscious Khmer were of their language's explicit exposition of differences of social status is illustrated in a novel set in the prewar era where an officious local governor cannot bring himself to speak politely to his subordinates by using /khɲom/ for "I" or "me," though he knows he should not now use the familiar /ʔaɲ/.[18] The result is that his underlings all become used to understanding what he says even with the pronouns "I" and "me" omitted!

In the immediate aftermath of Cambodia's independence from France, achieved in 1953, the wish to make the Khmer language capable of expressing modern ideas without using French was strong. It was sometimes expressed as an aim to make the Khmer language "the equal of any."[19] In fact, Khmer has a vocabulary of considerable richness. But for abstract terms, Khmer had, on the whole, either to build up compounds using verbs and a nominalizing device or to borrow from Sanskrit, Pali, and French. It thus seemed necessary to replace abstract nouns, as well as a great quantity of modern technical terms hitherto automatically adopted from French, with a new "Khmer" vocabulary. The existing Cambodian language could, with some difficulty, be manipulated to provide the new terms by the process of translating definitions. Compound neologisms such as *grāp'-paek-cheh* (seed-break-catch fire) for "incendiary bomb," could be absorbed if there was time for gradual growth; but a chemistry text book would not be easy to understand if it was full of such unfamiliar compounds of which, since there was no established practice of using hyphens or spaces between words, the boundaries would not be easily perceived. With regard to political terms, on the other hand, an aura of newness was a real advantage, since they were of paramount importance in those modernizing days. For all this novel, non-colonial vocabulary, abstract and technical, Khmer intellectuals turned to Pali and Sanskrit, the prestigious languages of older times, as naturally as the West turns to Greek and Latin. A "new vocabulary" of over 3,000 terms was thus created, one which is always regarded as being Khmer, but which we can legitimately view as a deliberate use of foreign vocabulary.

The creation of this New Vocabulary was the responsibility of a Cultural Commission, founded as a result of the difficulties encountered in composing the text of the Constitution of 1946. This body prepared lists of French words for which a translation was needed and received lists of French technical terms submitted to them by official bodies. The new translations, called "cultural words" (*bāky vappadharm*) were published in 1950 by the Ministry of Education as a short dictionary titled *Saddānukram pāramṅ khmaer,* and also appeared serially in *Kambujasuriyā*.[20] For each French word the commission either took an existing Indian loan, usually one long-established but infrequently used, and "matched" it to the relevant French word (e.g., *sundarakathā* [elegant discourse] with *discours*) or they "created," using Sanskrit and Pali, a new word (e.g., *sannisīd*, from the Pali *sannisīdati* [sink down, settle] for *conférence*). In some cases the new words were intended to cover only some of the meanings of the French word, while in other cases they were intended to translate all the meanings. Thus *sundarakathā* was to translate *discours* only in its meaning of "prepared, detailed talk to an assembly," while *sannisīd* was to cover both meanings of *conférence* ("meeting" and "lecture").[21]

With the rather sudden influx into newspapers and official documents of long, unfamiliar words, the Khmer public had to learn quickly. Radio talks by Sam Thang, a member of the Cultural Commission and later the author of a dictionary of the New Vocabulary, were subsequently published in *Kambujasuriyā*.[22] They explained just what the Cultural Commission intended a new word to mean and described how to go about pronouncing some of these 6- and 7-syllable words. The procedures and difficulties of the Cultural Commission may be observed by reading the articles by Neang Hu and Sam Thang published in various issues of *Kambujasuriyā* in 1960.[23] They show that the public was dismayed at the quantity of new words and grumbled openly. Teachers and officials wrote in, asking probing questions. What was the difference between the three words for "girl" (*kaññā, nārī* and *yuvatī*)? Why should *antara* be pronounced /ʔɔntərə/ in the new word /ʔɔntərəcì:ət/ (*antarajāti*) meaning "international" when it was pronounced /ʔɔndɔ:/ in the familiar /ʔɔndɔ:thì:ən/ (*antaradhān*) meaning "destruction"? What was wrong with calling a train /rətèh-phlɤ̀:ŋ/ (cart fire)? Neang Hu and Sam Thang had their answers ready. *Kaññā, nārī* and *yuvatī* were respectively "girl not yet of marriageable age," "woman" and "girl of marriageable age" (a distinction, one may add, which novelists of the period ignored). The different pronunciations of the same Indian prefix *(antara)* in the two Khmer borrowings was due to the naturalization of the older borrowing. The new word for "train" was invented because the Railway Board had asked for "translation into Khmer of equal status with the French word" of various technical words including "train." "However," declared the Cultural Commission through the medium of Neang Hu and Sam Thang, "people will not be wrong in ordinary speech if they continue to use /rətèh-phlɤ̀:ŋ/"!

The articles in *Kambujasuriyā* indicate that the Cultural Commission sometimes had difficulty in controlling its lexical offspring. They complained, for example, that they intended the translation of *indépendence* to be *issarabhāb* (powerfulness, condition of overlordship) but "everybody thinks it is *ekarājy* (single kingdom, one power)." The new word *paṇṇadūt* (sheet-messenger), a translation for the French *planton* (office-boy, orderly), had been produced independently of the Cultural Commission and become widely used. The Cultural Commission felt, however, that this term had an unfortunate association with *dūt* (envoy) and thus could not be tolerated. No offense was intended to office-boys. "We want you to have a title," it declared through the pages of *Kambujasuriyā* (to such office-boys as might read this learned journal), "but office-boys do not represent the government officially as envoys." Accordingly, the word *lekhahāri* (letter-taker) received the official blessing. In contrast to *issarabhāb*, it came into general use.

Fortunately for Khmer in official circles, who needed to acquire the New Vocabulary quickly, many components of the new words were already familiar as established loans. Thus *kamm* (fact, action) occurs in many compounds, e.g., *prati-kamm* (jet [plane], French *avion de ré-action*); *niyam* (to tend to) translates *-isme* in such words as *prākaṭ-niyam (réal-isme); vidyā* (study) is used for *-ologie*, e.g., *citta-vidyā (psych-ologie)*. It frequently proved possible to compose a new word by means of a straight translation of the components of the French term (itself often of Greek or Latin origin) into Sanskrit or Pali (as in the above instances), though some of the results, such as *ek-saṇthān* for the noun *uni-forme*, seem odd because we are no longer conscious of the two components of our own Western compound. (The new compounds naturally had no relationship with any attested Sanskrit or Pali compounds of the same form). As time went on, familiarity with the Indian components of the new compounds, such as those mentioned above as well as *pubv-* (pre-, fore-), *-āgār* (building, place), and *-ālay* (repository), increased. As a result, some interesting lexical changes took place. For example, the term *-bhāb* (state of affairs), from being used as a device to form some new abstract nouns, such as *sukhuma-bhāb* (detail-state of affairs) for "subtlety," later crept into use as the first component of compounds conveying the meaning "-ness,"[24] e.g., *bhāb l-a* (beauty). This method thus supplemented the two previous ways of turning an adjectival verb into an abstract noun—by infixation *(l-am-a)* and by using *sectī* (matter) before it.

The new requirements caused novel, specialized meanings to be conferred on some old-fashioned loans. *Siddhi*, for example, had long been naturalized as /sɤt/ (power), but it was now brought in as the new, unnaturalized /sɤtthì/ (rights). Similarly, *śilpa* had long been reduced to /sɤl/ (knowledge of the supernatural), but it was now reintroduced as the unnaturalized form /sɤləpa'/ (Art, the Arts). Some old loans retained the same pronounced form but acquired new meanings. Thus /samay/ (time, period) now obtained, through its occurrence in the much-used phrase /samay thmɤy/

(modern times), the meaning "up-to-date," or "fashionable" even when used without the word /thmɤy/ (new).

The process of implementing the New Vocabulary may be observed in newspapers and journals from the 1950s onwards. Frequently the French term which was being replaced would follow the new word in parentheses, e.g., *ādideb-ksatrī(y) (dieu-roi)*.[25] Soon words such as *ekarājy* (independence) and *mātuprades* (motherland) were familiar enough. Sometimes the metaphoric meaning of a French word was transferred to its replacement. Thus the Sanskrit *pariyākās*, adopted to translate *atmosphère*, acquired the latter's secondary meaning of "political (and social) atmosphere." The old Khmer word *amnāc*, denoting "power" in the abstract sense, took on the secondary meaning of *pouvoir* to refer to "a powerful state." Alongside these partial neologisms such old compound expressions as *dik ṭī* (water land) for "territory" and *cuḥ cūl* (go down enter) for "to submit to" remained in journalistic use, while vivid combinations of old words to express new political or technical conceptions were also developed: e.g., *phlīen kralai* (adulterated rain) for "poison gas," and *campāṃṅ chmak* (fighting one-who-catches) for "guerrilla warfare."[26]

As time went on the New Vocabulary was so much used in journals and official documents that it continued the process, started by French loans, of changing, through its predominantly nominal character, the syntax and literary style of modern news writing.[27] The long, involved sentences were so similar in construction to the sentences of French that they were easier to understand if French was borne in mind, and were probably a mystery to those Cambodians who knew no French.

Quite apart from the fact that Sanskrit and Pali forms were used in the postwar period to develop the New Vocabulary, the general prestige of these languages is visible in the continued use of the High Language in specific contexts. In the title of a well-known magazine of the 1960s, *Nagar Khmaer,* the literary word for "kingdom" appears. Freedom movements adopted Pali-derived names: for example, Khmer Serei (from the Pali *serīn* [independent]) and Issarak (from the Pali *issara* [master]). Norodom Sihanouk, however, did not adopt the New Vocabulary wholeheartedly. His self-bestowed title Samdech Eu *(saṃtec ū)* or "Prince-Father" was composed of native vocabulary, and he addressed the people in homely language as "brothers and sisters" *(paṅ p-ūn)*, while referring to them in the third person as "Khmer children" *(kūn khmaer)*.

Modern prose fiction started late in Cambodia by comparison with the rest of Southeast Asia. It was only in the late 1930s, several years after the installation of a printing-house in Phnom Penh, that the new genre really came into existence. The first published novel was Rim Kin's *Suphāt* ("Sophat") in 1938. In the 1950s, however, novels began to be published in quantity. In them two features of literary composition which had previously been characteristic of different genres are found together: the conscious use of the High Language, once mainly characteristic of Indian-derived themes retold in verse, and realism, found most in folklore and *cbap* (though there are some amusing and very colloquial passages in the verse-novels which cannot be ignored).[28] A novel was a literary composition, and therefore had to be dignified by the use of the literary language; yet, for the first time, there was now *carte blanche* for authors to write at length about what ordinary people said and did.

The influence of the French novel was strong. In the early years of *Kambujasuriyā* French fiction was regularly translated and serialized: Chateaubriand's *Paul et Virginie*, for example, appeared in the issues of 1955. Some authors, perhaps with nineteenth century French novels in mind, began every chapter by setting the scene with a long descriptive passage in the literary style, using, that is, both the High Language, associated previously with poetry, and some of the vivid vocabulary in which the Khmer native lexicon abounds. Modern Khmer social problems formed the subject matter of most postwar fiction but the descriptions of love-scenes, lacking in traditional Cambodian restraint, and of the heroes of adventure and crime detection stories owed much to Western novels and films. (For example, in the historical novel *Rīoeṅ Brāḥ Pad Bañā Yāt* ["King Ponhea Yat"], a hero arrives on the scene just as a heroine, bound and gagged by the villain, is about to undergo a fate worse than death. With finger poised, not on the trigger, but on the equivalent part of his cross-bow, he cries, "Turn around and hands up!")[29]

Some colloquial words in written form were now regularly needed and gradually they were spelled more consistently. It was now felt desirable to make it clear when direct speech was quoted and to indicate whether a sentence was a question, exclamation or statement; for these purposes, French punctuation was adopted.

The established literary language, as we have just seen, was still in use, especially in descriptive passages where authors attempted to attain as high a literary standard as possible; since literature proper had always been poetry, the language of poetry had to be used. Nonetheless, changes were at work in the type of Sanskrit and Pali borrowings. Since heroes and heroines were no longer royal now (except in historical novels), they were termed *mānab/mānavī* (young man/girl of marriageable age). The girl, no longer *debī* (goddess), could be called *yuvatī, kaññā* or *nārī* (young girl). Alternatively, she might be referred to as *kalyāṇ* (the beauty). At the same time adjectives tended to be indigenous Khmer words. The old-fashioned attribute of feminine perfection, *grap' lakkh(ṇ)* ([having] every virtue), very common in folktales and verse-novels, came to be replaced by simple Khmer phrases describing characteristics traditionally admired, e.g., *subhāb rāp sā* (of modest behavior), *santāp' dhnāp'* (docile) or *rūp s-āt* (well turned-out, neat and trim). Yet, many a heroine was still described by the use of one adjectival verb of clear Indian origin: *anāth* (defenseless)—for there was quite a vogue for rather Victorian-style abandoned heroines.

The earliest novels were generally free of the New Vocabulary. Some had been written many years before publication and were naturally not composed in the modern style. But gradually the new words infiltrated fiction.[30] Initially, novelists adopted the New Vocabulary for the special purposes of avoiding French vocabulary and of associating themselves with the approved language style of the new era of independence. The degree to which the New Vocabulary was used varied widely from author to author and, depending on the nature of the theme, from one work to another. Many novels, especially those appealing to the least literary of readers, were composed in conversational style throughout. Sometimes just the preface of a novel was full of New Vocabulary; a statement might be made there about one or other of the political *motifs* of the period—the new flowering of Khmer literature or the recently won independence under Sihanouk's Buddhist Socialist Republic. On the other hand, in historical novels, based on the legendary heroes of the Angkorean and post-Angkorean eras, such New Vocabulary words as *ekarājy* (independence), *serībhāb* (freedom) and *mātuprades* (motherland) often occur. In a play set in the post-Angkorean period, at a time when the Thai kings were fighting to extend their control into Cambodia, a Khmer who has deserted to the other side and now repents of his treachery describes himself as *"an imperialist to the bone" (khuor cakrabatti)!*[31] In the same play the Cambodians are said to be fighting, not for their country (*prades,* or *sruk*) but for their "nation" (*jāti*), a more fashionable concept. Novels concerned with class struggles in the pre-Sihanouk days brought on stage the farmers, now known as *kasikar,* and their work, *kasikamm.* The working man, never classified as such before, appeared as *kammakar.* And how could romantic novels be written without the new vocabulary for "feelings" (*manosañcetanā*), "duty" *(karaṇīyakicc)*, or the "scenery" *(desabhāb)* at which the lovelorn hero/heroine invariably gazes? In love stories, the heroine was often given the New Vocabulary title of *kaññā* (Miss), while hero and heroine were *yavajan* (young people or, in a political context, Youth).

Some authors brought in the New Vocabulary to an extent which seems excessive to the present writer. Very often the practice of going out of their way to use a more literary term spoils rather than embellishes the style. A neat little Khmer phrase such as *tāṃṅ bī kmeṅ* (ever since childhood) is clumsy when dressed up as *tāṃṅ bī kumārabhāb*.

The lively comedy *Saṃpuk it me pā* ("A Nest without the Parents") by Hang Thon Hak incidentally provides some lighthearted comment on the New Vocabulary. The curtain goes up at the beginning of the play to reveal the living room of a modest house. A voice exclaims, "*Phdaḥ! Gehaṭhān! Ramaṇīyaṭhān!*" ("A house! A residence! A stately home!"). Thematically, the narrator's voice is merely saying "home, sweet home!" but the use of the third word, a New Vocabulary term which indicates "place of interest to sightseers," is intended to raise a laugh. As this comedy of modern manners proceeds, the New Vocabulary supplies many key words. The young head of the family which has been deprived of its parents exclaims, "*I* have to look after the family finances—*I* can't [unlike the younger, modern members of the family] discuss religion *(sāsnā)*, science *(vidyāsāstr)*, art *(silpa)* and society studies *(saṅgamasāstr)*." The term used for "religion" here is not a new borrowing; religious vocabulary has hardly been augmented at all in the postwar period. But the words for "science" and "art" are new (though "science" *[vidyāsāstr]* was one of the earliest new terms). The form *saṅgamasāstr* suggests that the busy young head of the family confuses *saṅgamavidyā* (sociology) and the use accorded to -*sāstr* in the earliest 20th century formations for the names of fields of study. The rest of the family admire, using a new term, this *manuss karaṇīyakicc* (man of duty). A description of the typical Cambodian girl of tradition endows her with *iriyapath jā nārī khmaer* (the deportment of a Khmer young lady); she will "keep the Buddhist precepts, give alms, observe the established customs and be compassionate." The *nārī samay* (the modern miss), on the other hand, whistles, sits Western fashion (instead of on the ground with legs folded sideways), wears checked trousers, has her hair fluffed out (/bɔmbe:/ from the French *bombé*) and thinks she is allowed to choose her own husband. The argumentative, philosophizing, guitar-playing young brother teases the family head until the latter protests that he needs peace and quiet to think about the family's needs. He exclaims, using a verbose sentence full of New Vocabulary and with a syntactical construction worthy of journalism, "Give me the right *(siddhi)* to have the freedom *(serībhāb)* to fulfill my duty *(karaṇīyakicc)* with justice *(yuttidharm)*, boldness and heroism *(varabhāb)!*"

The extent to which the French language remained in use was limited but interesting. On the whole, such old familiar borrowings as /bùyro:/ (office), /ka:t/ (identity card), /lì:se:/ (college, high school), which continued (and continue) in oral usage in everyday situations, were replaced in the novels by the new words *kāriyālăy, paṇṇ,* and *vidyālăy*. Yet there are plenty of instances of the conscious use of French words for effect. The word /doktɔ̀ə(r)/ occurs in place of the old compound, composed of established Indian loans, *grū bedy*, when reference to a French-trained medical doctor is intended. The term /ma:dɤ:mu:əsael/ (Mademoiselle) occurs in a short story when a sixth form pupil addresses the girl he desires and wishes to impress her favorably. In some of the contexts in which they occur French words seem to be used because the French language is admired. In others, however, they are used maliciously: for example, in a detective novel, an undesirable character is referred to as /ʔa: msiə(r)/ (that [derogatory implication] Monsieur). Sometimes it is as though the characters (or authors) are merely showing off their knowledge of French. Why else would a character in the play mentioned above say /sù:e:/ (*jouer,* play) a children's game instead of /lè:ŋ/? We might note in passing that a residual awe of the French also appears in some untraditional uses of the old Royal Vocabulary. In one novel, for example, the young hero, a newly appointed provincial official, is said to have to *gāl'* the French Governor; this term is the "classical" word for attending upon, or appearing in the presence of, Khmer royalty.[32]

One word borrowed from Thai which was much used in the 1950s and 1960s was /sìvìlai/, a Thai loan from the English "civilized." It conveyed the idea of Western-style sophistication. Cambodians had taken a great interest in the superficial effects of modern developments in Thailand. In his novel *Mālā Ṭuoṅ Citt,* Nou Hach allows his hero to admire not only the nail varnish but also the friendly manner of a Thai girl who actually talks to an unknown man in a train. (To be sure, the same hero criticizes the widow of a Thai official who, though over fifty years of age, wears brightly colored sarongs and puts on face-powder.) A further comment on Thailand in this story, composed after Cambodian independence but relating to the previous period (actually 1939), is made when the hero says to the Thai heroine, with a certain lack of logic, "How could I aspire to your hand? *Your* father is a rich man in a country which is fully sovereign *(ekarājy beñ dī)!*"

The remaining language from which words have deliberately been borrowed in recent times is English. The English items are not always immediately recognizable in their adapted forms and spellings. It is easy to spot /ba:y-ba:y/ (bye-bye), but less so to catch /kho:v-baoy/ (cowboy) or /svì:ɲ kò:m/ (chewing gum).

Finally, a word is necessary on two languages which have had a strong influence on Khmer over a long period, but which seem never to be used in writing for deliberate effect: Chinese and Vietnamese. Chinese loans, chiefly connected with cooking, trade, finance and gambling,[33] have been steadily infiltrating for several centuries, at least since Angkorean times. They include such household vocabulary as /toʔ/ (table) and /ʔa:v/ (shirt). Chinese novels and plays have had enough local prestige to be translated into Khmer.[34] China has been regarded with awe in both ancient and modern times, yet this awe has sprung from an awareness of China's political and military power, not of its language and culture. It is interesting that, during the Khmer Rouge period, new words and new uses were still being coined by reference to the traditional source, India. Thus the new word *aṅgabhāb* (age, stage of physical development) was linked with the established Indian loan *kumār* (child) to mean "children aged 6–13," and in conjunction with a word from the New Vocabulary, *calat* (mobile), to denote "mobile young people (aged 14–18)." The Vietnamese language has also supplied everyday words which have become established loans, though to a much less extent than Chinese. Examples are /ŋùːə/ (Vietnamese *ngu* [to lie down]) in /kda: ŋùːə/ (bench) and /laɲ/ (glossy silk, taffeta, from Vietnamese *lạnh* [cool]). Once again, it seems that there has not been enough admiration of Vietnamese culture for deliberate citation of its vocabulary to take place.

Conclusion

We have seen that in different historical contexts the Khmer enjoyed using for effect vocabulary drawn from different foreign origins. In the pre-Angkorean and Angkorean periods, admiration of Indian culture led them to use Sanskrit for poetic expression and people were often given Sanskrit names. As the practice of Buddhism became better established, from the eleventh century onwards, this religious devotion was shown in the use of Pali vocabulary both as a source of names and in the form of citations of whole phrases. In the Middle period the continuing prestige of both these Indian languages is conspicuous in the deliberate use of Sanskrit and Pali words for simple objects in order to elevate the style of Khmer poetry. Finally, in the modern period, the Khmer have resorted to Sanskrit and Pali to compose new words for technological and other modern concepts.

Quite early in the period following the fall of Angkor the affectation of Thai vocabulary in Khmer poetry (again to replace very ordinary Khmer words) suggests an admiration of Thai culture. This tendency became particularly pronounced in the nineteenth century.

The conscious use of French vocabulary seems to have had contradictory implications. In some contexts it appears to indicate admiration, in others dislike.

Finally, there is a striking lack of evidence for the deliberate use of either Chinese or Vietnamese vocabulary. This avoidance may be reasonably interpreted as indicating a cool detachment towards these languages.

---

1. Here I am concerned with the literary unity of each period. For an account of the parallel social and political epochs, see, for example, David P. Chandler, *A History of Cambodia* (Boulder: Westview Press, 1983).

2. See my "Sanskrit Loanwords in Pre-Angkor Khmer," *Mon-Khmer Studies,* 6 (1977), pp. 151–68, at pp. 160–67.

3. For example, *prasiddhi,* meaning in Old Khmer "exclusive right" and in Modern Khmer "to cause to be successful"; or *puṇya,* in Old Khmer "foundation," "work of merit," in Modern Khmer "festival," "good."

4. See, e.g., K. 557, Est 33–34. References to pre-Angkor and Angkor inscriptions are given as in George Coedès, *Inscriptions du Cambodge,* 8 vols. (Paris: École Française d'Extrême-Orient, 1937–66).

5. In fact this corpus of inscriptions does include one long poem, No. 38.

6. These identifications are noted in S. Lewitz (1970–73)/S. Pou (1974–75), "Inscriptions modernes d'Angkor" [henceforth *IMA*], *Bulletin de l'École Française d'Extrême Orient* [henceforth *BEFEO*], 57 (1970), pp. 99–126; 58 (1971), pp. 105–23; 59 (1972), pp. 101–21 and 221–49; 60 (1973), pp. 163–203 and 205–42; 61 (1974), pp. 301–37; and 62 (1975), pp. 283–353.

7. The Middle Khmer words cited here are given their correct spelling. In this essay most Khmer vocabulary items are rendered in the Lewitz transliteration system (see S. Lewitz, "Note sur la translittération du cambodgien," *BEFEO,* 55 [1969], pp. 163–69). Only in cases where the modern pronunciation is of greater interest than the spelling is my own transcription employed (see my *Introduction to Cambodian* [London: Oxford University Press, 1968]).

8. See *IMA* 6.

9. *IMA* 4 and 17.

10. S. Pou, *Études sur le Rāmakerti (XVIe–XVIIe siècles)* (Paris: École Française d'Extrême-Orient, 1977), pp. 58–60, takes a different view, including the *Lpoek Aṅgar Vatt* in the epic category.

11. Many similes, some of them long and involved, were formed in imitation of Sanskrit originals. The shorter ones were often repeated by later poets: e.g., the vast army of the king was typically compared with the sea, *mahā sāgar;* the anger of heroes was compared with era-ending fire.

12. Kings and princes were described as "serene" even when some disaster threatened or when some great sorrow afflicted them. Such official serenity was regarded as befitting their station in life; note the typically serene expression of the royal heroes depicted in Angkorean sculptures, leather shadow-play puppets, dance theater masks and painted illustrations.

13. The vocabulary illustrated under (d) was already in everyday use by those people who had occasion to address or to speak about roy-

alty, since it formed part of the Royal Vocabulary. In all later literature writers had to use this Vocabulary (with its very lengthy terms) when royalty was referred to, even if they had no wish to use the High Language in general. This political necessity tended to give the (sometimes incorrect) impression that an elevated style was generally intended.

14. See Pou, *Études*, pp. 53–58, for a discussion of the dating of this work.

15. The admiration for the Thai felt by the Khmer was reciprocated. Everyday Khmer words regularly occurred in contemporary Thai poetry.

16. Saṅkh Silp Jăy is a personal name of the Buddha in a previous existence. The name literally means "victorious, supernatural shell," and refers to the fact that this Buddha was born with a shell enclosing his body.

17. *Kambujasuriyā* (1930), no. 1, p. 12.

18. Nou Hach, *Mālā Tuoṅ Citt* [A Garland for the Heart] (Phnom Penh: Samāgam anak nibandh Khmaer, Association des écrivains Khmers, 1952), p. 140.

19. Sam Thang, *Vākyaparivatt(n) khmaer-pārāmṅ. Lexique khmer-français* (Phnom Penh: Kim Ky, 1962), preface.

20. All the issues of 1961 and 1962 contained short lists.

21. Occasionally a French word was still retained; for example, the "translation" for *chancelier* was /sɔŋsɤ:li:e:(r)/.

22. *Kambujasuriyā* (1960), pp. 91–97; 221–26.

23. *Kambujasuriyā* (1960), pp. 331–35; 461–67; 580–88; 710–16; 829–34; 943–51; 1069–75.

24. *Bhāb* had occurred previously as a noun meaning "condition," "state," e.g., *bhāb satv* (the condition of being an animal), but it had not been used to form compounds.

25. *Kambujasuriyā* (1956), p. 828. Alternatively, a reduplicative phrase might be used combining a French-derived word and its Khmer quasi-synonym, e.g., *jā arpîtr jā majjhattakar* (as arbiter), in Nou Hach, *Mālā*, p. 183.

26. Nonetheless, some French loans for the vocabulary of politics remained acceptable, such as *plok (bloc)* and /plɔŋ/ *(plan)*.

27. An essay of mine on this subject is due to appear shortly in a volume of papers for Eugenie Henderson.

28. For example, the typically female conversation among the *kinnarī* as they vie with each other for the attention of the Bodhisattva, in *Rīoeṅ Saṅkh Silp Jăy, Histoire de Saing Selchey* (Phnom Penh: Institut Bouddhique, 1962), pp. 106–9.

29. Kuy Lot, *Rīoeṅ Brāḥ Pad Bañā Yāt* [King Ponhea Yat] (Phnom Penh, Kuy Lot, 1966), p. 54.

30. It is curious that the *Kambujasuriyā* refer only to the use of these new words in official documents and newspapers.

31. Tan Seng Ky, *Rīoeṅ Vira:jan khmaer* [A Tale of Khmer Heroes] (Phnom Penh: Bou Phally, 1966), p. 84.

32. Nou Hach, *Mālā*, p. 121.

33. See Saveros Pou and Philip N. Jenner, "Some Chinese Loanwords in Khmer," *Journal of Oriental Studies*, 9: 1 (1973), pp. 1–90.

34. For example, the novel *Sam Kok* was serialized in translation in *Kambujasuriyā* between the years 1946 and 1955, and also in the newspaper *Mātubhūmi* during 1962.

7

THINKER, THESPIAN, SOLDIER, SLAVE? ASSUMPTIONS ABOUT HUMAN NATURE IN THE STUDY OF BALINESE SOCIETY

Mark Hobart

> 'Tis evident, that all the sciences have a relation, greater or less, to human nature; and that however wide any of them may seem to run from it, they still return back by one passage or another . . . since they lie under the cognizance of men, and are judged by their powers and faculties.
>
> Hume, *A Treatise on Human Nature*, xv.

Monsignor Quixote, according to Graham Greene, believed his car, Rocinante, to run on prayer, care, and attention. Sadly enough, academics are seldom as fussy about what keeps their models going. Stopping every few miles to see if, and why, the engine is working is a silly way to drive. To have little clue as to what keeps one chugging along may be still less wise. It is worrying when scholars relax at the wheel, so to speak, with blind faith in the inexhaustible capacities of the academic machine and ignore what goes on under their intellectual bonnets.

In this essay I want to explore the problem of "meaning" in other cultures (Bali in particular) in view of the importance of context in interpreting speech and action, and the unspoken theoretical presuppositions about a universal human nature that inform much academic discourse.

THE BACKGROUND

A problem raised in the Introduction was, if meaning is partly contextual, how can the infinite range of possible contexts delimit a coherent object of study? Some answers take the form of cutting down the field of possibilities by selecting criteria of relevance.

One can try to focus on what is implied or presupposed in utterances,[1] although this has yet to be done successfully. One can filter possible contexts by appeal to human interests: people are treated as trying to maximize some goal. Apart from the well-known models of Man as an economic or rational animal,[2] two of the most popular are those of human beings as seeking to gain power, or to render the world meaningful.[3] So it is common to talk of "utility" being "maximized," social ties or interpretations being "negotiated," or "meaning constructed." It is in order to cut context down to size that such theories of human nature, or of human purposes and interests, are invoked. Hence confusion over context is intimately linked with confusion over appropriate models of human nature. The four images alluded to in my title are four of the more popular Western construals of who the Balinese "are." Yet we shall see that not only are the models of Western commentators and of the Balinese utterly different, but even their ideas of explanation may be incommensurable.

Contextualization in Bali

Much of the existing interpretation of Balinese culture is based on the assumption that language or meaning works in one particular way, so that the Balinese may be adequately explained from a single perspective. There are obvious weaknesses to such a stance and it may be fruitful to explore the possibility that language in its broadest sense has different uses. One might consider then the conditions under which statements seem to impute an essential meaning or close off the range of potential contexts.[4] Rather than assume that words must denote definitely, we might look at essentializing as a style or strategy. This approach opens the way for a more ethnographically sensitive recognition of the other styles or strategies which may be found. Contextualizing in some form would then be an obvious alternative; so might pragmatizing (after the pragmatic theory of truth) where it is regarded as necessary to take action without the time, or need, to consider the intricacies or the fuller contextual implications. From the speaker's, rather than the listener's, point of view there is also a whole battery of loosely "rhetorical" devices to attract attention and persuade an audience.

One of the seemingly simplest kinds of situation which Balinese villagers encounter in everyday life is considering how to apply terms for the groups and institutions which make up their immediate frame of reference and action. How far can such groupings be unambiguously defined, thereby circumscribing the context of their use?

Balinese settlements are often known as *désa*.[5] The term commonly suggests a physical village and its territory, and is opposed taxonomically and in practice to a ward, or *banjar*, the group responsible for organizing the daily affairs of the residents. In Tengahpadang, as in many other areas, the *désa* tends also to be considered as a group with mainly religious functions, the foremost of which is the observance of religious law and practice to ensure the ritual purity of the traditional settlement land, the *tanah désa*. Difficulties naturally arise from these divergent conceptions. *Désa* members are heirs to individual compounds on village land, and as such are collectively under the protection, and authority, of the village's guardian deities, whose sphere of influence is thought of as defined by the boundaries of the *tanah désa*. On the other hand, the *désa* may equally be viewed as the broader area where the villagers live and work (which may extend into fields beyond the *tanah désa* proper). As people migrate, the nature of their ties to, and membership of, the *désa* becomes more complicated. On different occasions, then, the *désa* may be defined as a bounded territory in which certain people live or work, as the zone of influence of a set of deities, or as a place of origin. Which aspect comes to the fore depends on the circumstances, especially when disputes over *désa* jurisdiction occur.

In order to define Balinese village structure, Geertz has attempted to circumvent the ambiguities in terms like *désa* by an appeal to "planes of social organization" which are "a set of invariant fundamental ingredients," the possible combinations of which define the parameters of Balinese society.[6] His aim was to escape from the misapprehension that a society can any more be epitomized by a "representative" unit than by a synthetic amalgam of materials depicting "social structure." Unfortunately, in steering clear of one essentialism, Geertz has fallen into another.[7] He writes that the *désa* is part of the "shared obligation to worship at a given temple."[8] Defining the *désa* as a group of worshippers, however, conceals significant differences in what "worshipping" implies. One may *nyungsung* ("support") a temple, which means to be a full member of a temple group with accompanying ineluctable rights and duties. One may *maturan* ("make offerings, give to a superior"), which refers to the daily offerings each household takes along when its members go to pray. (Many members of the *désa* are expected to *maturan*, but are not required to *nyungsung*, the latter duty falling only on owners of compounds on the traditional village land.) Finally it is possible to pray (*muspa* in high Balinese; *mebakti* in low) without making large offerings. *Maturan*, and certainly *muspa*, may be done by people with no formal membership of the group, across all sorts of social and even caste boundaries. Boon has suggested that the plane of temple organization is better understood as "a meta-mode to index the other modes."[9] It is certainly of a different logical order than some of the other principles, but if its function is an index, cognitive map, or "simplified model of Balinese social structure,"[10] then it fails abysmally. For the sheer range and diversity of temple congregations is far more complex than the reality of which it is supposed to be the index.[11]

The confusion is due partly to there being more than one criterion involved in the principles of incorporation.[12] The same holds for the other "planes of social organization." *Subak*, often glossed as "irrigation association," is defined by Geertz as about the "ownership of rice land lying within a single watershed."[13] It is quite possible, however, to own rice land within a watershed and not belong to the local, or indeed any, *subak*. Moreover, their charters (*awig-awig*) commonly define such groups in terms of control not of land, use of land, nor labor, but of water, although not necessarily from a single source. On different occasions, and according to circumstance, their sphere of competence may be quite differently interpreted.[14] Similar observations can be made about other Balinese social institutions.

How far one can conclude that one feature of an institution is essential and the others ancillary emerges from a brief look at the definition of marriage in Bali.[15] The *sine qua non* of marriage appears to be the rite of *mesakapan* (a term which also means "to work someone else's land"—but not as an in-law) between two partners. The practice of low-caste girls undergoing the rite, not with a prince, but with his sword or housepillar, can be accounted for by metonymy. By this criterion, however, it is not just human beings who marry: pigs, slit gongs, and drums pass through an identical rite. In what sense would one wish to state these to be married? The point is not as trivial as it might seem. Whether the union of human beings is the essential feature of marriage and everything else metaphoric "extension," or whether, for instance, we are dealing with culturally appropriate forms for the conjunction of complementary opposites— of which humans are one example—is hardly by the way.

The serious difficulties really begin when we consider what "marriage" involves. The rites themselves vary in degree. So the distinction between becoming a secondary wife or a concubine may be hard to fix, and could lead in the past to confused legal claims. It is also possible for a ceremony to occur but still be overlooked. Balinese may engage in "marriage by capture" (*melegandang*, as opposed to mock capture, *ngambis*).

If a girl is taken by force, at least from her own and her family's point of view, the rite may be ignored. Matters become still more complex in that what constitutes "agreement" is open to dispute. What one side may consider elopement, the other may treat as capture and act accordingly. In other situations marriage may be a necessary criterion of membership in certain groups. For instance, the unit of membership in the ward is normally the *kuren*,[16] comprising an able-bodied male and female, usually but not necessarily married.[17] It is, of course, perfectly possible to tidy all the exceptions away and maintain that there are essential characteristics to Balinese marriage. The result, however, is pretty vacuous, and ignores the kinds of confusion in which Balinese villagers often land and the problems they face in interpreting these confusions. Such an approach might be valid if it could be shown that the Balinese acted as if there were essential features, but no one seems to have asked.[18] It is implicitly assumed that ideas contain consistent essences. What would happen, though, were certain notions contradictory or contrary (as Quarles van Ufford, for instance, has suggested, of the idea of authority in Java)? For what is the essence of a contradiction?[19]

One of the most common ways of circumnavigating the complexities of what people actually do is by recourse to the "rules" which inform their activities. Regularity is not then to be explained at the level of actions, but in terms of the rules or ideals which guide these actions. The device is as popular as it is pernicious, for it appeals to a questionable epistemology and commits a category mistake by confusing the analyst's and actors' (asymmetrical) frames of reference. There is also a hidden contextual clause in much reference to rules. For is a rule a categorical, or a hypothetical, imperative? Is it an unconscious structural determinant, a legal injunction, an expectation, or a regularity? It is common to find different senses being put forward in different contexts by precisely the people who deny that context is important at all.

Such analytical assumptions beg the question of how the Balinese regard and use such rules. A simple example will make the point. One of the few rules on which ethnographers seem to agree is the Balinese ban on sister-exchange, which is usually represented as an absolute prohibition.[20] Unfortunately the Balinese have different interpretations of their own kinship "rules." What is an absolute prohibition on one reading, is merely undesirable on another. Different castes, and people expressing different aspects of identity, tend to adhere to different versions of what is proper or possible. So the proscription of sister-exchange may be treated simply as a ban, or it may be seen as a means of protecting people from dangerous liaisons. Since sister-exchange is usually classified as a "hot" *(panes)*, as opposed to a "cool" *(etis)* union, it risks damage to the people concerned and to their social ties. In Tengahpadang one man did contract such a marriage. He was politically opposed to the then-dominant local elite, who stressed the religious and social value of observing what they saw as "traditional" kin ties. Was his action then merely the result of ignorance (as the establishment claimed)? Was it deliberate defiance? Or was it that the girl was attractive? His action could be, and indeed was, interpreted differently by different people in different contexts. Rules do not just exist as cast-iron commands constitutive of "culture" as such. They may be a matter for contemplation, interpretation, and rival assertion and challenge under different circumstances. Perhaps we are dealing not with the determination of "fundamental invariant ingredients" but with the circumstances under which some people assert and others deny different interpretations in different ways.

This rather open view is at odds with most of the conventional accounts of Balinese marriage. Boon, for instance, notes the existence both of negative injunctions of the kind mentioned above and positive marriage standards.[21] Marriage may be romantic, by elopement or mock capture, and is then most likely between kin groups not in alliance.[22] The other kinds of marriage are more likely to be arranged. They may be strategic and designed to forge alliances between groups, or sacred and cemented within a kin group, although this is also "hot" and dangerous among very close kin like first cousins, unless one is strong enough to ward off the peril.

There are serious problems with Boon's model, however. For a start it is ethnographically inadequate. There is no simple connection between ways of contracting unions and the three kinds of relationship he outlines. Important forms, like real capture, are omitted. (It may be illegal, as Boon states, but the illegal is not the impossible and merely gives capture greater impact.) *Mepadik*, formally asking for a woman in marriage, is conflated with the negotiation of agreement between all concerned (*adung-adungan rerama*), and with *atepang rerama*, where the parents impose their will on the children. Externally they may seem the same but, as the last involves coercion (*paksa*), to the Balinese the psychological implications are starkly contrasted. The link of ideals with social consequences suggests a mechanical relationship which overlooks the extent to which ideals are always asserted contextually.

Boon implicitly assumes that marriage is essentially the same cross-culturally (otherwise his reference to alliance theory would make little sense), even if its specific cultural forms differ. There is little consideration of the possibility that, as marriage involves at least two persons, we might require recourse to Balinese ideas of personhood and human nature. In describing romantic marriage based on love (for which Boon incidentally is obliged to use the *Indonesian* term *cinta*),[23] Boon appears to believe that there is an emotion or inner state commensurable cross-culturally. He appeals to literary traditions, like the tales of Prince Pañji, for collateral evidence. This appeal is shaky on two grounds. First, it may be tautologous: how do we decide to translate the motivation of characters in literature as "love" in the first place? Second, the robust sexual flavor the Balinese are wont to read into personal attraction fits ill with the usual Western connotations of "love." Romantic lust might be a better gloss!

The dangers of simplistic translation come out clearly in Boon's handling of "sacred" marriage. As Hooykaas has noted, what constitutes "the sacred" and what Balinese word would even roughly correspond to this English term are questions fraught with difficulty.[24] The nearest term is probably *suci*, which is often glossed as "pure." The two are clearly not coterminous. *Suci* is understood by the Balinese in very different ways: it may be used descriptively as an attribute, it may be prescriptive as an ideal, it may be treated at times almost as if substantial (although one should note the Balinese generally avoid imputing the existence of "matter," preferring to speak simply of particular objects as existing and events as occurring). Introducing a notion of "the sacred" merely distracts attention from the serious question of indigenous ontologies and styles of argument and interpretation.

Contextualizing and Essentializing

The examples discussed so far have hinged on the ambiguity inherent in institutions which are defined in terms of more than one feature. Which feature is to the fore depends upon interpretive style, context, and personal perspective. Obviously life is carried on despite different readings being given by people on different occasions.[25] Some collective representations, presuppositions and words, however, may be asserted to be more critical, axiomatic or necessary to a postulated hierarchy of values, than others. Such closure of possibility is arguably an aspect of power. So in this section I would like briefly to consider some of the conditions under which closure is more likely to happen or not.[26]

For example, the Balinese have a system of ranking similar in certain respects to the Indian caste system. Kings, as warriors (*satriya*), were at the apex of the hierarchy, being ranked in purity above everyone except the *brahmana*, a caste of priests. Many of the diacritica of caste status were held to be transmitted by birth. For *satriya* these included courage, loyalty, and honesty. Members of other caste groups were regarded as relatively lacking such attributes. To speak of someone as being a *satriya* implied he had these characteristics. (It will be noted that the word may be used as a title, or name, and as an adjective.) If being a *satriya* implied being brave and so on, being brave implied one was a *satriya*. Here we seem to have an example of how qualities may be prescribed for a title, so that the proper contexts of use are circumscribed.

In practice, however, not all princes were brave by Balinese standards; and some brave men were not *satriya*. The assertion "(all) *satriya* are courageous, loyal and honest" had two non-identical applications. The one through which the caste hierarchy was celebrated in dynastic chronicles and other texts was an ascriptive reading. It was the official version, an authoritative discourse on how the world should be seen. Yet enough princes were palpable cowards and enough members of other castes were gifted with *satriya* qualities that realities could not be ignored. The scribes of dynastic histories not uncommonly had to face the violent rise and accession to the throne of capable upstarts who could not be passed over in silence. On such occasions the official explanation was usually that the upstart was "really" of *satriya* ancestry, that the gods had intervened, or something similar.[27] In this way the essentializing of the attributes of *satriya* could be maintained, though the actual events were far more fluid than such ideological assertions made them seem.

This brief outline should make it clear why it is useful to talk of essential and contextual meanings as being styles or strategies, and not as the ways words in themselves mysteriously relate to the world. Being able to essentialize the "meaning" of *satriya* and to minimize unwanted contextualizations has both epistemological and political overtones. Relevance is not an attribute intrinsic to language so much as a variable aspect of discourse.

Some Balinese terms have been subjected to so high a degree of cultural elaboration that their contextualization in novel ways might seem effectively ruled out. One of the most systematically and consistently developed distinctions in Bali is the directional axis of *kaja* and *kelod*. *Kaja* roughly denotes "towards the interior," "upstream"; *kelod*, "towards the sea," "downstream." These, rather than Western compass points, frame the dominant system of spatial representation, according to which the structure of villages, shrines, temples, houses, the layout of offerings and much else is oriented. The result is a totalizing classification, because the extremes of the axis have come to be linked with qualities which are of great independent importance. *Kaja* is associated with ritual purity, and *kelod* with pollution. The two are often expressed metaphorically (and used metonymically in ritual) in the flow of water: pure water comes from mountain streams and reaches the sea bearing the detritus of human existence with it.

The *kaja-kelod* classification encompasses a great deal. For example, the arrival of foreign merchants and later tourists could easily be fitted in. Contact with traders was conveniently on the coastline; and more recently most tourist hotels have been built around the few sandy beaches on the island. Both sides, working with quite different models of space, seem to have been happy with this arrangement. Tourists sunbathe, swim and step on stonefish—and the traders push their wares—in the zone of impurity, while the Balinese hold the high ground. Since demons are often thought of as large, red, hairy, and uncouth—just the attributes that Balinese tend to ascribe to Westerners—it was in strict accordance with the classification that the latter should prefer to live by the sea, the cesspit of pollution. In this region of tourist money, fashion, and the vast political resources of the Indonesian state administration (much of it concentrated in tourist areas and the geographically peripheral provincial capital), reprehensible desire runs riot: a gloomy picture, which fits, however, with Balinese and Hindu theories of the entropy of the world.

The *kaja-kelod* axis is described variously in the literature as: towards and away from Gunung Agung, the highest volcano; mountain-sea; inland-sea; interior-exterior; and upstream-downstream. It is linked with the propitious and unpropitious, purity and pollution, life and death, and so forth. Part of this flux is simple scholarly inexactitude, part is variations in Balinese contexts of use. One of the most common referents for this spatial axis is the path of water (parallel to the familiar Malay axis *ulu-muara* [headwater-rivermouth]). Because most water comes from volcanic lakes and springs, *kaja* may refer to the direction of the mountains; but as it is associated with the pure and auspicious, there are contexts in which it can be used for any propitious direction (although I have not met it actually referring to "seaward"). Similarly the attributes of life and death often associated with east and west may be mapped onto the upstream-downstream axis and vice versa. Compared then to our polar axis around notionally fixed points, the Balinese axis is more like the dial of a clock around the island's center.

The classification is not neutral, however, since many types of values are linked to it. In so far as the political and religious hierarchy in Bali is underwritten by the presupposition that ritual purity is graded, a differentiated spatial grid may be more or less tied to hierarchy. The seemingly neat closure of the system is prey however to problems of consistency, and allows for unexpected contextualization. If water is identified in some way with purity, then what about the largest body of water of all, the sea? On one interpretation, it is polluted; on another, it is so extensive in its purity that it is able to absorb all the impurities of the world. Demons may be identified with pollution and the periphery, but they are partly divine beings and so probably purer than human beings; moreover, they are identified with the dangerous aspects of high gods. And while the traditional centers of Balinese culture and excellence lay inland, new wealth, new possibilities and new sources of power emerged on the coast. Even the most entrenched classification cannot ensure closure.

Another simple but elegant example of the problem of context comes out in discussion of which is the proper, desirable, or ritually ideal direction of motion. Almost all Balinese agree that the proper direction for movement for processions, ritual lustrations, the order of eating in ritual meals *(nasi agibung)* and even the erection of houseposts, is to the right.[28] Usually this practice is recorded in Western ethnographies as "moving clockwise." Observation of Balinese temple ceremonies, however, shows that people quite frequently circumambulate the temple anticlockwise. The link seems not to be to Hindu ideas of *pradaksina* (and reverse movement, *purwadaksina* in Bali), but to different ideas about the context of "right of." Is it to the right of the speaker, or to the right of the subject or object being circumambulated? (The problem is familiar to students of Javanese shadow theater, where the question of right and left, Pandawa and Kurawa, victors and losers,[29] is usually defined relative to the puppeteer, not the audience.) So quite different emphases are suggested by motion to the right when seen as egocentric and when seen as focused on the other.

If such classifications are tied to others, could it be that part of the closure is linked with key cultural assumptions, absolute presuppositions, which somehow lie behind, or govern, surface manifestations? Were it possible to show there to be such a hierarchy of values, one would have strong grounds for arguing that context can only play at the feet of the towering structure of culturally essential beliefs. There is evidence aplenty of hierarchies being referred to in Bali, but we must be careful before leaping to conclusions. In order to see how a hierarchy of values may be invoked, we may turn to a brief case study.

> A problem arose in one of the wards of Tengahpadang. A woman who owned no riceland used to be one of several traders in cooked meals on the main square. Her stall was an expensive brick building, sited, as it happened, directly beneath a *waringin* tree, the Balinese equivalent of the Indian banyan. Various misfortunes had befallen the village, including the devastation of many families following the abortive Communist coup in 1965. It was remarked by a number of villagers that, unlike many other wards, there was no shrine in the square, and perhaps this accounted for the spate of troubles which had happened.
>
> It was also recognized, however, that erecting a shrine would probably require destroying the woman's stall. Against this view ran the argument that the calamities were sufficiently grave that so serious a step might well have to be taken. In addition, the stall happened to be located on land belonging to the *désa*. Among the issues at stake were whether the misfortunes were connected with the absence of a shrine; whether their continuation would be prevented by building one; whether such a shrine should be erected underneath the tree; and whether the spiritual benefits to the community outweighed the loss of livelihood for a villager, or at least the loss of that part of her capital which had gone into building the stall; and even whether putting a place for making profit in a pure spot had contributed to the misfortunes in the first place.
>
> A high caste geomancer[30] was called in, who was celebrated for his knowledge and mystical power *(sakti)*. At a full meeting of the local ward he agreed that there might be a link between past troubles and the lack of a shrine, and that further misfortune might be mitigated by building one. He confirmed, after geomantic measurements of several possible sites, that the ideal place was where the stall stood. But he also offered other places, especially one behind the ward meeting-pavilion. Seeing that the woman's stall was beneath the *waringin*, he warned the village against the wrong-doing which would be wrought by ruining the source of the woman's income. The meeting, however, promptly voted that, to be on the safe side, the shrine should be put up; and, as the stall was on public land, the responsibility for its removal was the woman's and that she should bear the costs of pulling it down as well.

It is striking that the link between the shrine and the misfortune was accepted on the geomancer's authority (it is not unusual to seek several different opinions), while his suggestion of alternative sites was ignored. In any case, as discussion wore on over the weeks before and after the consultation, the main issue became phrased in terms of the relative priority of an individual being allowed to pursue her (or his) livelihood and the possible threat thereby created for public welfare. (In addition, the widely accepted principle that the interests of disadvantaged members of the community, such as widows [which the woman was], should be protected wherever possible, had to be weighed.)

In the course of the arguments, hierarchies of values were referred to by several parties. All seemed to operate on the assumption that a correct hierarchy existed, or at least that some principles had greater weight than others. But there was no agreement on which was central. It was apparent that hierarchy did not exist as a fixed system of reference; various elements in it were variably invoked to interpret the situation.

Context was vital in other ways which demonstrate the inadequacy of an analysis in terms of cultural ideals alone. I note merely the most salient. The woman's personal life was an ummentioned issue, as were the political party aspects of the whole affair. She had left her husband for the man who had been responsible for his death in 1965; and then deserted the latter for a man deeply embroiled in local politics, who had carried out the savage beating of her lover on political, and probably personal, grounds. (It was this lover who, while he still wielded political influence, had ensured that the building of her stall slipped through quietly.) The last man was an outsider, bitterly hated for his brutality, and sufficiently infatuated with the widow that it was widely thought that he would pay the costs of demolition and rebuilding the stall for his new mistress.

Several points emerge from this (highly truncated) story. First, any appeal to a definitive hierarchy of values would ignore how such values are actually used. Second, almost everyone did imply, but not always state, that there was such a hierarchy. If some claimed to know the proper order of priorities, others pointed out the issue had further aspects, questioned the essential principle at stake and suggested another, or left the matter open. Essentializing and contextualizing were obviously part of various political strategies, but was this all? Different participants seem to have understood and argued the dispute in quite different ways. For the geomancer there was an ideal, as well as possible alternative sites according to the criteria laid down in his manuals. For some who were deeply concerned at the spate of inauspicious events, it seems to have been a matter of finding an immediate remedy regardless of the niceties; others were seeking the most fitting, *manut*, solution to conflicting interests. A minority, by their own private account, were as interested in humiliating the woman as in the shrines and were using the latter as an acceptable cloak for publicly unavowable motives.

Yet are there perhaps some presuppositions in Balinese culture which are absolute for any group at any one time? If there were, would they be free of context for their exposition? It is one thing to trace logical presuppositions (assuming that the logical operations of a culture, in theory and in practice, have been studied) in an intellectual tradition which stresses formal consistency as highly as ours; it is another to explore such presuppositions in cultures where a premium may be placed elsewhere. While inference or empirical evidence may be used to show that the Balinese do recognize and appeal to presuppositions, it remains a matter for research how systematically, and under what conditions, "absolute presuppositions" are actually found (as opposed to how fervently they are asserted).

Context and Human Agency

Is it possible to infer a model from the Balinese material which would account for the ways context is invoked? I think not, for several reasons. One obvious approach is to try to establish a set of presuppositions so central that any change in them would produce massive conceptual confusion or endanger the structure of authority. To do so, however, would be to reify what I have called essentializing and contextualizing styles. Neither is the exclusive prerogative of any group or caste; rather they are two ways of attempting to work out how collective representations should be applied to events and actions.[31]

Relevance and context seem then only to be establishable empirically. If it is not possible to circumscribe the relation between cultural representations and actions in terms of a theory of meaning, might one not instead focus on the agents?[32] In other words, can we provide an account of human interests or action which would delimit the goals, and so the effective means, which the Balinese seek?[33] To pull off such a feat, however, would involve postulating a theory of human nature and human agency.

As Collingwood argued long ago, the various philosophers on whose thought much anthropological theory is based

> ... assumed that human nature had existed ever since the creation of the world exactly as it existed among themselves ... that *our* reasoning faculty, *our* tastes and sentiments, and so forth, are something perfectly uniform and invariable, underlying and conditioning all historical changes.[34]

Furthermore, models of "society" generally rely on some truth, palpable or implicit, about human nature. Lukes observes:

> Durkheim sides with Hobbes and Freud where Marx sides with Rousseau and the Utopians. For the former, man is a bundle of desires, which need to be regulated, tamed, repressed, manipulated and given direction for the sake of social order, whereas, for the latter, man is still an angel, rational and good, who requires a rational and good society in which to develop his *essential* nature.[35]

The point is not whether Lukes's characterization does justice to these thinkers, nor which of them may be right, but that a vision of human nature is an unacknowledged part of the academic's baggage. The humble ethnographer, panning his chosen backwater for nuggets of empirical truth, cannot safely dismiss the problem as part of the paraphernalia of the armchair theorist. What we find in the field depends largely on what we use to sift our facts.[36]

The problem may be seen in the seemingly contradictory ethnographic accounts of Bali, which portray its inhabitants as wildly different kinds of human beings. The Balinese variously appear as driven to establish order and meaning in the world; as fey actors strutting the proscenium of life, worried over stage-fright; as belligerent men of action, poised to attack their neighbors, enslave other islanders, or loot Dutch ships; as slaves to tyrannical rules or to established social and moral conventions. At times, of course, some Balinese may be thinkers, others thespians, soldiers, slaves or much else besides; but there is little point in asking "would the real Balinese stand up?" For the question assumes the Balinese to have an essential nature and thereby begs the interesting question.

THE NATURE OF CULTURE IN BALI

What kinds of model of human nature have been suggested to explain Balinese society? There are, of course, about as many as there are commentators. As Boon has argued, much of the early work on Bali should be seen in the light of Western, here especially Dutch, constructions of "the Other."[37] To the extent that in the first half of the twentieth century the stress was on a "neutral" description of social institutions, the assumptions about human nature and society tended to be those of various schools of anthropology, such as Dutch structuralism. Enough has been said elsewhere about the kinds of assumptions made as to require no further comment here.[38]

A rather different model of social action has recently been suggested by Geertz, which he claims can explicate the Balinese ethnography. It is worth considering as a text in its own right, because it is the most explicit formulation of a problem that other accounts have tended to take for granted. Geertz places the Balinese within a general theory of culture which " ... is essentially a semiotic one ... [where] man is an animal suspended in webs of significance he himself has spun."[39] He takes it for granted that a key aspect of human nature everywhere is man's need to make sense of the world, and of his place within it. Accordingly, the focus in analysis must be "an interpretive one in search of meaning."[40]

How is the relationship between human beings and culture-as-meaningful described? On this point Geertz's language becomes strikingly metaphorical. A fascinating gradual shift occurs in the images by which this relation is represented. We start with something close to culture-as-a-kind-of-building.[41] "Our data are really our own constructions of other people's constructions" which are, however, "structures of signification" erected on a given "social ground." Once the point has been made that culture is man-made, the images shift to various natural scientific techniques for observing and preserving it: anthropological interpretation is said to consist in "tracing the curve of a social discourse; fixing it into an inspectable form." It attempts to "rescue the 'said' of such discourse from its perishable occasions."[42] When cultures have been "inscribed," their study becomes archaeological (if of the object) or archival (if about our inscriptions); for we must "uncover the conceptual structures that inform our subjects' acts." In other words, we eventually arrive at the meaning, a "pseudoentity" which some anthropologists have "fumbled with" because they ignore the "hard surfaces of life" and "the biological necessities on which those surfaces rest." From all this the anthropologist gleans the answers that those he has studied have given, in order "to include them in the consultable record of what man has said."[43]

Geertz's metaphors might seem a little out of place in what purports to be a "scientific" approach to culture.[44] But the real difficulty lies in describing culture as manmade, for such a view is circular, since ideas about what human beings are like are themselves in part culturally formulated. Stress on biological and physical necessities also raises the interesting question of whose idea of biology and the physical world are we dealing with? Arguably a cultural account should consider indigenous ideas rather than postulate our contemporary views as universal.

The unexceptionable grounding of Geertz's argument is in ethnographic detail:

> Behavior must be attended to, and with some exactness, because it is through the flow of behavior—or more precisely, social action—that cultural forms find articulation.[45]

Already we have two transformations: behavior becomes action, and from this a specific category of "social action" is somehow extrapolated. The next step introduces a significant framing of what anthropology is about. For "anthropological interpretation is constructing a reading of what happens."[46] In the following flood of metaphors, however, the ontological nature of social action, or culture, undergoes a series of further reinterpretations. We are evidently now committed to a particular relation of society and the individual in which culture is created, or invented, by people, through "symbolic interactions" (with all the dubious assumption of voluntarism entailed).[47] This invented culture in turn takes the form of an inscribed text (Geertz cites Ricoeur approvingly).[48] (One might note here that Ricoeur's sense of "text" refers to specific inscriptions, not the general presuppositions and conditions of possibility of social action.[49] It is apparent that however subtle compared to previous views, Geertz's outlook on objects of study remains firmly positivist.) Furthermore, these man-made inscriptions are, it seems, the surface of conceptual structures. By this point we are asked to accept the "existence" of abstract entities we call "concepts" and their having a "structure." Starting with the idea of culture as behavior, then as something manmade, then as inscribed, then as a readable document, which later reveals an underlying conceptual essence, we have made an odd and questionable journey.

One of the most intriguing silences in this progression is the absence of discussion of exactly how the impressions of the anthropologist are related to those of the native. While it is obvious in one way that we are concerned with "our constructions of other people's constructions" (in the sense that interpretation, but *not* all behavior, is construction), it does not follow that their and our constructions are of the same logical or empirical order—even if ours depends on theirs—nor that they are even commensurable.

The *deus ex machina* here is, unsurprisingly, an assumption about human nature. It is that people everywhere in the world (by virtue, one assumes, of the assertion that people make culture) engage in actions for the same reasons or causes; they may interpret actions in different cultural styles, but they share essential features of humanity which enable them to do so with identical logics, perceptions, and semantic processes. As Hollis has pointed out, however, these are at best epistemological, and more likely metaphysical, presuppositions, certainly not empirical truths.[50] In effect, the psychic unity of mankind is assumed. Unfortunately, those who appeal to such a principle interpret it in such different ways that it can underwrite approaches as far apart as hermeneutics and truth-conditional semantics. In Geertz's case, it means incorporating in his view of culture the idea of "the knowing subject."[51] This idea gives his interpretation that flavor of individualism and freedom so popular in Western metaphysics of self. Nonetheless, it has not been established that the same idea holds for other people. The fact that we may find his interpretations appealing does not mean they are true; it merely means they fit our present prejudices.

The danger in Geertz's image of culture as being "inscribed" is that it leads too easily to assuming a mechanical relation between a collective representation and its interpretation by members of a society. Brief reflection on the presuppositions behind his argument about the working of symbols shows what is at issue. In attributing meaning to cultural constructs, one requires a theory of mind, and the relation of individuals to society, such that they construe collective representations in one way rather than another.

TIME, PERSON, AND LANGUAGE

In Geertz's *Person, Time and Conduct in Bali* we are presented with notions of time and their significance from a reading of indigenous calendars.[52] In the Javanese-Balinese calendrical system a 210-day year consists of ten concurrently running weeks from one to ten days long. Each week has differently named days and different uses. As Geertz quite reasonably notes, this tends to give particular "combinations of days" an individual flavor. To infer from this, however, that the nature of Balinese time-reckoning is necessarily, or even preferentially, permutational, let alone that it reflects "the very structure of reality," is oddly mechanical.[53] Might one not equally read from the system, among the main features of which is the mathematical regularity of combinations, a model of complex order distinct from the variability of human affairs? Such a model would be peculiarly fitting for describing the doings and prescriptions of divine agencies which are apart from human contingency. Geertz chooses not to inquire into the vast number of ways in which the Javanese-Balinese calendar is actually used every day, and seems instead to assume that calendars have essential features which may be read out by the analyst independent of, and prior to, detailed study of their contextual use.

There is no space here to enter into the largely sterile and ethnographically uninformed debate about the nature of time in Bali.[54] Suffice it to say here that all the accounts represent time catachrestically.[55] That is, it is approached through constitutive metaphors, often spatial—time as "linear," "cyclical," "zig-zag," "punctuated," "durational"—of a kind which Balinese explicitly eschew. Perhaps part of the problem derives from the assumption that there is some essential "time," which is then measured in different ways. In one sense time is peculiarly contextual, in that it is referred to relative to the situations of its use. For example, the Balinese recognition of stages of the sun's movement across the sky is particularly appropriate if it is a matter of going to the fields or finishing work, before sunset or before it gets too hot. To say that Balinese set off for the fields at 5 a.m. and return at 10 or 11, is far less informative. Much of the confusion about time in Bali might be avoided, I suspect, if, instead of asking what time really "is," we were to look at how it is actually used and the relations which its use implies.

In similar fashion Geertz infers a "depersonalization" of Balinese from their notionally distinct "orders of person definition."[56] Teknonymy, for instance, denotes a person in terms of parenthood of members of successive generations, and so stresses successors rather than predecessors. Geertz's interpretation again depends upon a very literal, formal reading of the bypassing of autonyms (personal names). As Feeley-Harnik rightly notes, teknonymy may equally permit a focus upon ancestors and the domination of the ascendant generation.[57] (Her point is that the "inscriptions" of culture should not be read simplistically.)

Once again we find the habit of postulating the essence of a system in isolation from its semantic context and the situations of its use. In fact the Balinese have a perfectly workable system, and use it, to refer to ancestors, with kin terms reaching at least the fifth ascendant generation. Furthermore, teknonymy is not used equally by all social groups. In Tengahpadang it was characteristic of kin groups identifying themselves as smiths *(pandé)*, who strove to keep themselves apart from others and to limit the range of their exchanges (including names?). One wonders if it is coincidental to Geertz's model of naming that his research was largely done in Tihingan, one of the few villages in Bali dominated by smiths. In developing his model of Balinese depersonalization, Geertz goes on to suggest that:

> as the virtually religious avoidance of its direct use indicates, a personal name is an intensely private matter . . . when [a man] disappears it disappears with him.[58]

This may be fine in theory but in the roll-call for village meetings not the teknonyms but the personal names of distinguished old men (even if each is "but a step away from being the deity he will become after his death") were yelled out across the village square! Whatever the idealized reading of collective representations, villagers in Tengahpadang invariably referred to their dead ancestors by the personal names they are supposed not to know.[59]

Before rushing to order Balinese means of referring to others, we might do better to consider Balinese ideas about naming. There is a set of texts, known as Dasanama (literally "Ten Names"), which indicate the various names by which heroes in the literature are known in different roles, at different stages in their lives, and in different aspects of their personalities or incarnations. It thus appears that the applicability of names is a matter of context. As the Balinese use Dasanama, the implications of naming are often the reverse of ours. People and things are not essentially tied to any one label; rather the labels are used to indicate different perspectives on the same phenomenon. Names may denote, but they do much else besides.

Behind the model of the unfortunate "detemporalized" and "depersonalized" Balinese lie several questionable presuppositions. The same assumptions come out in

Geertz's method of interpreting symbols in his recent work on the "theatre state" in Bali.[60] Having extrapolated from the ethnography certain symbols as definitive, constitutive or descriptive of kingship, he brings his analysis to a close.[61] The assumption is that, having laid out the symbols, we are in a position to grasp how the Balinese understand and use them. This procedure, however, presumes an unstated theory of the relation of symbols to action. First, the argument relies on a denotational model too crude to pick up the nuances of use in utterances. Second, the implication is that collective representations are the necessary, or indeed sufficient, conditions of "ideas" or of some kind of "inner state" (in Needham's terms):[62] but whether they are the reasons or causes of action (or some less Cartesian relation) is unclear. Third, there is an implicit theory of the relation of society and the individual, since describing some of the socially available symbols is thought in some way to describe their meaning for people in that society. Fourth, in using the notion of "symbol" (which is so broad as to be meaningless)[63] a specific theory of human action has already been presumed and the ontological problems of the analysis of Balinese culture neatly pre-empted. How Balinese collective representations and Balinese culture are to be interpreted has been determined *a priori* by implicit assumptions about what culture and humans are—in other words, by a theory of human nature.[64]

HUMAN NATURE IN BALI

How is Geertz's general model of human nature and culture worked out in Bali? He approaches Bali with the general assumption that it is through symbols "upon which men impress meaning" that "man makes sense of the events through which he lives."[65] In different cultures, man's relation to society may be structured in terms of different metaphors. In Bali, as Geertz sees it, the image is somewhere between play and dramaturgy. There is a "playful theatricality" at work, for "Balinese social relations are at once a solemn game and a studied drama."[66] This trait is epitomized in the Balinese cockfight, which is a "melodrama," a kind of "art form" or "text," because it is "a Balinese reading of Balinese experience"—in this instance that social life is "a status bloodbath."[67] Perhaps the most elaborate use of this metaphor is in his picture of Balinese politics where "statecraft is a thespian art."[68] For the state in Bali "was a theatre state in which the kings and princes were the impresarios, the priests the directors, and the peasants the supporting cast, stage crew and audience."[69] The metaphor could hardly be made plainer. If human beings in general are thinkers, in that they ponder the conditions of their existence, Balinese human beings act this thinking out by being thespians.

Geertz's notion of "meta-social commentary" has rightly attracted attention. It is a timely reminder that cultures may engage in reflexivity. But Geertz believes that one can read meaning more or less directly into the cockfight and learn "what being a Balinese is really like."[70] The intensity of Balinese involvement is described as "deep play" (a phrase borrowed from Jeremy Bentham), through which they portray their status battles to themselves. The link is through the double meaning of "cock" which, we are told, is the source of much cultural imagery about machismo, and the commentary hinges on complex levels of cock-based metaphor (e.g., "the underdog cock").[71]

It is unclear why the recondite image of an English philosopher should provide the key metaphor for Balinese gambling. The parallel may be illuminating to us, but in what sense is it valid? It corresponds with our ideas of the use of metaphor, but does it do so for Balinese? The Balinese, after all, have a very complex vocabulary to describe the relation of signs and symbols to their referents. The term most appropriate here is *pra(tiw)imba* (derived from Sanskrit, via Old Javanese, meaning "image, model;

shadow"),[72] which is widely used in Bali in the sense of "model," "metaphor," or "analogy." The crucial point about *praimba* is that metaphors, by comparing something to something else, are inherently false, and are therefore treated with great suspicion when encountered.

It is true that people in Bali are also often described in the literature as "playful." One should not assume, however, that "play" refers to the same class of phenomena in different cultures.[73] Where the one English word links the activities of children, relaxation, story-telling, sport, joking, theater and so on, Balinese designates each by a separate term and, so far as I can tell, these are not treated as deriving from any core, or essential, set of characteristics. Care is therefore required in using such preconstrained terms in depicting other cultures.

Geertz has no way of establishing that the cockfight is *ipso facto* a meta-social commentary, nor that its object is really a precarious status battle. It is surely unnecessarily Durkheimian to assume that status relations somehow constitute the reality of which something else is a dramatic representation (especially if one takes Goodman's point that representations are of something as something else).[74] One might note that much Balinese theater and literature develops the theme of fighting, whether it be interpreted as dualistic, agonistic, Manichaean, or metaphysical. The characters in the shadow-theater, and orators in public meetings, are often caught in conflicts of potentially lethal outcome. What is a commentary on, or reflection of, what?

The themes of conflict or contradiction (both rough glosses of the Balinese *miegan*, which is also "fighting") and violence are too complex to be dismissed as the idiom of status claims. It is noticeable that Western commentators seem to have great difficulty with the role of violence in Balinese society. The editors of the *Śiwarātrikalpa*, an Old Javanese text found in Bali, felt it necessary to excuse "the gruesome methods of warfare which the poet's imagination conjures up" and remarked more generally that:

> Another compulsory feature of almost all *kakawin* is the elaborate, and to our taste exaggerated, descriptions of wars and battles between armies of heroes and demons.... The Western reader struggles through these endless scenes with difficulty—in comparison with these the fighting in the Iliad seems mere child's play.[75]

Ignoring what we see as violence in Bali because we do not like it does not seem a good way of approaching Balinese culture.

In other words, I am suggesting that however interesting Geertz's argument about the cockfight is, it has been seriously essentialized.[76] Apart from failing to consider cockfighting against the background of violence, the argument also omits other possibly significant contexts.[77] We are not, for instance, given any idea of Balinese views on psychology to understand what watching or bringing about bloodshed implies. Instead we are offered an implicit Freudian imagery of *thanatos* in the butchery and *eros* in the sexual identifications. The idea that the cockfight is about status or prestige is taken largely as an unanalyzable fundamental.

Perhaps the most serious contextual omission is any reference to the Balinese "Chain of Being." In most versions animals are scaled according to their enslavement to bodily urges as against their capacity for control (see below). Accordingly, animal classifications do not rank mammals above birds, but take each species on merit. So doves, regarded as peaceful and pure, are placed higher than pigs (which are thought to be stupid and to eat their own kind), while cocks, being inclined to fight, are notoriously low. They fight not because they are forced to, but because that is what they tend to do. The homonymic identification of bird and penis to us is made in quite a different classificatory context among the Balinese. Not only were cocks and genitals never analogized (to the best of my knowledge) but they were held to lie near opposite taxonomic poles.

What should we then make of Geertz's elaboration on the identification of man and animal essential to this meta-commentary? As he puts it:

> The language of everyday moralism is shot through, on the male side of it, with roosterish imagery. *Sabung*, the word for cock (and one which appears in inscriptions as early as A.D. 922), is used metaphorically to mean "hero," "warrior," "champion," "man of parts," "political candidate," "bachelor," "dandy," "lady-killer," or "tough guy."[78]

The difficulty is that "cock" is usually *siap* in low Balinese and *ayam* in high, while "cockfight" is *tajèn*. *Sabung* is certainly not everyday Balinese. It does not occur in any of the classic dictionaries in Old Balinese, Old Javanese,[79] or archipelago Sanskrit.

This presents us with a problem. For the word is Malay, the language of trade, and has been incorporated into official Bahasa Indonesia, both being little known until recently by most Balinese. Not only does it seem then that the Balinese managed the remarkable feat of expressing their tender sentiments of love in a language which most of them did not speak, but they chose to pun on private parts in an erudite way! Furthermore, in writing about Balinese personal names, Geertz describes as "arbitrarily coined nonsense syllables" what are in fact mostly common everyday words.[80] The linguistic foundations of Geertz's symbology start to seem somewhat shaky.

If we now turn to look at other modern anthropological views of the Balinese, we find Boon distinguishing between two styles of culture, the epic and the romantic:

> Epic posits constant, consistently principled, heroic familial aristocracies, whose leaders establish the lawful and the just at the expense of the enemies of right. Romance portrays vulnerable disguised protagonists, partial social misfits who sense surpassing ideals and must prove the ultimate feasibility of actualizing those ideals often against magical odds.[81]

So sweeping is the classification that Bali, if one can pigeon-hole a culture, might by turns be both, either, or neither. To assist us, however, we are offered further bearings in the form of a "syllogism" *(sic)*:

> If pre-Islamic Java were Renaissancelike in its elaborate schemes, certainly rivaling Plotinus or Plato, of the interrelation of cosmos, art, and society, then Bali was and is more loosely mannerist.[82]

Where Geertz offers an extended image of Bali as thespian, Boon places it in a classification of literary genres. Either people are heroes battling in soldierly fashion for the good and right, but as slaves of their culture; or they are misfits questioning the system they have inherited and in search of higher (extra-cultural?) ideals. Reference to Western models of man is hardly accidental, for elsewhere Boon elaborates his image of Balinese as Eastern Romantics. Rather than draw any link between the world views of Indian and Balinese literati, he suggests that

> a more apt comparison would link Balinese Brahmanas with German romantics: Both have sought to inform their sense of themselves and their exclusive role in

society and literature by referring to Sanskrit texts and to Indic ideals of literary priesthood. In a way the Herders, Schlegels, and Novalises of Germany occupy a position vis-à-vis India analogous to that of the *Ida Bagus*es and the *pedandas* of Bali.[83]

How the Balinese combine such different centuries and traditions in being at once Mannerist and Romantic is not explained. But indirectly Boon makes an important point: the German Romantics did use current ideas about India to formulate their vision of their place in the world. Needless to say, they had a curiously Western view of "the Other." Showing that our own tradition once pictured itself in terms of its image of others is not, however, a very good reason for repeating the mistake; this time by reconstructing an entire people in terms of someone else's ideas of how the world, and human nature, ought to be.

There is a final model of Balinese society which we need briefly to consider. It has been put forward by Bloch in a criticism of Geertz's views on definitions of person and time in Bali.[84] He argues that while there is evidence that cultures define persons, like interests, goals and even time, quite differently, at another level there are shared conceptions of the way the world really is; otherwise we could never translate or speak across cultural boundaries. What we have here is a dual theory of human nature. There is a culturally specific model underwritten by a necessarily universal account. Bloch objects to the absence, in cultural accounts such as Geertz's or Boon's, of any way of explaining much of the practical action and political manipulation recorded in the Balinese ethnography. This is indeed a difficulty in Geertz's model of culture and human nature, but it does not follow that the only alternative is a universal account. For Bloch's vision of human nature looks remarkably like Utilitarian Man writ large and it is just as cultural in another sense as is Geertz's, and grounded on equally *a priori*, if different, assumptions. Instead of one account of human nature we have two, such that whatever does not fit in the universal model (determined largely by what the analyst can make sense of) fits in the other. In place of thinker and thespian, we are given shopkeeper or mercenary.

BALINESE VIEWS ON HUMAN NATURE

The degree to which explanations of action in Balinese society rest upon imported views of human nature should, I hope, be clear from the foregoing account. Yet how much does it matter if we import explanatory theories or metaphors? Apart from involving us in a dubious epistemological exercise, it tends to make nonsense of the ethnography.

For example, we have seen that Balinese social life is widely portrayed as a kind of theater in which the actors strive to maximize control over the presentation of self, as it were in fear of forgetting their lines, or giving in to "stage fright."[85] Now whose idea of self and theater is this? The Balinese themselves speak of theater as about reliving *tattwa* (historical truth), whether grand or squalid, and not as representing something as something else. Geertz is using a vision of theater from his own culture to explain what he argues to be Balinese ideas of their roles. This is simply a category mistake.

One also wonders how wise it is to define the proper subject matter of inquiry prior to an investigation of Balinese categories of speech and action. The point is not that we must be confined to their explicit accounts (for no one is suggesting these necessarily explain why they do what they do) but that, as these are the categories in terms of which Balinese evaluate their own and other's speech and actions publicly, they form part of any full ethnographic account. To conclude, I would therefore like to outline Balinese representations of speech, action and human nature, and suggest that they

148   Context, Meaning, and Power

are sufficiently different as to vitiate explanations based on alien presuppositions.

The Balinese distinguish between two kinds of speech which people use in everyday life. The differences are important, as they determine the kind of interpretation which is put upon their "meaning" (arti). Young, stupid and uncontrolled people are likely to speak straightforwardly what is on their minds or, as the Balinese put it, speak "the contents of their stomachs" (isin basang). Such immature speech (raos nguda) stands in contrast to raos wayah, which is what mature adult men and women should properly use. Such wiser, more controlled people speak less and enfold the point (tetuwek) beneath the surface—which is just what the young and the foolish will read. Those who are more reflective understand how to unravel from hints, structured according to fairly well known cultural standards, what the true reference or purpose (tetujon) is. It is thus not a question for them of projecting various kinds of image, as Geertz's theatrical metaphor suggests, but rather of expressing degrees of self-control in the kind of language used.

The Balinese also have well-developed views on meaning and communication. For instance, terms like *sekadi* or *satmaka*, normally glossed as "like" and "as if," may be used explicitly, not as part of a referential use of language, but metalingually, to express the degree of the speaker's commitment to the truth of what he or she is asserting. These expressions are much used in reporting speech or claims by others, when the speaker needs to make clear that the accuracy of the account is uncertain, and to suggest the degree of likelihood that he or she places on the statement. As noted above, the Balinese express a strong dislike for any avoidable use of metaphor and analogy. It is remarkable that so much of the Western work on Bali happily assumes the Balinese have the same penchant as we, without considering the kinds of truth conditions the Balinese use in evaluating one another's statements.

What kinds of assumption do Balinese then make about human nature? The formal framework owes much to an adaptation of classical Hindu models. Three schemes are in general circulation.

Triguna:	sattwa	raja(h)	tamas
	purity	passion	desire
	knowledge	emotion	ignorance
Triwarga:	darma	art(h)a	kama
	disposition	pursuit of	enjoyment of
	to do good	material	sensual
	one's duty	utility	pleasure
*Tiga-jñana:**	idep	sabda	bayu
	thought	speech	energy

*The last triad is normally given in reverse order: energy, speech, action. I have altered it here, because of the connection between the qualities in each column. The last triad is also generally unnamed, although as Hooykaas (from whom the term is taken) notes, it is of great explanatory importance in Bali (see "Sarasvatī, the Goddess of Learning," in *Āgama Tīrtha*, p. 26). It provides the basis, among other things, for a classification of "nature" (in our terms) of a quite non-Aristotelian kind. Other names used for the triad include *tritattwa*. The glosses in English are crude and designed only to give a rough idea of the kinds of quality at issue (for a helpful translation see Zoetmulder's *Old Javanese-English Dictionary*).

The *triguna* are the three constituents of human nature; the *triwarga* are the three aims of human life; and the *tiga-jñana*, the three forces manifest in various degrees in living things, as well as the three kinds of knowledge associated with different living forms. The possible connections between the three sets allows many exegeses. The system offers, among other things, a comprehensive account of the Balinese Chain of Being. At one extreme, animals (and plants) are capable only of acting as systems of energy, or at best, of simple speech, seek sensual pleasure in eating and sexual intercourse, and live in a state of ignorant desire. At the opposite pole, gods approximate pure thought, are motivated only by a disposition to do good and epitomize knowledge and purity. The higher they are the more remote and ineffectual they become, since they lack the capacity for speech and energy. The Balinese give this set of schemes, which they seem originally to have imported, a twist of their own. For they link this model with their own transformational view of the universe. Everything is thought to be in a state of continuous transformation *(metemahan)*. For human beings, therefore, to stress only purity or knowledge is dangerous since it easily leads to excess and madness (or darkness, ignorance). Balance should be preserved between each of the three states in each system (although the precise point of balance depends upon what is fitting for people from different castes and for different personalities). In this way the entire scheme is run through with contextual clauses.

We have here a fairly thorough-going theory of human faculties, goals and "natural" processes. Yet this theory is determinedly tripartite and fits badly with Western dichotomies like pain/pleasure and altruism/egoism or with psychoanalytical models. It is therefore unwise to transcribe our distinctions, dual or otherwise, onto the Balinese without careful prior consideration. Since the scheme is common knowledge, not an esoteric priestly model, and is presupposed—if often unreflectively—in Balinese interpretations of disputes and action in daily life, we ignore their relevance at our peril.

How are such schemes actually used? At this point the possible ways of contextualizing presuppositions become important. Among the more common renderings has been the linking of *triwarga* with caste. For each caste notionally has a different *darma*, or set of appropriate caste duties, which are laid out in various texts offering an authoritative view of proper relations between the different estates. Once again, however, such schemes are open to multiple interpretation. For *darma* is seen as the moral duty incumbent upon all human beings and as an ideal associated with brahmana and priests, whether of high or low caste. In addition, *darma* is characterized in everyday life as reflective thinking (*pemineh* or sometimes *manah*, from the Sanskrit *manas*, the organ, or faculty, of thought) as opposed to thinking about how to fulfill one's desires instrumentally *(keneh)*. In these ways *darma* may be linked to caste duties of different kinds; it may be seen as the ideal of a few specialized, and dedicated, persons; it may be seen as a legitimate goal for all human beings; or it may be the classification of one kind of thinking. Similar styles of contextualizing the classifications are found for each of the other terms. Hence, on the one hand, terms may be contextualized singly; on the other, their interconnections or their possible links with other schemes, like that of a transforming world, may be stressed. When a scheme like the *triwarga* is contextualized in this way, however, its authoritative aspects, stressed in the caste model, may undergo great change. As we have seen, an excessive stress on purity, or duty, may lead the personality to a state of imbalance and the commission of gross acts.

Use of Balinese representations of human nature can thus lead to a quite different interpretation of institutions than those usually given. Cocks fighting for dominance might more easily be examples of what humans should *not* do. Rather than offering an extended theatrical play on Balinese society, they may equally be seen as a dramatic representation of how not to behave. It is instructive that cockfights occur obligatorily at temple festivals and other rites when the destructive and atavistic, expressed as *buta* (demonic, but also what is blind and ignorant), have their moment.

Just as it is possible to specify the cultural forms that ideas of human nature take, so we can give a preliminary specification of the styles or strategies of interpretation. So far I have treated these as labels, not as universal essential processes, as they obviously take different forms in different cultures and periods. We noted early on four commonly used ways of structuring and interpreting collective representations: essentializing, contextualizing, pragmatizing, and elaborating. It may be useful to link these provisionally to popular Balinese words widely used in evaluating words and action. First, Balinese commonly use the term *tattwa* when they wish to indicate how things really are, the true account behind appearances.[86] So *nattwain* is to work towards the truth of something. *Tattwa* is generally not directly accessible for human beings, who must work through texts, inference, or revelation; and it is often maintained that the Supreme Being, or Intelligence, Sang Hyang Wid(h)i alone knows this truth. In Old Javanese it had the implication of "the essential," "the actual" (as contrasted with the apparent or incidental). On this reading, even if it is one that village Balinese do not often seem to make (as they tend to work in a world of actuality, not of essences), *tattwa* is directly linked to essentializing.

Often, however, things are to be understood in context to ensure they are appropriate *(manut)*—a common word to hear in meetings, and in discussion of interpretations of theatrical performances. Contextualizing is then *nganutang*, "fitting"; and since ensuring that things are fitting is central to making pragmatic judgments, *manut* has very practical overtones. There is another word, *pasti* ("definite," "certain"), which picks up some of the English connotations of "necessity" or "making sure." So *mastiang* may be used with the implications of "making certain that," "determining," or "stating." While theater should be about *tattwa*, it is recognized that most people are sufficiently weak in *darma* that is is necessary to appeal to their *kama*. So *tattwa* must be elaborated and decorated *(kaiyas)* in words and action to make it palatable. It would be possible to refine and add to these terms, but they should be adequate here to make the point that these strategies or styles are not pure analyst's importations.

The advantage of characterizing the Balinese in terms of their own cultural idioms rather than the literary genres of Europe or America, of which they know nothing, is that we do not run the danger of creating a *bengkiwa* ("sterile hybrid," taken from the monstrosity born of mating two local breeds of duck). There are also many occasions on which the Balinese themselves appeal to such models in explaining the actions of others. However, this still remains an essentializing strategy. Other constructions may be put upon events. Accepted roles may be contextualized in all sorts of different ways. After all, is an orator a thinker, a human version of a fighting cock, a shadow-puppet of some patron, or a man who likes the sound of his own voice? He may be any one, all or none.

Representations of human nature in Bali bear directly on the kinds of interpretation we may legitimately put upon their actions. If we wish to use the image of "negotiation," which is currently a popular image for how social relations are to be understood, then it might be well to include indigenous ideas of what negotiation is about. One might reasonably expect the Balinese to express the actions of others in terms of styles of transaction which are culturally available. For instance, the bartering image for human relationships, present in so much of the literature, would seem *prima facie* out of place in a society where court intrigue plays so great a part in everyday life and in the theater. I am not saying that there is some mechanical relationship between representations and action: merely that such representations are part of the circumstances under which Balinese act and interpret the actions of others. Omitting such points is to omit a critical part of the ethnographic record. Reflecting on our own presuppositions is also a first step away from a pervasive ethnocentrism which scholarly studies may subtly perpetuate by searching for an essence, at worst imported outright, at best contrived, by reifying what happens among the people with whom they work.

Despite—or even because of—the amount of research on Bali, it is becoming clear how little we know. The plethora of unexamined, but relevant, indigenous treatises and the degree of local variation alone suggest that generalizations are rather dubious. Much of the material has reported assertions in particular situations as fact, and fact as truth. What we have mostly is a smattering of textual sources, partial dynastic chronicles and legal codes, the opinions of well-informed informants (priests, headmen, and marginal men; but rarely women) taken out of context and mapped onto nebulous paradigms of Western intellectual history, without regard for Balinese epistemological criteria. Balinese culture remains largely an invention of its commentators. There is much in Daniel Heinsius of Ghent's motto: *Quantum est quod nescimus!*

AFTERTHOUGHTS

In taking issue with some of the presuppositions we borrow to account for other peoples' doings, I am only hinting at the tip of an iceberg. When scholars extrapolate a set of symbols, or when they describe another culture in terms of how people there "construct" or "negotiate" their culture, what precisely are they doing? Is the implication that the existence of symbols or evidence of negotiation explains why people do what they do? To assume this would be to import further presuppositions of our own, about the relation of collective representations and events, and about the link between thought and action, as well as ideas about what constitutes an explanation, all far from fixed and all dependent on our own cultural fashions. The explanation of action is a notoriously tricky business.[87] The sheer difficulty of providing an account of ordinary everyday behavior in terms of the available models of intention, reason, cause and motive suggests the potential weaknesses of our own ideas and another good reason not to impose them on others.

We need the kind of detailed knowledge of how people use their cultural representations which to date has rarely been considered necessary. There is evidence to suggest, for instance, that the Balinese use their ideas of human nature in different ways than we might be led to expect. The schemes they elaborate are not generally used to provide an efficient, or final, causal explanation of particular actions. Instead the models are used to provide a general account of the conditions under which actions take place. The Balinese—suitably in the light of recent Western tendencies in the philosophy of mind and action—are inclined to treat the question of intentions or the reasons for doing something, as private, if indeed knowable at all. Where we develop ever more sophisticated techniques for the examination and exposure of the person, under psychoanalysis and legal definitions of responsibility, the Balinese draw a polite veil. Some things they still leave to the person. There may be good professional grounds for our doing the same. For our illusion that we can explain the actions of others is a product as much of our tendency to essentialize and simplify, as it is of any realistic possibility of being able to do so. Context is too complex to allow such certainties. If I am right, then the business of explaining others is likely to be much harder than we like to make out. If I am wrong, then, like Monsignor Quixote's illustrious ancestor, I am tilting harmlessly at windmills.

1. See, for example, Dan Sperber and Deirdre Wilson, "Mutual Knowledge and Relevance in Theories of Comprehension," in *Mutual Knowledge*, ed. Neil V. Smith (London: Academic Press, 1974), pp. 61–85.

2. Anthony Heath, *Rational Choice and Exchange Theory: A Critique of Exchange Theory* (Cambridge: Cambridge University Press, 1976); and Martin Hollis, *Models of Man: Philosophical Thoughts on Social Action* (Cambridge: Cambridge University Press, 1977).

3. Compare Edmund R. Leach, *Political Systems of Highland Burma: A Study of Kachin Social Structure* (London: Bell, 1954), and Clifford Geertz, "Religion as a Cultural System," in *Anthropological Approaches to the Study of Religion*, ed. Michael Banton (London: Tavistock, 1966), pp. 1–46; reprinted in his *The Interpretation of Cultures* (New York: Basic Books, 1973), pp. 87–125.

4. A *caveat* obviously applies to my use of terms like "culture" and "the Balinese." I do not wish to suggest there is any essential Balinese culture. There are only the myriad statements and actions in which people living on the island of Bali, and calling themselves Balinese, engage. In speaking of "the Balinese" I am really referring to those in the settlement of Tengahpadang, North Gianyar, where I did field research; they include both men and women of high and low castes, unless otherwise stated. How far usage varies between communities in Bali is an empirical issue and is still far from clear. Rather than hypostasize an entity called "Balinese society" and postulate its structural principles, I shall look instead primarily at how the people in one area set about interpreting their own collective representations.

5. The word seems to be from the Sanskrit for country, countryside, region, or place. Petrus J. Zoetmulder, S.J., *Old Javanese-English Dictionary* (The Hague: Nijhoff, 1982), p. 393.

6. Clifford Geertz, "Form and Variation in Balinese Village Structure," *American Anthropologist*, 61 (1959), pp. 991–1012, at p. 991.

7. For example, he asserts that "clues to the typologically essential may as often lie in rare or unique phenomena as they do in common or typical ones; ... essential form may be seen more adequately in terms of a range of variation than in terms of a fixed pattern from which deviant cases depart." Ibid., pp. 1008–9. Essentialism also lurks within his ambiguous idea of "social organization," whether one reads this in a Firthian sense, or as a "plane of significance." Cf. Raymond Firth, "Social Organization and Social Change," in his *Essays on Social Organization and Values* (London: Athlone, 1964), pp. 30–58; and James A. Boon, *The Anthropological Romance of Bali* (Cambridge: Cambridge University Press, 1977), p. 59.

At the same time, there is an intriguing parallel between Geertz's definition of "planes" and the variety of "substance-codes" Inden has suggested are to be found in Bengal. (See Ronald Inden, *Marriage and Rank in Bengali Culture: a History of Caste and Clan in Middle Period Bengal* [London: University of California Press, 1976], pp. 13–14.) But Inden carefully locates these principles in an indigenous metaphysics, whereas in Geertz's case it is quite unclear how far these are the analyst's notion or a distillation of native constructions.

8. Geertz, "Form and Variation," p. 992.

9. Boon, *The Anthropological Romance*, pp. 61–62.

10. Clifford Geertz, "Tihingan: A Balinese Village," in *Villages in Indonesia*, ed. Koentjaraningrat (Ithaca: Cornell University Press, 1967), pp. 210–43, at p. 239.

11. See my "A Balinese Village and Its Field of Social Relations" (Ph.D. thesis, University of London, 1979), pp. 123–31.

12. Michael G. Smith, "A Structural Approach to the Study of Political Change," in his *Corporations and Society* (London: Duckworth, 1974), pp. 165–204.

13. Geertz, "Form and Variation," p. 995.

14. At times there may well be discussion about what *désa* and *subak* are, or should be; but in the main practical demands require action. Coping with conflicts requires adjustment with other institutions, as does resolving perceived contradictions between collective representations.

15. In the essay on "Polyandry, Inheritance and the Definition of Marriage: With Particular Reference to Sinhalese Customary Law," in his *Rethinking Anthropology* (London: Athlone, 1961), pp. 105–13, Edmund Leach argues the impossibility of providing a universal definition, on the grounds that the

plethora of legal rights which may be conferred is in itself too complex and diffuse.

16. Geertz, "Form and Variation," p. 998, curiously renders *kuren* as "kitchen"—which is properly *paon*.

17. Both sexes are required because of the sexual division of labor in collective tasks. A person's opposite sex sibling may well be an acceptable alternative to a wife or husband. The *kuren* is not, incidentally, "the basic kin unit from the point of view of all superordinate social institutions" (Geertz, "Form and Variation," p. 998). At the same time, owners of compounds on *désa* land are members of most groups regardless of their marital status.

18. A counterargument might run that although marriage may take different forms, it still constitutes a *rite de passage* with the classic features of separation, transformation, and reintegration. Without disputing that these may be a feature of *mesakapan*, as of many other rites, the universalism often claimed for such rites of transition is a good instance of circular argument: what is transition if not separation, change and reframing?

19. Quarles van Ufford, "Contradictions in the Concept of Legitimate Authority: Processes of Local State Formation in Indonesia," *Bijdragen tot de taal-, land- en volkenkunde* (forthcoming).

20. Boon, *The Anthropological Romance*, pp. 131 ff.

21. Ibid., pp. 120–30.

22. Boon (ibid., pp. 121–22) glosses mock capture as *ngerorod*, a term used for "moving place" and so colloquially used for elopement (*melaib*, "running away"). *Ngerorod* is in fact part of every marriage rite, when the couple are secluded in someone else's house prior to *mesakapan*.

23. *Cinta* comes from the Sanskrit for thought, care, anxiety.

24. See Christiaan Hooykaas's review of Clifford Geertz and Hildred Geertz, *Kinship in Bali* in *Archipel*, 11 (1975), pp. 237–43, at p. 241.

25. Anthony F. C. Wallace, *Culture and Personality* (New York: Random House, 1961), pp. 29–44.

26. I am here arguing, partly on the basis of my reading of the Balinese ethnography, that ideas do not always come singly, but are usually part of more complex, changeable, semantic sets. In other words I am not using a Popperian model, but one closer to the position of Quine, who speaks where possible of words, or terms, to avoid imputing a questionable reality to ideas, concepts and meanings. (Willard V. O. Quine, "Two Dogmas of Empiricism" in his *From a Logical Point of View* [Cambridge, Mass.: Harvard University Press, 1953], pp. 20–46.) When I use expressions like "meaning," "idea" or "statement," these are my glosses of Balinese words, here *arti pemineh* (opinion) and *sané kebaos* (what was said) respectively.

27. See Christiaan Hooykaas, *The Lay of Jaya Prana* (Oxford: Luzak, 1958); and Peter J. Worsley, *Babad Bulèlèng: A Balinese Dynastic Genealogy* (The Hague: Nijhoff, 1972).

28. Leopold E. A. Howe, "An Introduction to the Cultural Study of Traditional Balinese Architecture," *Archipel* 25 (1983), pp. 137–58.

29. The gloss was first suggested to me by Alice Dewey and is preferable to the crude "good" or "bad" traditionally ascribed to the two sides. Good and bad tend to be (logically) attributive adjectives; that is, they are attributes of a predicate, not full predicates themselves. (For example, a good cricketer is not good and a cricketer.) To gloss the camps in the Mahabharata in the common way is effectively to preempt discussion of the complex issue of what kind of world and what image of humanity is being portrayed in shadow theater. For a more detailed discussion, see my "Is God Evil?" in *The Anthropology of Evil*, ed. David J. Parkin (Oxford: Blackwells, 1985), pp. 165–93.

30. In fact a *balian usada*, an expert in medical texts *(usada/wisada)*; but by virtue of the effects of space on health and welfare, such an expert needs to understand architectural and geomantic treatises as well.

31. Nor is it simple to extrapolate criteria of relevance from such core presuppositions. The latter do not exist in a timeless Platonic world, they are asserted. One would be assuming consistency in the postulated core, such that alternative criteria of relevance could not be found. And, as the definition of essential meaning is reached through Balinese usage, relevance would have to be inferred *a posteriori*.

32. Another way might be to examine indigenous theories of meaning. We are still left with the problem of the relation between such a theory, if it exists (and the Balinese have some shared ideas about meaning which there is no space to discuss here), and how it would be used.

33. Unfortunately two different issues often get confused here. Are we trying to explain why people actually did or said what they did? Or are we looking at how they represent such actions and motives? It is one thing to postulate a model of interests or agency, it is another to assume that this provides the necessary and sufficient conditions of all possible action.

34. Robin G. Collingwood, *The Idea of History* (Oxford: Clarendon Press, 1946), pp. 82–83.

35. Steven Lukes, "Alienation and Anomie," in *Philosophy, Politics and Society*, ed. Peter Laslett and William G. Runciman (Oxford: Blackwells, 1967), pp. 134–56, at p. 145. Emphasis added.

36. There are two further problems in our own representations of human action and nature which should be considered in a fuller analysis. First, is it possible to produce a model of human nature independent of society? Second, might there be universal aspects of human nature, independent of culture, such that we could produce a two-part model of human interests, one universal, one culturally specific? These are important issues in any general explanation of action, but are not immediately relevant to the topic of representations of action in Bali. For my concern is less with the ultimate explanation of action than with the presuppositions used in existing accounts.

37. Boon, *The Anthropological Romance*, passim.

38. See, for example, Geertz's review of Willem F. Wertheim, ed., *Bali: Studies in Life, Thought and Ritual*, in *Bijdragen tot de taal-, land- en volkenkunde*, 117 (1961), pp. 498–502; and Raden Mas Koentjaraningrat, *Anthropology in Indonesia: A Bibliographic Review*, Koninklijk Instituut voor Taal-, Land- en Volkenkunde, Bibliographic Series 8 (The Hague: Nijhoff, 1975).

39. Geertz, "Thick Description: Towards an Interpretive Theory of Culture," chapter 1 of *The Interpretation of Cultures: Selected Essays by Clifford Geertz* (London: Hutchinson, 1973), pp. 3–30, at p. 5.

40. Ibid.

41. Ibid., p. 9.

42. Ibid., pp. 19 and 20.

43. Ibid., pp. 27, 29, and 30.

44. There are, however, grounds on which they can be justified. Kuhn and others have argued that most scientific paradigms rest upon implicit metaphors. (See Thomas S. Kuhn, *The Structure of Scientific Revolutions*, 2nd enlarged edition [London: University of Chicago Press, 1962]; and Margaret Masterman, "The Nature of a Paradigm," in *Criticism and the Growth of Knowledge*, ed. Imre Lakatos and Alan Musgrave [Cambridge: Cambridge University Press, 1970], pp. 59–89.) Furthermore, the depiction of "theoretical landscapes" in terms of sustained progressions of metaphors is a quite common, if dubious, practice in writing about cultures. (See Anne Salmond, "Theoretical Landscapes: On Cross-Cultural Conceptions of Knowledge," in *Semantic Anthropology*, ed. David J. Parkin [London: Academic Press, ASA Monographs No. 22, 1982], pp. 65–87.)

45. Geertz, "Thick Description," p. 17.

46. Ibid., p. 18.

47. See Roy Bhaskar, *The Possibility of Naturalism: A Philosophical Critique of the Contemporary Human Sciences* (Brighton: Harvester, 1979), pp. 39–47.

48. Paul Ricoeur, "The Model of the Text: Meaningful Action Considered as a Text," *Social Research*, 38 (1971), pp. 529–62.

49. Cf. Roland Barthes, "From Work to Text," in *Textual Strategies: Perspectives in Poststructural Criticism*, ed. Josué V. Harari (Ithaca: Cornell University Press, 1979), pp. 73–81.

50. Martin Hollis, "The Social Destruction of Reality," in *Rationality and Relativism*, ed. Martin Hollis and Steven Lukes (Oxford: Blackwells, 1982), pp. 67–86.

51. Cf. Ian Hacking, *Why Does Language Matter to Philosophy* (Cambridge: Cambridge University Press, 1975), pp. 159 ff.

52. His account is taken from Roelof Goris, "Holidays and Holy Days," in *Bali: Studies in Life, Thought and Ritual*, ed. Willem F. Wertheim (The Hague: van Hoeve, 1960), pp. 113–29. The text is reprinted in his *The Interpretation of Cultures*, pp. 360–411.

53. Geertz, "Person," p. 392.

54. On this debate, see Geertz, "Person"; Maurice Bloch, "The Past and the Present in the Future," *Man* (New Series), 12: 2 (1977), pp. 278–92; Michael F. C. Bourdillon, "Knowing the World or Hiding It: A Response to Maurice Bloch," *Man* (New Series), 13: 4 (1978), pp. 591–99; and Leopold E. A. Howe, "The Social Determination of Knowledge: Maurice Bloch and Balinese Time," *Man* (New Series), 16: 2 (1981), pp. 220–34.

55. See Max Black, "Metaphor," in his *Models and Metaphors: Studies in Language and Philosophy* (Ithaca: Cornell University Press, 1962), pp. 25–47.

56. Geertz, "Person," p. 368.

57. Gillian Feeley-Harnik, "Divine Kingship and the Meaning of History among the Sakalava of Madagascar," *Man* (New Series), 13: 3 (1978), pp. 402–17.

58. Geertz, "Person," p. 370.

59. The only exception was one high caste man and, on Geertz's view, such names are caste titles, not autonyms. There is no evidence local usage is recent or some strange "degeneration." Boon suggests that if anything teknonymy may be on the increase, as Balinese adapt status relations to new political ends. See his "The Progress of the Ancestors in a Balinese Temple-group," *Journal of Asian Studies*, 34 (1974), pp. 7–25.

It is almost as if names and words have some very special essence. We are in danger of entering a world where digital watches imply a different sense of time from the old analog ones; or classical Romans have tripartite orders of person definition and Englishmen bipartite since they were/are referred to respectively by three and two names. The implication seems to be that the Balinese are not just "depersonalized," but have the misfortune to have diffused identities in contrast to our unified persons. If this is so, it is not clear how they can be "knowing subjects" in the same sense as we are, nor how their "constructions of the world" could be the same as ours. If not, then what are the implications of personal names? How misleading a rigid and decontextualized linking of words and ideas can prove may be seen in Wiggins' attempt to grapple with Geertz's model of selfhood. David Wiggins, "Locke, Butler and the Stream of Consciousness: and Men as Natural Kind," in *The Identities of Persons*, ed. Amélie Rorty (London: University of California Press, 1976), pp. 139–73, at p. 155. (Rorty's "A Literary Postscript," in the same volume [pp. 301–23] is far more sensitively contextual.)

60. *Negara: The Theater State in Nineteenth-Century Bali* (Princeton: Princeton University Press, 1980).

61. The analysis draws heavily on two texts of Christiaan Hooykaas: "Padmâsana, the Throne of God," and "Śiva-Liṅga, the Mark of the Lord," in his *Āgama Tīrtha: Five Studies in Hindu-Balinese Religion* (Amsterdam: Noord Hollandsche Uitgevers Maatschappij, 1964), pp. 95–140 and 143–89. A close reading of Geertz's interpretation of Hooykaas's cautious and scholarly account is revealing.

62. Rodney Needham, "Inner States as Universals," in his *Circumstantial Deliveries* (London: University of California Press, 1981), pp. 53–71.

63. Geertz, *Negara*, p. 155.

64. This said, I should add that I am broadly in sympathy with Geertz's argument for examining the culturally specific forms that human action takes, as against Victor Turner's universalism. (Compare Geertz's "Person," for example, with Turner's *From Ritual to Theater: The Human Seriousness of Play* [New York: Performing Arts, 1982].) My criticism is that his argument has not been pushed far enough towards a recognition of the possibility of radically different metaphysical systems.

65. Geertz, "Person," pp. 362 and 363.

66. Ibid., p. 400.

67. "Deep Play: Notes on the Balinese Cockfight," in *The Interpretation of Cultures*, pp. 412–53, at pp. 423, 443, and 436. The latter phrase is taken from Erving Goffman's *Encounters: Two Studies in the Sociology of Interaction* (Indianapolis: Bobbs-Merrill, 1961), p. 78.

68. *Negara*, p. 120.

69. Ibid., p. 13, which quotes from Geertz's earlier "Politics Past, Politics Present: Some Notes on the Uses of Anthropology in Understanding the New States," reprinted in *The Interpretation of Cultures*, pp. 327–41, at p. 335.

70. "Deep Play," p. 417.

71. Ibid., p. 426.

72. See Zoetmulder, *Old Javanese-English Dictionary*, p. 1141.

73. Johan Huizinga, *Homo Ludens* (London: Routledge & Kegan Paul, 1949), pp. 29–45.

74. Nelson Goodman, *Languages of Art* (Brighton: Harvester, 1981), pp. 27–31.

75. Andreas Teeuw, et al., *Śiwarātrikalpa of Mpu Tanakuṅ*, Bibliotheca Indonesica 3 (The Hague: Nijhoff, 1969), pp. 31–32.

76. Boon, *The Anthropological Romance*, pp. 31–34, observes that the cockfight can take on all sorts of significances in different contexts. Other texts exploring the complexities of status and caste include: Andrew Duff-Cooper, "Hierarchy, Purity, and Equality among a Community of Balinese on Lombok," in *Contexts and Levels: Essays on Hierarchy*, ed. Robert H. Barnes, Daniel de Coppet, and Robert J. Parkin (Oxford: JASO Occasional Paper No. 4, 1985), pp. 153–66; Leopold E. A. Howe, "Caste in India and Bali: Levels of Comparison," in ibid., pp. 139–52; and my own "Is God Evil?"

77. A curious omission is Balinese ideas about chance. Instead of treating cockfighting in isolation, it would have been interesting to consider the links with well-developed techniques for cutting down uncertainty and manipulating the world for personal ends, like magic, charms, love potions and so on. The role of trickery and cunning in outwitting chance is so widespread as to suggest that overlooking it says much about the moral background of ethnographers.

78. Geertz, "Deep Play," p. 418.

79. Rutger van Eck, *Balineesch-Hollandsch Woordenboek* (Utrecht: Kemink, 1876); Herman N. van der Tuuk, *Kawi-Balineesch-Nederlandsch Woordenboek* (Batavia: Landsdrukkerij, 1897); I Wayan Warna, *Kamus Bali-Indonesia* (Denpasar: Dinas Pengajaran, 1978); J. Kersten, *Kamus Kecil Bahasa Bali* (Singaraja: privately published, 1978); Jan Gonda, *Sanskrit in Indonesia* (Naghpur: International Academy of Indian Culture, 1952); and Zoetmulder, *Old Javanese-English Dictionary*.

80. "Person," p. 369.

81. *The Anthropological Romance*, p. 3.

82. Ibid., p. 6.

83. James Boon, *Other Tribes, Other Scribes: Symbolic Anthropology in the Comparative Study of Cultures, Histories, Religions, and Texts* (Cambridge: Cambridge University Press, 1982).

84. Bloch, "The Past."

85. Geertz, "Person," pp. 401–2.

86. *Tattwa* has complicated philosophical roots which seem to affect its popular usage in Bali. In Indian Nyāya-Vaiśeṣika it is "the nature of things" (Karl Potter, *Indian Metaphysics and Epistemology: The Tradition of Nyāya-Vaiśeṣika up to Gaṅgeśa* [Princeton: Princeton University Press, 1977], p. 240). In Sāṃkhya it is the principles or basic categories of reality (Jan Gonda, *Visnuism and Śivaism: a Comparison* [London: The Athlone Press, 1970], p. 44). In Old Javanese texts found in Bali, the senses of *tattwa* include "what makes something what it is," "the actual facts of the matter, how it really happened, the true story." "Sometimes *tattwa* is the concrete object in its essence, *katattwan* the abstract essence of the concrete object" (Zoetmulder, *Old Javanese-English Dictionary*, p. 1962).

87. See Gertrude E. M. Anscombe, *Intention* (Oxford: Blackwells, 1957); and Alan R. White, "Introduction," to his *The Philosophy of Action* (Oxford: Oxford University Press, 1968), pp. 1–18.